── PRAISE FOR ──
A Gentle Clash of Cultures

"*A Gentle Clash of Cultures* is a cogent look at the experience of travel, culture shock, and adventure in the Philippines during the late 1970s. The Claytons, as Americans abroad, share both their disappointments and triumphs. Each chapter is a revelation, from the first . . . to the last. . . . Be prepared to be informed, challenged, and entertained by what you read here."

—**TERESE THONUS**, PhD, Applied Linguist and Professor, Director of the University Writing Program, Klein Family School of Communications Design, University of Baltimore

"Insightful, sensitive, and a great read! Anyone interested in travel or cultural anthropology will find perceptive insights into Philippine life astutely chronicled by an expat family who lived for three years on Luzon."

—**DON H. ABBEY**, PhD, Retired Professor of Biology, Retired Field Director, Adventist Frontier Missions

"It was fun for me to be back in that world. It is no surprise that as an MK (missionary kid), I relate to the chapter on Jeff and Kimberly. '*Mamaya* Means By and By' was my favorite chapter; the dialogue is great and does an excellent job of expressing culture through conversations. 'The Farmer's Daughter' is a gem—the most missional part of the entire story; Jesus did after all spend significant time with prostitutes. I enjoyed the book. [The authors] capture the culture well."

—**LUKE GRAY**, Author of *Three Ring Circus: Life as a Missionary Kid in a Family of 11*

"A traditional American family plunges into the Philippines, creating an Asian fusion of cultures that surprises the palate and always satisfies. The authors take turns creating a striking portrait of a country few of us know. Dale works with an assortment of students from around Asia [and] explores stories, islands, jungles, and cities while pursuing science with a [hodgepodge] of tools and a cadre of colorful characters. Kay leaves campus to barter for goods, travel by Jeepney, participate in local fests, and find a job. This is a book of substance, well researched and honest. A gentle clash of people and places that results in finding home within oneself and the wider world for each of them. The work is terrific! [The authors] have really shown why [their] information is of use to readers in the 2020s."

—**INA ORME**, BS, MA, Teacher, Writer of Children's Literature, Member, Oak Harbor Writers' Group

"[The authors'] writing is delightful; I love the description of how the roads 'made senile wrecks of vigorous young cars, and we had an old resuscitated Holden.' [The] description of taking photographs is refreshing, learning that [the authors] took photos of folks who didn't own a camera, being cautious not to offend, then sharing the photos with some of them. Describing things new to [the authors] in local biology is crucial to the reader's understanding of [their] experiences; and the politics specific to university committees needing to include the three basic Filipino people groups is insightful."

—**BILL WALKER**, MBA, Blogger, Author of *Diamonds and Dirt*, Screenwriter, Oak Harbor Writers' Group

"As [the authors] described [their] first landing in the Philippines, noting the mountains and evidence of volcanic activity, it's clear [they] felt [their] family was going through its own continental drift. Later when Mr. Malagit fixed the heating tank . . . and he said his daughter had two kids 'made in America' and then encouraged [the authors] to increase [their] family so [they] could have kids 'made in the Philippines!' I found it hilarious and delightful!"

—**ERIKA JENKINS**, BA, MA, Teacher, Blogger and Writer, Oak Harbor Writing Group

—PRAISE FOR KAREN J. CLAYTON'S OTHER WORK—
Demystifying Hospice: Inside the Stories of Patients and Caregivers

"[Clayton's] stories address when hospice is appropriate, how and where hospice care is given, the needs of the dying and their caregivers, how care is personalized, and most importantly the benefits of meaningful relationships between all involved—patients, families, and their lay and professional care providers. An added benefit of the story format is that it demonstrates through examples how to establish meaningful relationships, making the book valuable not only to people and families approaching the end of life but also professional healthcare providers, who often lack experience giving end-of-life care and who may themselves be grappling with their own uncertainties."

—**CHOICE MAGAZINE**

"'Hospice is extraordinary!' With this opening line, Clayton, a social worker and sociologist, declares her advocacy. In what she calls 'a gentle book about a difficult subject,' she spells out the benefits of compassionate care for people who can't get more 'curative' treatment, or who don't want more of it. . . . Clayton offers useful advice, including good tips on how to make last days more pleasant for both the patient and caregivers. Deepened by Clayton's feeling that it is an honor to find ways to help people say goodbye to their loved ones, this guide is invaluable."

—**BOOKLIST**

"*Demystifying Hospice* is an excellent addition to the hospice literature. Clayton has detailed wonderful stories about the hospice experience. It is well written and filled with compassion. I strongly recommend this book for all those who are interested in hospice and learning more about the hospice philosophy of care."

—**ROBERT W. BUCKINGHAM**, Professor of Public Health, University of Michigan-Flint, Pioneer in the development of hospice programs in the US and worldwide

A Gentle Clash of Cultures: Filipino Students and Colleagues, Martial Law and Civet Cats

by Karen J. and Dale L. Clayton

© Copyright 2024 Karen J. and Dale L. Clayton

ISBN 979-8-88824-352-7

All rights reserved. No part of this publication may be reproduced, stored in a retrieval system, or transmitted in any form or by any means—electronic, mechanical, photocopy, recording, or any other—except for brief quotations in printed reviews, without the prior written permission of the author.

Some names have been changed to offer privacy to some persons.

On the cover: Silhouettes showing the Baguio Rice Terraces

Published by

◢ köehlerbooks™

3705 Shore Drive
Virginia Beach, VA 23455
800-435-4811
www.koehlerbooks.com

A Gentle Clash of Cultures

Filipino Students and Colleagues, Martial Law and Civet Cats

Karen J. Clayton and Dale L. Clayton

VIRGINIA BEACH
CAPE CHARLES

Also by Karen J. Clayton

Demystifying Hospice: Inside the Stories of Patients and Caregivers

Dedicated with love and honor to our children, Jeffrey and Kimberly, who shared these adventures, helped make the memories, and were shaped by the joys and the challenges.

TABLE OF CONTENTS

Map of the Philippines xiii
Frequently Used Words and Phrases xiv
Foreword - A Slice in Time: 1977–81 (Karen) xvii

Chapter 1 - Coming Home (Dale) 1

Chapter 2 - Two Invitations (Karen) 5

Chapter 3 - The Other Side of the Earth (Karen) 12

The Baesa Campus, Caloocan City, Metro Manila

Chapter 4 - New Country, New Campus, New Home (Karen) 22

Chapter 5 - *Mamaya* Means "By and By" (Dale) 34

Chapter 6 - New Ways to Do Things (Karen) 38

Chapter 7 - Getting into It! (Dale) 44

Chapter 8 - The Baesa Campus, Students,
and the Classroom (Dale) 49

Chapter 9 - Israel Was No Egghead (Dale) 58

Chapter 10 - Early Journaling: New Friends and
Women Who Taught Me (Karen) 62

Chapter 11 - An Embarrassment of Riches and Fear (Karen) 68

Chapter 12 - The Silang Campus: No Longer a Mystery (Karen) . 76

Chapter 13 - Becky, Extraordinary Helper and Friend (Karen) 80

Chapter 14 - Education Challenges and Insights (Dale) 89

Chapter 15 - Being Needed Made All the Difference (Karen) 95

Chapter 16 - No Cats for Cat Lab (Karen) 99

Chapter 17 - Jeepneys: Carnivals on Wheels (Karen) 104

Chapter 18 - A Visit from Our American Family (Karen) 110

Chapter 19 - Polillo Island Graduation (Dale) 115

Chapter 20 - A Working Holiday (Dale) 125

The Silang Campus, Puting Kahoy, Silang, Cavite

Chapter 21 - Time to Move to the Side of a Volcano (Karen) 132

Chapter 22 - The Expatriates and
     Culture Shock Reflections (Karen) 139

Chapter 23 - A Time for Everything (Karen) 149

Chapter 24 - "Can't we stop this killing?" (Dale) 152

Chapter 25 - Differences Are More Interesting (Dale) 158

Chapter 26 - Beauty Is What Works (Dale) 164

Chapter 27 - Easter Celebrations:
     People Look for Answers (Karen) 174

Chapter 28 - Independence Day, July 4 and June 12 (Karen) 184

Chapter 29 - Mom and Dad Clayton and Other Visitors (Karen) 187

Chapter 30 - Jeffrey and Kimberly (Dale and Karen) 195

Chapter 31 - Flight Attendants of 004 (Dale) 209

Chapter 32 - Civet Cats, Owls, and Other Critters (Karen) 213

Exploring the Countryside

Chapter 33 - The Elusive Tamaraw (Dale) 220

Chapter 34 - Study Tour by Ship (Dale) 231

Chapter 35 - String Beans and Other Tales (Dale) 251

Chapter 36 - Some of Our Favorite Places and Things (Karen) ... 255

War Experiences and Other Difficult Stories

Chapter 37 - They Came Ashore Right There (Karen) 264

Chapter 38 - Richard Hammill, POW (Dale) 271

Chapter 39 - The Farmer's Daughter in Makati (Dale) 277

Another Adventure – Another New Home

Chapter 40 - Where Do We Go Next? (Karen) 282

Chapter 41 - Reverse Culture Shock (Karen) 285

Postscript - A Slice in Time: 1978–1981 (Karen) 293
Postscript and Disclaimer (Dale) 296
Bibliography and Suggested Reading 298
Appendixes 305
    A. Demographics 306
    B. How to Learn about Another Culture (Karen) 308
    C. Challenges Doing Cross-Cultural Work (Karen) 310
    D. Historical Timeline: The Philippines and SDA Work 312
    E. A Brief History of the Philippines 321
    F. Taking Folks Back to Their Roots: Making Coconut Soap .. 323
Acknowledgments 325
About the Authors 328

Map of the Philippines

Frequently Used Words, Phrases, and Pronunciation Guide

Banca: A dugout canoe with bamboo supports or outriggers.

Barong: A formal shirt of lightweight material, with panels of embroidery.

Barrio: The primary unit of government, rural or urban; average of 2,500 people.

Barangay: A 1975 law replaced "barrio" with "barangay" (Source: Wikipilipinas).

Calesa: A small cart used for transportation, pulled by a small horse.

Carabao/Tamaraw: Water buffalo; the tamaraw is a small variety indigenous to Mindoro.

"*Conte lang*": Little bit only.

"*Diyan lang*": Just nearby.

Filipino/Filipina, alternatively Pilipino/Pilipina: male/female; also the language.

"*Hindi*": No.

"*Kumusta?*": How are you?

"*Mabuti naman*": I'm fine [with respect].

Maganda: Beautiful.

"*Magandang umaga*": Good morning.

"*Magandang hapon*": Good afternoon.

"*Mainit*": Very hot!

"*Magandang gabi*": Good evening.

"*Masyadong mahal*": Very dear/expensive.

"*Magkano*": How much?

"*Oo*" or "*Opo*": Yes, or Yes [with respect].

Pakikisama: A spirit of sharing (objects, services).

"*Po*": Added to words or phrases to show respect, especially to elders.

Sala: Living room.

"*Salamat*": Thank you.

"*Salamat po*": Thank you [with respect].

"*Sayang*": What a pity!

"*Talaga?*": Really?

"*Walang anuman*": You are welcome.

Pronunciation Guide

- The sound of Tagalog, the national language, is similar to Spanish. "A" is pronounced as "ah," "E" as "ay," "I" as "ee."
- There are more than eighty-six dialects. English is widely used.
- Each vowel is pronounced separately: e.g., Bataan pronounced "Bah-tah-AHN."
- Emphasis is usually on the second or third syllable, as in Baesa (Ba-EE-sah); Silang (see-LANG).

English Words Added to Tagalog

Sometimes new words do not have Tagalog words created for them, but are used in abbreviated form: e.g., air con (air-conditioning), ball pen (ballpoint pen), CR (comfort room/restroom).

Useful Translation Tools

- Tagalog Lang/Learn Tagalog online! "Tagalog-English Dictionary": https://www.tagaloglang.com/ang

- 90+ Useful Tagalog Phrases for Everyday Conversation: https://owlcation.com/humanities/Tagalog-Phrases-For-Everyday-Use

Identifying Tagalog Words

Tagalog words will be italicized the first time they are used.

Learning a Foreign Language

Learning a people's language helps in understanding values, relationships, history, and their worldview. It is also a courtesy to the native speaker and shows you honor them and their country and want to understand and be involved in life as they know it.

— FOREWORD —

A Slice in Time (1978-81)
Under the Marcos Regime and Martial Law

Karen

"Every slice in time is important."
—*Literary Agent*

My parents gifted me with the interest, excitement, and the opportunity to travel. We always had *National Geographic* magazines in our home. We drove to interesting places near and far and attended lectures and films about worldwide travel at the W. K. Kellogg Auditorium in Battle Creek, Michigan; what I learned inspired me to want to know more about my world and understand other cultures.

Dale's home was in Killmaster, a tiny town in the center of Michigan's lower peninsula. His early adventuring in biology involved fishing and trying to create four-leaf clovers in the fields near his home. He learned about ethnicities there (local Native Americans and a Hungarian community), then went away to school to pursue his curiosity about animal behavior and becoming a "teacher doctor"—not a "fixer doctor," as I explained it to our children, Jeffrey and Kimberly, when they were very young.[1]

Dale's educational and professional interests took us to Oregon, California, back to Michigan, then to Walla Walla College (WWC) in College Place, Washington. Then in 1977 he was invited to teach

---
[1] Dale Clayton. In preparation: *Killmaster Kids*.

at Philippine Union College (PUC) near Manila. A small school on the other side of the earth, it was part of the second-largest Christian education system in the world, operated by the Seventh-day Adventist Church. Filipino dynamo Doctora Rasa told us that most biology students studying there wanted to be nurses, doctors, lab technicians, or biology teachers.

Our 1960s *Encyclopedia Americana* and the WWC library didn't offer much current information about the Republic of the Philippines (RP); and in 1977 there was no World Wide Web. We learned the Philippine archipelago formed about fifty million years ago, and it is believed the earliest inhabitants came from the Asian mainland. Later we learned that Filipinos were the first Asians to come to America, arriving in California as early as 1587. They "worked on a Spanish ship as part of the Manila galleon trade which sailed from Mexico to the Philippines," and nearly two centuries later, in 1763, these sailors "settled in a Louisiana bayou, and became the first Filipino immigrants to settle in the United States, known as 'Manilamen.' ... [They] made many contributions including revolutionizing the shrimping industry."[2] That was not a part of any history we had learned in school.

We were aware of the US military involvement with the country during WWII, and we knew of President Ferdinand Marcos and his colorful wife, Imelda. When we talked with the political science professor at WWC, he said Ferdinand Marcos was a "benevolent dictator" and that we should be safe there. We were excited to embark on this adventure with the plan to live there for three—and possibly six—years. If we'd known more, we might not have gone.

We are glad we did go. Our time in the Philippines was a high point in our lives. As an artist, social worker, and sociologist, I began studying cultures—especially belief systems—while we were there. I was an administrative assistant in the Far Eastern Division Seminary

---

[2] "Manilamen: The First Asian American Settlement," The Asian American Education Project, Accessed February 11, 2024, https://asianamericanedu.org/manilamen-first-asian-american-settlement.html.

of the Seventh-day Adventists, and I took classes. Dale, the biologist, began thinking sociologically and culturally, especially after electricity challenges thwarted his circadian rhythms research. He taught, directed research, and traveled the length of the archipelago with a few students; and he and Jeff adventured to find a small water buffalo, the tamaraw, which lives only on the island of Mindoro. Jeff and Kimberly went to a one-room, multigrade school for expatriate children. After grade 8, the plan was that they would go to a small boarding school in Singapore.

We lived on two different campuses: the first, Baesa, was at the edge of Metro Manila, with armed guards at the gates and squatters making their homes against the broken-glass-topped walls of our campus; the second, in Silang, was built halfway down the side of the still active and occasionally threatening Taal Volcano and surrounded by pineapple fields, coconut groves, and coffee plantations. We both wrote long letters home on our Remington manual typewriter, keeping carbon copies for our own files.

After we'd been back in the States for a while on other academic and family adventures, Dale and I began to write about our Philippine experiences. We enjoyed remembering our time there and realized the stories might interest others—especially those who want to travel or are considering living and working in another part of the world. We wrote and wrote; then I took a formal proposal for this book to the Whidbey Island Writers' Conference.

"When were you in the Philippines?" a literary agent asked.

"It's been a long time," I replied.

"It doesn't matter when you were there. Every slice in time is important. It's a slice in time like no other. It's valuable and interesting. Go for it!"

Several businesses use the phrase "a slice in time" to sell the idea of exotic locations around the world, enticing folk to travel. My mind is filled with memories of intriguing places. Dale and I have explored twenty-two countries, and we travel every other year to Australia to see Kimberly and her family. Jeff is a construction supervisor for huge projects, lives in California, and has worked across the United States and in Haiti and Kenya. His kids and grandkids enjoy the stories of his travels.

Recurring themes in today's Philippines reflect parts of our experience: Martial law is occasionally threatened, the son of benevolent dictator Ferdinand Marcos has won the presidency, and his vice president is the daughter of the recent crime-fighting Rodrigo Duterte.[3] Freedom of the press remains vulnerable; journalist Maria Ressa, who challenges corruption in the Philippines and cofounded an online-only newspaper named *Rappler*, shared the 2020 Nobel Prize for Peace with Dmitry Muratov, a Russian journalist.

The most important treasures of the Philippines are its fascinating people and the beauty of the islands. Our attempts to understand and value other people, places, and ways of thinking presented a enthralling challenge. We hope you enjoy and learn from our adventures.

Why write this book?

- To describe what it's like to step outside your comfort zone.
- To share what we learned and provide insights for learning about other cultures.
- To inform and entertain.
- To show firsthand that people are more alike than they are different.
- To reveal that differences are fascinating and result in understanding, growth, and acceptance.

Here's who we think will enjoy our stories and insights:

- People who like to learn about others and wonder *Why do they do that?*

---

[3] The candidate with the most votes becomes president; the person with the second-most votes becomes the vice president.

- People who are already travel or just love to read about travel.
- People who will live in any culture different from their own.
- Anthropologists, biologists, missionaries, political scientists, readers, sociologists, theologians, travelers, and NGO employees.

— CHAPTER 1 —

Coming Home

Dale

"I'm coming home to a place I've never been before."
—*John Denver, Songwriter, Performer, Environmentalist*

The shimmering blue sea beneath the China Airlines 727 gave way to sparse white clouds floating above serpentine shorelines and the varied greens of tropical plants and browns of Philippine hardwoods. This island, Luzon, would be our home for some years. Luzon is one of the more than 7,100 islands forming the Philippine Archipelago; only 466 of these islands have an area of more than one square mile. The Philippines has the fifth-longest coastline in the world and is the world's fifth-largest island country.[4]

An old Filipino legend explains the origin of this archipelago. A long time ago, so the legend goes, there was only Sea where the islands now stand. Bird had been flying between Sky and Sea for many hours and could find no resting place, so Bird incited an argument between Sky and Sea. The argument revolved around which was the mightiest, Sky or Sea. In answer to insults, Sea threw huge waves at Sky, and then Sky, angered, hurled rocks at Sea, until finally Sea was pacified. The rocks became the many islands of the

---

[4] Ian Fulgar, "How Many Islands Are in the Philippines?" June 19, 2023, https://www.ianfulgar.com; The National Mapping and Resource Information Authority (NAMRIA), Accessed February 12, 2024, https://www.namria.gov.ph/.

archipelago. Bird, at last, did rest![5]

Modern geologists tell another story, equally astounding. On a map, you can follow the rim of the Pacific Basin from Alaska west to Kamchatka and south to Japan, Taiwan, the Philippines, Indonesia, and around to New Zealand, then eastward to the coast of South America. If you continue north along the west coast of Central and North America to where you started in Alaska, you have traced the rim of the Pacific Basin, often called the Ring of Fire.

Some geologists believe that this fiery circle of volcanic activity and mountain uplift represents the edges of a huge crater created when cosmic forces tore the moon from the Pacific Basin and, in so doing, unbalanced the earth. As a result of this imbalance, the continents have been slowly drifting toward the void, now filled with water. The crumpled edges of the Pacific Basin bear the scars of continental drift, faulting, folding, mountain uplift, and much earthquake and volcanic activity.

Theory and legend offer vivid pictures of the scenes passing beneath our plane on that sunny day in May. The hundreds of tiny islands did conjure visions of rocks hurled into a raging but now pacified sea; and the rugged terrain of larger islands is nicely explained by the folding, faulting, and volcanic activity—the great crustal movements that make and move mountains. I realized our family was experiencing its own continental drift.

Mountain streams, an occasional road, and, less frequently, a farmer's field peeked through the clouds where the trees parted, but on the whole, the mountains seemed little disturbed by humans. This picture changed slowly but markedly as we approached Manila International Airport (MIA) and mountains gave way to the plains of central Luzon. A yellow mist—smog—moved steadily toward the plane, and I thought of the travel brochures that said, "Manila is

---

[5] D. L. Ashliman, Editor. "Creation Myths from the Philippines," University of Pittsburgh, Accessed February 13, 2024, https://www.sites.pitt.edu/~dash/creation-phil.html.

the most Westernized city of the Far East." That statement misled me to believe that Filipino and American cultures would be similar. Filipinos are truly "people of the East" and not simply a "little brown brother" left longer in the Creator's oven, as another legend suggests.

Fasten Seat Belts: No Smoking signs flashed, and the plane went through the slightly erratic movements of pilots correcting for direction, descent, and speed of approach. The landing field moved lazily toward us. A boundary fence of wire and rough concrete block raced below the plane's window. Tight against the concrete wall, using the blocks as the back wall, stood several shacks of cardboard and tin. Most seemed about ten by twelve feet—or three by four meters, as I would soon grow accustomed to saying.

People swarmed about the shacks. Children waved at our plane.

Why, I wondered, *does the Federal Aviation Administration [or its Philippine equivalent] allow this? What are those shacks used for?* Many questions ricocheted around my mind, but the salient one should have been *Why do people live so near this noise and ever-present danger?*

It didn't occur to me to ask that question because I did not see the shacks as homes. I did not believe people lived there. I had seen adults, children, a dog, a mother sitting in the shade and nursing a baby. It all passed swiftly beneath as I looked out the window. I only sensed what it meant.

Later, after days of observing the same things in other parts of Manila, reality registered and brought on the first mild pangs of "culture shock." Those were people's homes. But the Philippines and I were on a honeymoon, and some realities had difficulty intruding on what I could understand. Now I know that when I hear of hundreds of homes destroyed in typhoons, many are likely homes like those, made of cardboard, tin, and plywood if it can be obtained.

Many things happened that first day. We departed the plane, collected our baggage, and were greeted by smiling faces. Doctora Rasa—chair of the Biology Department—and other science and nursing teachers from PUC used the Nursing Department's new twenty-two-passenger bus to transport us from MIA to the campus. There we met other teachers, PUC's president, Dr. Roda, and his wife, Lydia, who warmly welcomed us with an excellent feast. Then we were taken to our new home; but that's a whole other story.

On this day, we were coming home—to a new home in a land we had never seen before. Coming home to a people we would learn to love but never totally understand. Karen would contract the first and most severe case of culture shock and homesickness, then recover to suffer occasional minor relapses, not unlike the recurring chills and fever of malaria. Our children would be less affected in the beginning but not immune. There were challenges for both of them, now and then.

I would enjoy six months of bliss and immunity, but when culture shock surfaced, it was chronic, never severe. Once back in the States, I missed the "Hey, Joe!" greeting, which seemed to connect me to, not separate me from, the people whose land I had invaded.

— CHAPTER 2 —

Two Invitations

Karen

"The doors we open and close determine the lives we live."
—Paraphrase of Flora Whittemore, Author[6]

Engracia Arguelles Rasa slipped into our lives during a 1977 science conference at Andrews University in Michigan.[7] She told Dale she wanted to visit our campus in Washington State and asked if he would give her a tour around the Biology Department. She said she was gathering information to improve the Biology Department of her small college in the Republic of the Philippines. We made plans for her to visit our campus.

Dra. Rasa was a delightful, diminutive powerhouse, friendly and businesslike at the same time. She had taken her undergraduate training in the Philippines and her graduate work for her doctorate in botany at the University of California, Davis. She was the chair of the Biology Department at Philippine Union College (PUC) and was respected nationally.[8] The University of the Philippines (UP),

---

[6] Flora Whittemore, writer, proofreader, and bookkeeper; for some time, she had a column, "Grams Corner," in the *Idaho State Journal* and reported for the *Post Register* in Idaho Falls. https://www.findagrave.com/memorial/26037850/flora-permelia-whittemore (Accessed February 11, 2024).

[7] A Christian school established in 1847 in Battle Creek, Michigan, operated by the Seventh-day Adventist Church (SDA). It was named for J. N. Andrews; he and two of his children were the first SDA missionaries. http://www.andrews.edu (Accessed February 11, 2024). Currently located in Berrien Springs, Michigan.

[8] Now Adventist University of the Philippines (AUP). https://www.aup.edu.ph (Accessed February 11, 2024).

the most prestigious university in the country, extended annual invitations for her to join their faculty. Each year, she declined the offer, saying, "Who would take care of biology at PUC if I left?"

When Dra. Rasa arrived at Walla Walla College, we invited her to stay at our home. Dale took her on a tour of the Biology Department, where they examined the equipment and talked science.[9] We also shared some Northwest history and culture with her, taking her to Whitman Mission and to a play in Walla Walla's outdoor amphitheater, which dramatized the story of the valley's Indian conflicts, cattle trails, and Gold Rush activities in the 1800s.

We raved about WWC's Rosario Marine Biology Station on Fidalgo Island in Puget Sound, 340 miles northwest of Walla Walla. She wanted to visit there, too. Early one morning, Dale took her to catch the train and arranged for someone to meet her in Mount Vernon, Washington, and take her to the biology station. On their way to the train, Dra. Rasa surprised him with a request: "Dale, why don't you come over to the Philippines and help us?"

It sounded to Dale like a modern Macedonian call, reminding us of Paul's dramatic vision described in Acts 16:9 of a man pleading for him to travel to Macedonia and help the people there. Always one to keep an open mind, Dale said he would consider the idea.

We both grew up hearing stories about living and working in other countries, about "the mission field." We sang songs with Jeffrey and Kimberly about one day being "a missionary teacher, or doctor, nurse, even a missionary mommy." Still, we'd been in College Place for nine years and were happy there. Dale enjoyed his students and colleagues and loved teaching; he was now a full professor, involved in fascinating research and publishing on circadian rhythms. WWC was a small, intimate, quality university; both WWC and PUC were operated by the Seventh-day Adventist church system.

I found the classes I took each semester toward my bachelor's degree stimulating. I was still deciding what I wanted to be when I "grew

---

[9] Now Walla Walla University (WWU). https://www.wallawalla.edu (Accessed February 11, 2024).

up"—an artist, social worker, or sociologist. Jeff was eleven, Kimberly was eight; they rode their bikes to Rogers Elementary, a few blocks from our home, and had a full life with their activities and friends. Going to the other side of the earth had not been in our playbook.

We sought out what information there was about the Philippines, first poring through our encyclopedia. We and the children were used to regularly bringing books home from the library; but it was frustrating not to find more helpful material about the Philippines.[10]

Several weeks later, I answered our home phone, and the caller announced: "This is Johnson from Washington, and I'd like to speak to the Clayton that teaches theology."[11]

That took me aback! "Hello, this *is* the Clayton home, but my husband teaches biology. If there's a Clayton who teaches theology, we don't know him. I'll give you Malcolm Maxwell's phone number. He will likely know *that* Clayton, wherever he teaches."

The next day, there was another call, and a familiar voice again said, "This is Johnson from Washington, and I'd like to speak to the Clayton that teaches theology."

Déjà vu. Does this man not know he said the same thing to me yesterday? I assumed that, since we lived in Washington State, "Johnson from Washington" was calling from there.

Dale was at home, and I handed the phone to him, standing close by to hear the conversation. Soon we learned that Mr. Johnson was from Washington, DC, and secretary for the Global Missions department, responsible for sending 3,420 workers to various sites around the world.[12] He asked if we had ever considered foreign service and where we might like to work outside the US.

Dale said, "Do you mean the Philippines?"

"Oh, you know about that!" Mr. Johnson responded.

---

[10] See bibliography for samples: e.g., Anne Schraff and a Globe Trotters Series; Climo re: animals of the Philippines.

[11] Johnson is not the actual name of the dear man doing his best to fill many mission spots all over the world.

[12] Adventist Mission sent 3,420 workers/missionaries in the 1970s. https://www.adventistmission.org (Accessed February 2, 2024).

He then explained that there was an opening at Philippine Union College in Manila and wondered if Dale would be interested. Dale explained that he taught biology, not theology, and Mr. Johnson said, "Well, we need biology teachers, too!" We told him we'd consider it, and he promised to send us detailed information.

A few days later, we received a formal-looking letter in the mail. When Dale came home that evening, I asked him to come out to our new family room with me. We sat on cushions in the bay window seat, and I said, "I love this new room. You've done a beautiful job on the brickwork around the antique stove and creating this huge bay window seat. The barn you've built is amazing, and I love the garden, the corral, the horses, and chickens. I'm not sure we want to open this," hesitantly handing him the letter. Of course, he opened it, and then it was all very real.

We were being offered an extraordinary opportunity; we knew that. But deciding whether to go or stay involved many other decisions: about our home, our animals, the kids' education and what they wanted, and supporting our aging parents. We learned there would be an American teacher for children of the expatriates, a term I didn't like because it felt negative, even though it's a perfectly good word meaning a person who works outside their home country. We did need more information. Mr. Jenkins told us the "term" was six years, and we'd have a three-month furlough at the end of the first three years—*and* that we could come home permanently then if we wished to.

We were made to feel that we were wanted there—needed, even—and that the college would accommodate us. It was all quite exciting. We also knew we needed more information.

We thought, analyzed, and prayed for guidance. I felt a bit like Dr. Doolittle's pushmi-pullyu critter. Crucial considerations involved our children. When we came to Walla Walla in 1969, Jeff was three and a half and Kimberly only nine months, and this was the only home they'd known well. They would be faced with a new culture, hot and humid weather, widespread poverty, different foods, and a language and dialects unknown to them. Their formal schooling would be in small classes; informally, they would likely learn more about geography and culture than in Washington State. When they returned as teenagers, they would need to adjust to the US culture and schools. We knew some children have mixed experiences living abroad; they have a tag, MK (missionary kid), which means they might face some of the same problems and advantages of a PK (preacher's kid), such as positive and negative expectations.[13]

Memories intruded: we all loved the summers we spent at the biology station, snuggled in a tiny cabin on a picturesque bay in north Puget Sound. There was no guarantee that a position would be available for Dale at WWC when we returned. Also, our parents were all in their late sixties. My mom, four years past her breast cancer diagnosis, was dealing with metastasis to the bone. She was very active and doing well—and my parents were planning an eight-week trip to Europe. I'm an only child and didn't like the idea of our being far away from her. Already we were states apart, speaking often on the phone. I reasoned that looking forward to traveling to the RP to visit us, sending us "care packages" with items we couldn't find in the RP (e.g., chocolate chips), and knowing we were having an amazing adventure and missionary experience could be beneficial to her physical and emotional health, keeping her forward looking.

When I mentioned my mom's illness to Mr. Jenkins, he stunned me by saying, without hesitation, "Take her with you." I thanked him and said I didn't think my dad would appreciate that, explaining that they were settled and happy in Battle Creek, Michigan. He told us that the Global Mission office would help my parents and Dale's with

---

[13] Research reports mixed consequences for the kids, with a wide range of positives and negatives. https://www.dictionaryofchristianese.com/missionary-kid-m-k (Accessed February 11, 2024); there is even a special ministry for MKs: MK Ministries, said to exist "to minister to missionary kids by helping to reinforce them while on the field spiritually, socially and emotionally, reintegrate them smoothly into their 'home' culture, reestablish their foundations of faith, and reconnect those who have lost touch with others in the missionary community, while promoting spiritual enrichment in the life of all MKs, for the Glory of God" (Accessed February 11, 2024).

reduced-fare airline tickets so they could visit us. What a blessing!

We again scoured the college library and found Leon Wolff's book *Little Brown Brother*.[14] Stunned by the title, we believed it reflected an outdated perspective. Surely we would not have to deal with that kind of racism or xenophobia. We didn't even check out the book. That was unwise of us; we have it on our shelf now, and its information and insights could have helped us understand important aspects of early US–Filipino interactions, which continue to affect how Filipinos view American intervention.

"Jeff, Kimberly, your feelings are a very important part of our decision," we told our children in a serious discussion, "and we won't go if you don't want to." We shared what we knew: "There will be other American kids and an American teacher. We'll travel to different countries and see wonderful new things: Taiwan, Japan, animals, beaches. It can be a huge adventure!"

They thought a bit and said they wanted to go. Of course, at their ages, what could they really know or understand?

We filled out the lengthy application, answering questions about why we wanted to go overseas and what countries we'd prefer. The country was already decided for us based on Dra. Rasa's invitation. There were questions about what climates would be difficult for us and much detailed personal information; however, no psychological testing was required. That should have been included—not for us, of course, but for those *other* crazies who pick up and leave everything to move to a foreign country on the other side of the earth with small children.

References were required. Former friends and colleagues were asked about our professional capabilities, our financial responsibility, and our characters (some said yes, we were characters), and soon it was determined that we were appropriate material for an overseas assignment. And we decided to go. We are usually positive, so our reaction was "How exciting!" And then: "Oh my goodness, what have we done?"

---

[14] Leon Wolff. *Little Brown Brother: How the United States purchased and pacified the Philippine Islands at the century's turn* (New York, NY: Doubleday, 1961).

2020s Update:

—**Walla Walla College became Walla Walla University** (WWU) in 2007. It is one of 142 Seventh-day Adventist (SDA) colleges and universities worldwide. WWU historian Terrie Aamodt writes of how mission fields have changed and now have a broader meaning. Student volunteering includes service in domestic and foreign locations; they are known as "Christian service volunteers" and may be on assignment for a year or a few weeks (e.g. summer camp).

—**PUC, now Adventist University of the Philippines (AUP),** offers several degrees in their College of Science and Technology Program: biology, chemistry, engineering, library and information science, mathematics, and physics. There are six faculty in the Biology Department; one is an American.

—A lovely **elementary school** is now operating on the AUP campus.

— CHAPTER 3 —

The Other Side of the Earth and Traveling with Buckminster Fuller

Karen

"Coming out of your comfort zone is your biggest challenge."
—*Manoj Arora, Engineer*[15]

How do you decide what you will need for the next six years in a tropical country? We quickly had to consider 1) what to take, 2) what to do with the chickens, the horses, and the dog, 3) what to give away, 4) what to store, and 5) where to store it. And I'm well known for taking too much wherever I go.

While I was contemplating our options, we received an encouraging and helpful letter from Barbara Van Ornam, who identified herself as an American mom living on the PUC Silang campus. Her practical advice included the following:

- Bring clothes for hot and humid weather. They should be at least 65 percent cotton because the temperature will be in the nineties and the humidity about 85 percent year-round.
- Bring very few men's dress shirts. Most men wear the popular Philippine barong shirts, which you can buy in the markets and have made to your specifications very reasonably.

---

[15] Manoj Arora from *The Rat Race to Financial Freedom* Quotes, https://www.goodreads.com/author/quotes/7152775.Manoj_Arora (Accessed Mar. 21, 2024) https://www.goodreads.com/work/quotes/254708137-from-the-rat-race.

- Bring Simplicity or other dress pattern books. Material can be purchased at the markets, and local seamstresses or tailors will create the clothes for you, also very reasonably.
- Bring your favorite spices in jars with tight lids; garlic and ginger are available fresh.
- Bring Jell-O and packs of gum to give as gifts to hostesses and kids in the countries you'll visit in Asia.
- Don't bring wire hangers; they rust and stain your clothes.
- Bring sheets, pillow slips, lightweight blankets, dishes, pots and pans, silverware.
- Be sure to get lots of good Tupperware. It keeps the moisture and bugs under control.[16]

One huge consideration was whether to sell or rent out our home. We reasoned that if we sold it, our banked or invested money would be earning interest; and if we rented it, it would increase in value in the meantime. But how would the new carpeting, the carefully prepared landscaping, and our new family room survive if we rented it? If we kept property in the States, we realized we would need someone to oversee it.

The SDA Office of Global Missions sent us a letter with the form we were to sign and send back indicating we had sold our home. They reasoned that selling would mean one less thing to worry about far away in the States. And we decided: *That is what we will do.*

We sold our home and bought a fourplex at a favorable price, then left that new multiple-dwelling property in the capable hands of our friends Larry and Linda McCloskey. We completed a property management contract with them that spelled out the agreement for a monthly fee, including money for advertising and commissions for showing, renting, and managing the apartments. One more decision was taken care of. We did not reply to our sponsor's letter about selling; thankfully, they didn't pursue the issue.

---

[16] I often think of that recommendation when I take brown sugar, flour, or cornmeal out of my yellow/gold Tupperware containers still in use forty years later!

The father of our friend Andy Dressler worked at Subic Bay; Rosemary, Michelle, and Jamie would be coming to see them and us. They were some of our closest friends in College Place, and Andy, business teacher and businessman, offered to help us with tax issues while we were abroad.

Then, yet another phone call came from Mr. Johnson's office: "It will be necessary for you to attend the Missions Institute at Andrews University in Michigan."

"Great, we'd love to. What are the dates?"

"January 15 through February 28."

"Oh, that's a problem. We'll be beginning our second quarter here, and we're already going to miss the third quarter entirely. We can't leave the college in that kind of a bind. Sorry, we won't be able to attend."

"But you have to go. It's a requirement."

"Sorry, we just can't."

"Okay then."

So that potential time problem was solved, and we were relieved. Later we would be *very* sorry we didn't receive the benefit of that training. Previous missionaries, including Gottfried Oosterwal—professor, anthropologist, missionary, and director of the institute—taught the courses, and they knew what we would need to know. Topics included travel tips, culture shock, anthropology, sociology, geography, comparative belief systems, SDA history in that area, and much more. That kind of head start in learning how to live in and value a new culture and work effectively for the best long-term results could have helped us manage or avoid some culture shock experiences.[17]

We went back to the library for more books about the Philippines.[18] Most of what we found concerned US involvement there, beginning with Admiral Dewey's defeat of the Spanish forces in Manila Bay in

---

[17] It is no longer possible to go on an overseas assignment through our sponsor without attending that institute. See notes on cross-cultural training in the appendixes.

[18] Writing about the Philippines is easier today than researching it was then.

1898 and progressing to the American occupation and a bit about the Philippines gaining independence from the United States in 1946. We found no kid-friendly books about the Philippines.

Wolff's *Little Brown Brother* book would have helped us understand the history that brought about current attitudes. William Howard Taft, first governor-general of the Philippines (1901–1904) before he became the twenty-seventh president of the United States, is quoted as using the term. He suggested that "our little brown brothers" would likely need "fifty or one hundred years" of close supervision "to develop anything resembling Anglo-Saxon political principles and skills." Historian Stuart Creighton Miller, who uses the term "benevolent assimilation," describes the comment as "enlightened" for his time, while journalist Carmen N. Pedrosa calls it a reflection of "paternalist racism."[19] General MacArthur's initial reactions were not much kinder.[20] We found the attitudes appalling; surely things were better now.

We talked much too briefly with a historian on our campus, asking his perspective on the Philippines; his response was "Marcos is a benevolent dictator. And you're likely safe going there." We wish we'd spent more time quizzing him. Expecting to focus on teaching and service, we found those comments comforting and did not ask for more information. Today, perhaps, the Marcos regime might be labeled an "illiberal democracy"—where citizens can vote but are kept unaware of actions that take away rights and freedoms.[21]

It was a much happier experience reading *Flying Doctor of the Philippines*, about William Richli, an adventurer, innovator, craftsman, physician, and pilot who worked on the islands of Luzon

---

[19] Stuart Creighton Miller. *Benevolent Assimilation: The American Conquest of the Philippines, 1899-1903* (New Haven, Connecticut: Yale University Press, 1984); Carmen N. Pedosa, "Paternalist racism," *The Philippine Star,* September 20, 2009.

[20] Bob Welch. *Resolve: From the Jungles of WWII Bataan, the Epic Story of a soldier, a Flag, and a Promise Kept* (New York, New York: The Berkeley Publishing Group, 2012).

[21] Fareed Zakaria, "The Rise of Illiberal Democracy," Accessed February 11, 2024, https://fareedzakaria.com/columns/1997/11/01/the-rise-of-illiberal-democracy.

and Mindanao.[22] While under construction, the Adventist Manila Sanitarium and Hospital had been hit by a naval torpedo, which destroyed the elevator shaft. Dr. Richli rebuilt it.[23] He was dubbed "an angel of mercy, complete with wings" by some and was also known for being the "first individual to cross the Pacific in a solo flight in a single-engine plane."[24] Dale and I also read a book popular at the time about healing by psychic surgeons and other cautionary tales some called "cruel deceptions" of promised healing.

Decisions and packing continued, and we learned that our shipment wouldn't reach us for about three months after we arrived. I felt it was essential to make our house there feel like home, so I packed two large boxes with special items. In one I put the quilts Grandma Clayton had made for our kids; a leaded-glass cardinal to hang in my window given to me by my best friend, Nan; a sofa cushion hand-painted by Dale's sister Carol; and a pair of ceramic doves gifted to me by my mother. In the second box I placed basic cooking items, a set of dishes, tableware, and sheets and towels for four people, and then contacted the transportation coordinator and said we wanted the boxes air-freighted even if we had to pay for them.

"No problem," he said. "Actually, we could send the whole shipment by air freight for no more money than being shipped by sea."

"What? Really? Then why . . . ?"

"Because the man who will get your shipment through customs knows the right people to pay at the shipyard. He doesn't know the right people at the airport."

---

[22] Raymond H. Woolsey, *Flying Doctor of the Philippines* (Hagerstown, MD: Review and Herald Publishing, 1972). Note: R&H Publishing was absorbed by Pacific Press Publishing in 2014.

[23] When we lived there years after those events, the elevators had been working for a long time. Still, I thought about that torpedo story every time I rode the elevators, and especially the time I was stuck there for a short time. The others on the elevator, used to frequent "brownouts" in Manila, relaxed and planned to stay until it was fixed. I was due in a meeting on the third floor and said, "Let's try it again." That time it responded appropriately. Most of the time I took the stairs at the San!

[24] Mountain View College Facebook page: https://www.facebook.com/groups/200339663383734/.

Dale had mixed feelings about leaving WWC. In addition to his classes, he mentored several graduate students; it would be hard to leave them midproject. One student, Heather Roberts, had met Dale at an animal behavior convention. She was interested in his study of circadian rhythms and decided to attend WWC. They had been working on a project with bluegill fish she caught in the Columbia River. Heather came to our home with a gift: a beautiful glass oil lamp from her parents in Ohio, famous for its glassworks.

"My parents said they believe you are likely to have problems with electricity in the Philippines, so they've sent a way for you to always be able to read and study and see what you are eating." Thoughtful!

A few days before we left, WWC teachers Lucille and Carl Jones invited us for supper. Their family had been on the Baesa campus for several years in the 1940s. She told of finding shell casings on her kitchen window. "Our boys learned Tagalog and got along very well. In fact, John is teaching at the Far Eastern Division Seminary. His wife, Pat, is teaching in the nursing school; the girls are in the American school there. So, you'll get to know them." Dessert was mango ice cream to help us get in the mood for the exotic fruits we'd enjoy.

As our departure neared, we viewed Walla Walla Valley, our friends, our home, and our schools with a new perspective. When would we see them again? We asked friends to store items for us—books, furniture, art, my piano; and we arranged for the care of our three horses with three different friends. I was astounded they would commit to that care for three, possibly six years. The horses were a long-term investment, and we loved them: American quarter horse Trinket had been bred to a gorgeous Appaloosa and given us two foals. Apache Music ("Zeke"), now a beautiful young gelding, and our filly Sweet Music ("Sweetie") had each won first-place ribbons in different years at the Walla Walla County Fair. Dale had built a barn and corral for them. They were a treasured part of our family.

Friends offered to care for our apricot poodle, Pumpkin, until we got settled, and then they would ship her to us. Quite amazing! We sold our car, and early one morning we took a last look at our home as friends drove us to the Walla Walla airport.

About forty friends came to see us off and wish us well. Some were envious, some incredulous. All were encouraging. We were so touched to have them there, giving us final hugs and comments, especially "Keep in touch. We'll miss you!"

We flew north to Spokane on a twelve-passenger plane operated by Cascade Airlines—not a good omen—during terrible weather. We tipped and tilted and bounced and were jolted until we felt ill. Jeff said he was not sure he wanted to go on any more planes. Thankfully, the flight from Spokane to Chicago was much more comfortable, and we looked forward to two weeks of visits with family and friends.

Physical exams and immunizations were required, so while visiting Dale's parents, we went to their family doctor in Alpena, Michigan. Things were going well as the four of us gathered in an exam room for the procedures. Nine-year-old Kimberly came face-to-face with an intimidating needle—and slid to the floor in a dead faint. She woke up almost immediately and was confused for a bit, then went on with the injections and did just fine. She said she'd been dreaming about the Flintstones. However: "When I woke up, I felt I couldn't move, talk, or open my eyes. I could only hear the nurse—who lied about it *not* hurting—say to Mom and Dad that if it was okay, they'd give me a wake-up shot if I didn't come around soon on my own. I remember thinking: *Wake up! Wake up! Wake up! They don't know I'm trapped!*"

We reveled in the goodbye parties, luscious food, and warm hugs with friends and family in Killmaster and Battle Creek. Then, finally, we were leaving on our adventure.

One of my favorite photos from that time was taken at Chicago's O'Hare Airport: of Jeff in his silky, blue-and-white Dolphins football jacket and hat, silhouetted against the huge, plateglass windows, gazing at the immense Northwest Airlines DC-10 that would take us to San Francisco. Whenever I see that picture, I wonder what was going on in that twelve-year-old mind—what questions, what happy anticipation, what fears. The world was opening for all of us.

Our first stop was Hawaii, where we vacationed for several days, visiting the American cemetery, the beaches, the Blowhole, and pineapple plantations and eating our first papaya. In the airport, waiting to leave for Tokyo, we purchased the last American edition of *TIME* magazine we would see for a while. On the cover was a clever drawing of Buckminster Fuller, engineer, architect, and pioneer of the future. The artist had drawn the top of Fuller's head as a geodesic dome, which Fuller had helped popularize. Inside the front cover were photos of him being honored at the White House, along with many other *TIME*-cover honorees.

That China Airlines flight from Hawaii to Tokyo was the first of our many international trips, and we were excited. Dale and Jeff sat in the middle of the six-person center bank of seats; Kimberly and I were in the row behind them. We settled in and watched the film *Oh, God!* starring John Denver. When the movie ended, the elderly gentleman on my left, dressed in a three-piece tweed suit, asked, "Do you like John Denver?"

"Yes, very much," I said.

He then said, "He is my friend."

Yeah, right! I thought. The gentleman and I talked a bit more about who lived where—he the East Coast, we on the Northwest Coast.

He asked, "Do you know Robert Fuller?"

I said, "Sorry, I don't know him."

"Yep. Robert Fuller. He's my brother. He has a museum in Seattle."

"Ah, I love museums," I responded enthusiastically. "We'll be in the Philippines for three years, but when we get back to Seattle, I'll find and visit his museum."

"Have you ever heard of Buckminster Fuller?" he then asked.

"Yes! Definitely! The man who created the geodesic dome!" And I turned to look at him more directly.

"Yep! That's me."

Wait, what? I'm talking to the *Buckminster Fuller!*

"Oh my! I'm so pleased to meet you."

We began a delightful and animated conversation; I excused myself for a moment to nudge Dale and Jeff in the seats ahead of us, urging them and Kimberly to listen carefully. I introduced them. We talked about his island on the East Coast, his windmills, his ideas about energy. We pulled out our *TIME* magazine, and he signed the cover and drew a sketch depicting one of his upcoming design ideas. And he showed us his four watches: one in each vest pocket, one on each wrist.

"So I know the time on my island, the time where my daughter lives, the time zone I've just left, and the time in Japan, where I'm going to give my lecture." And he asked what we would do when we finished our overseas assignment.

"We hope to go back to Washington State and maybe build our own home. I love to design houses," I said. "My dad is an engineer, and he taught me how to draw to scale. It's been a hobby of mine since I was thirteen."

Mr. Fuller urged us not to make too many detailed plans before we got back.

"The world and the possibilities will change so much between now and when you get back home," he said. "Just wait. It's going to be very exciting!"

Our sponsor, the SDA World Church, was very generous and encouraged us to visit SDA schools and hospitals on our trip east. They provided a week of room and board in Yokohama, Japan, and in Taipei, Taiwan, and we enjoyed museums, temples, restaurants, and shops. We were shocked to see armed guards at the Taiwan beaches, in Taiwan highway tunnels, and elsewhere; the folks there were on constant guard against Chinese invasion. It was 1978.

Those explorations gradually introduced us to Asia. We learned how to use public transportation and order meals while not understanding the language and began to understand more about the Far East.

Far East: "far" from where? Far from America, the center of our world, of course. It was all otherworldly and thrilling.

2020s Update

—**The Institute of World Missions** sessions are offered three times annually in either the US, Thailand, or Turkey. The "missionaries are introduced to a variety of resources, tools and activities that develop skills and attitudes" about working with various people groups.[25] Age-appropriate orientation for MKs is held concurrently with the institute. Online courses and reentry retreats are also offered. Workers are required to attend.

—**The people of Taiwan continue to be wary of the threats from China**, which sees three roads to unification: persuasion, coercion, and compelling "unification through direct military action."[26]

—**The Manila Sanitarium and Hospital (MSH), now Adventist Medical Center Manila,** was opened as a clinic in 1919 by Dr. Horace A. Hall, a medical missionary. The MSH School of Nursing opened in 1930, the first School of Medical Technology in 1954, and the School of Medical Arts in 1993. The mission is "Sharing Jesus Christ's Healing Ministry."[27]

—**R. Buckminster Fuller** was an engineer, architect, inventor, and futurist. Primarily remembered as the popularizer of the geodesic dome, he was an early environmentalist. President Reagan awarded him the Presidential Medal of Freedom.

---

[25] Institute of World Missions (IWM); provides cross-cultural training for SDA personnel working outside their cultural milieu. https://www.instituteofworldmission.org/mission-institute/ (Accessed February 11, 2024).

[26] Dan Blumenthal and Fred Kagan, "China has three roads to Taiwan: The US must block them all," *The Hill*, March 13, 2023, https://thehill.com/opinion/national-security/3896916-china-has-three-roads-to-taiwan-the-us-must-block-them-all/.

[27] Adventist Medical Center Manila - About https://www.amcmanila.org (Accessed February 11, 2024).

CHAPTER 4

New Country, New Campus, New Home

Karen

> *"Travel is fatal to prejudice, bigotry, and narrow-mindedness. . . . Broad, wholesome, charitable views of men and things cannot be acquired by vegetating in one little corner of the earth."*
>
> —Mark Twain in *The Innocents Abroad*

Even the oppressive heat and humidity were exciting as we descended onto the hot black tarmac and continued to the main terminal at Manila International Airport. We collected our luggage, adding it to our carry-ons, then walked into the enormous public reception area and beheld dozens of cardboard signs with travelers' names printed in large letters, held by taxi drivers, family members, friends, and sweethearts. And there, surrounded by twenty beautiful, smiling faces, was *our* sign: WELCOME CLAYTON!

Dra. Rasa, already a friend and now Dale's biology chairperson, said, "Welcome, welcome! Thanks to God for your safe trip. These are our teachers from Biology and Nursing. It's good you are here! Come, our ride is just there," gesturing with her chin toward a small white bus outside.

The welcoming words, the smiling faces, and the sweet, enthusiastic greetings were a joy! We thanked them. But I couldn't help thinking, *It's so hot!* I'd never felt such wet heat. It was oppressive, smothering, just as we'd been warned. Ray Holmes, an American colleague, writes about his arrival, "I felt like I'd had a wet blanket thrown over me; it was hard to breathe."[28] Jeff remembers it as "a full-body punch"!

Trying to ignore our moist underarms, we focused on our hostesses as they corralled us and our wide-eyed children into the, thankfully, air-conditioned minibus. They were happy and proud to tell us the Nursing Department had loaned it so they could bring us to campus in comfort. "It's the best vehicle at PUC," they told us. I found it comforting that almost everybody around me was my height (five feet) or shorter.

The driver headed toward a wide expanse of water, and someone said: "Manila Bay! So beautiful! *Maralig*!"

We knew it was a natural bay off the South China Sea—one of the best-known and best-loved features of the Philippines and one of the world's great harbors. Very soon, we were on Roxas Drive, a wide boulevard paralleling the shore. Through the tall palms we saw at least a dozen huge ships waiting to dock. Our companions pointed out the buildings of the Cultural Center of the Philippines Complex. They said, "Imelda Marcos had it built on land reclaimed from the sea."

A vast, well-manicured park sprawled along the other side of the road. I blurted out, "That statue must be Rizal!" Our hosts expressed shock and amazement that I knew about their national hero, José Rizal. Of course, I could have let them tell me. Perhaps I should have, but I wanted to impress and was excited to connect printed information with reality.

Just before we turned off the boulevard, someone pointed out the elegant Manila Hotel, telling us that it was designed by an American architect hired by President Taft and that General MacArthur and his family had lived there.[29]

---

[28] C. Raymond Holmes, *Boiled Rice and Gluten* (Self-published, 1972).
[29] The man hired by William Howard Taft was New York City architect William El Parsons; it is said he envisioned California mission-style architecture. Taft was the twenty-seventh US president from 1909 to 1913. MacArthur and his family lived in the penthouse throughout his time in the Philippines during World War II.

Then we were on busy city streets, surrounded by noisy vehicles—buses, cars, bicycles, and tricycles. Horns blared and music played from inside the brightly colored jeeps running alongside us. My first sight of a jeepney! I'd read about these leftovers from WWII, repurposed for travel everywhere in the Philippines. I briefly wondered—thankfully to myself—what the brown cloth objects with straps and stiff, cuplike things hanging from the roof of a cart parked on the sidewalk road were, then recognized their purpose. *Of course, bras! Bras for Filipinas!*

Tiny shops lined the city streets. These were not for tourists; most were fitted with roll-up metal doors now fully open to the sidewalks packed with people. The whirl of colors and crafts displayed in the sidewalk shops, restaurants, and vendors' carts was intriguing: woven baskets of all sizes, batik tablecloths, colorful dresses for adults and children, and pastel-colored men's shirts with elaborate embroidery down the front. Vibrant fruits, vegetables, and woven strings of garlic were abundant.

Our hostesses pointed out some features of their enormous capital city of eight million, and, yes, that *was* a hog with a pole skewered through its snout and out the other end, hoisted over a roaring fire, juices dripping.[30]

"Ah, *inihaw na* suckling *baboy*. Roasting baby pig!" the sweet young woman beside me said with embarrassed giggles. It was a given that they didn't eat it themselves because their religion—our religion—forbids the indulgence in pork.

After about forty minutes of slow inner-city driving, our little bus turned left onto a two-lane street with gray, cement-block buildings close to the road on both sides. These were primarily homes above small shops—all with windows open to the heat and the noise of the many people living so closely together. The sounds were somewhat

---

[30] The hog turns rotisserie fashion and roasts for several hours, usually producing a very crisp skin. The term the woman uses in the next sentence above conveys the idea of a suckling pig, but adult pigs are also used.

muted inside the bus, but we still heard horns honking from small trucks and jeepneys, children laughing, babies crying, customers talking with shop owners, pots and pans clanking in cafés and tiny markets known as *sari-sari* stores. I was told the phrase means "variety." The houses and shops continued to our right. To our left appeared a tall cement block wall. Suddenly we were driving through a gate, past the campus guardhouse and uniformed men with conspicuous guns.

Our hostesses announced, "We are here. Welcome to PUC!"

Guns are a mystery to me. I think the guards were holding rifles, but there were also smaller guns (pistols or revolvers, I assumed) in holsters hanging just below their waists. We already knew Manila had been under martial law since 1972. The regulations were reportedly less restrictive now, though; there was no longer a curfew, and habeas corpus was in place again, so there had to be actual charges before folks were arrested and imprisoned. Still, I had noticed armed, uniformed men outside shops on our drive through the main streets and was surprised to see them at the school. We learned this was one of only two points in the walled campus where persons could legally enter or leave.

The sight was jarring, and I felt a pinprick of fear. Twelve-year-old Jeffrey found the scene intriguing; Kimberly, busy chatting with the lady next to her, didn't seem to notice. Dale and I exchanged looks, silently agreeing to talk with the children about the guards and the guns later.

The campus felt like a quiet oasis, with flowering shrubs, tall palms, and many other varieties of trees. There were beautiful, weathered, one- and two-story wooden buildings. The bus stopped, and we were escorted upstairs to a sizable second-story room. Someone told us it was the only air-conditioned one on campus. Many people awaited us there, along with an unbelievable spread of food.

We first met PUC's president, Dr. Alfonso Roda, his beautiful wife, Lydia, and then other faculty and staff. Hands reached out to hold ours, and folks greeted us enthusiastically. So many warm and welcoming people. *Lovely*, I thought. *It feels like we are in another world.* It seemed strange to be the center of all that attention, wanting and needing to do and say the right things.

After many warm greetings and much delicious food—fruits, vegetables, pancit, lumpia, and much more, all well prepared and artfully displayed—our entourage urged us back onto the bus. We rode under tall palms and flowering bushes and past several wooden structures forming the campus: a store, two-story classrooms, labs, administrative buildings, and homes. A shift in scenery occurred as we drove through the opening of a fenced area, no gate, into the world of the overseas workers: the missionaries, the foreigners—us. *Dayuhan* is Tagalog for "foreigner, alien, immigrant." I don't remember being called dayuhan, but we would grow accustomed to *Kano*, shortened from "Americano."

Colossal trees and sprawling yards on our left surrounded three one-story, pastel-colored, cement-block homes. Ominously, the fourth home down that gentle slope was missing its roof and doors. We were told that over the course of a few months, the pipes, doors, windows, electrical wires, and other features had disappeared. An open field lay to our right.

"The campus has been sold to a company that is converting it to a cemetery," one of our companions explained. "Then we will be moving to the new campus." She gestured across the field toward two large, rather modern buildings. "Those are the Philippine Publishing House and the Food Factory, and"—pointing to the left—"this is your home."[31]

The little bus turned into the driveway of the third house, its many floor-to-ceiling windows protected by white burglar bars. We entered, and—*Delightful!*—it was cooler inside, thanks partly to smooth, cool, terrazzo floors, high ceilings hung with slowing-turning fans, and the screened windows.

---

[31] Now called Country Vegefoods, Inc., and situated in Bgy. Putingkahoy, Sillang, Cavite. https://www.facebook.com/people/Country-Vegefoods-Inc/1000640 (Accessed February 12, 2024).

"This room is your *sala*," our new friend Tessie said.

"That means 'living room,'" Dra. Rasa explained.

It was large and furnished with cushioned rattan furniture. To one side was a huge dining room table and chairs. *Oh my goodness! There's also an organ! Surely that's not ours.* On the far wall, a set of French doors opened into a large, tiled room with more floor-to-ceiling screened windows on three sides. Lining the edges of the tile floor were planters filled with lush ferns, small palms, and colorful flowers. There was no furniture on the porch. *That's going to be my dining room*, I mused.

The kitchen and bathroom were very nice, with all the needed appliances and many cupboards, also floor to ceiling; the bedrooms were off a hallway, each quite large, airy, and comfortable with overhead fans; there was a box air conditioner in one window of the master bedroom. We all walked back down the hall to the kitchen, through a screened door, and down two steps into the one-car garage with a washer and dryer. We were told that the little room in the left back corner was the helper's room. We'd already decided we would not have servants; it seemed too upper class to our American mindset.

Maybe Dale can use this for an office, I thought.

"The water heater is not working," someone said. "But Mr. Malagat will be by to fix it very soon."

I didn't feel the need for hot water anytime soon. Cold water to drink was what I wanted—and a cool bath. After the entire welcoming committee proudly showed us through our beautiful new home, they prepared to leave so we could settle in.

"We will all be back with a potluck dinner after church on Sabbath," Dra. Rasa explained: "An American family, the Kleins, with a boy and a girl, live next door, but they are on a three-month furlough in the States. A Canadian family, the Knellers, is living there for the summer. The elementary teacher for the American children lives in that first house."

Yes, the pastel-pink cement-block palace.

Dra. Rasa continued: "One of the rooms there is used for the school. She's away right now, too. You'll meet the other overseas families soon. They have already moved to the new campus being built thirty miles outside Manila."

Dra. Rasa shared some important information: "Dale, you will be teaching mostly on this Baesa campus, and two days a week you will commute to the Silang campus. Someone will drive you the first week; you will drive yourself there after that. Soon the entire school will be operating on the Silang campus."

This information about another campus was entirely new to us.

"But you must see the Biology Department and your office," she continued. "You both meet me there tomorrow at 10 a.m. Just go back through the gate. Someone will direct you."

We thanked them all profusely for meeting us at the airport, bringing us to the campus, and for the marvelous meal. Then they left. Dale and the kids investigated the house and yard. The first thing I wanted to do was take a cool bath. I started the water in the large tub and went to find fresh clothes. When I returned, I saw, swimming on the surface of the water, hundreds of variously sized, glistening cockroaches. They must have crawled out of the drainpipe when the water began flowing. I *hate* cockroaches. Who doesn't? But I scooped them out the best I could and climbed in.[32] Yes, the weather and the bathroom were *that hot*, and I was so sticky, and the bath was refreshingly cool. The ambient heat had taken the chill off the water before it left the pipes. It was just what I needed! Most of the cockroaches skittered out of sight. *We'll deal with them later*, I thought.

The children settled into their rooms with the few things we'd carried with us on the plane, and after my cool bath, I unpacked my suitcases. Late in the afternoon, our Canadian neighbors, the Knellers, came to the house and invited us for supper. What a delight and a blessing it was getting acquainted with them. During

---

[32] The cockroach problem went away for the most part; we did see a lot of geckos on the walls and ceilings.

the school year, they lived in Singapore at the Far Eastern Academy, a grades 9–12 boarding school for SDA missionary kids from all around the Far East. Ralph taught biology, and Marie taught home economics and was the girls' dean part-time. They had two children, Julie, age eight, and Jimmy, age six, which meant Kimberly would have English-speaking children to play with.

"We're here just for our summer holiday," Marie said. Ralph explained that each summer, he volunteered to help one of the Adventist campuses in the Far East. He continued, "I'm working on both Baesa and Silang campuses. About thirty other Americans are out there at the new campus. Some of them are a part of Philippine Union College, some teach at the Far Eastern Seminary there, some are helping to plan and construct buildings on that campus, and one, Don Van Ornam, is the business manager."

Good to know.

"It's thirty miles to the new campus," Marie said. "First you go back down Balibago Road, then take the main highway skirting Metro Manila; then you hit the dirt roads with their bumps and holes and travel through several interesting barrios. It takes ninety minutes to get there! Yes, ninety minutes to go thirty miles. Each way, of course."

We asked about living under martial law with armed guards.

Ralph said they had gotten used to that. "Not to worry! We've found it doesn't affect our lives much. And it's likely a good thing. There have been incidents on campus which make people fearful, like people climbing over the wall to get fruit from our trees. Then they have opportunities to take other things, too. I don't know of any stealing from houses. We are having a good holiday—working and having time to travel. I'll take you on some jeepney adventures."

The next morning, Dale and I walked to the main campus to meet Dra. Rasa at the Biology Department. Everything felt new and exciting. The trees and flowers were gorgeous. Students we passed greeted us: "Hello, ma'am. Hello, sir." In their pronunciation of "ma'am," the "a" sounded like "ah," so it sounded like they were saying "Mom." *That will take some getting used to*, I thought.

Dra. Rasa awaited us outside a large wooden structure.

"Good morning. Here is your classroom. It has lots of big open windows so you can stay cool," she said with a twinkle in her eye.

It was 10 a.m., and already the air was hot, and so were we. And indeed there were many huge windows—and no glass panes or wooden shutters.

"You can see we have nice, big, overhanging eaves that keep out most of the rain and some of the wind. The winds can be big, and the air blowing through can be a blessing."

We had already learned as much during our Eastern Washington summers, when we drank hot tea to feel a bit cooler. Anticipating the heat, we had brought tea with us and planned on following the example of the British, who, when in India, drank lots of hot tea to speed the personal "air-conditioning" process, stimulating perspiration to better appreciate the breeze from handheld or overhead fans.

She guided us inside: "These tables are for classes and labs. And"—she lifted her chin and pursed her lips, using them to point toward a door to the side of the classroom—"just there is the lab setup room. That little building out to the side is for storage of specimens."[33]

"Dale, your office is just there," she said, again using the chin gesture, and led us from the main class building to a smaller two-story structure, up one flight of worn, narrow stairs, and into a tiny room. The room was crowded with all three of us inside. A small desk, a straight-backed wooden chair, and a couple of simple, wall-hung shelves for books were the only furnishings. We heard people talking and what sounded like kitchen utensils rattling. Following the sounds, we walked to an open window and looked down. This building was tucked between the biology building and a portion of

---

[33] Soon we adopted the efficient chin gesture, often saying, as she did, "Just there [points chin] is the kitchen."

the ten-foot-high wall surrounding the campus. On the other side of the wall were small, rough lean-tos made of board planks, metal sheets, cardboard, and occasionally pieces of plywood. The campus wall served as the only solid part of their small homes.

"Your neighbors—squatters."

The family just below heard us, looked up, and smiled broadly as they waved: "*Magandang umaga*, sir, ma'am." (Good morning.)

We smiled and waved back. I vowed that next time I'd reply with the appropriate greeting. Back downstairs, we sat at one of the classroom's long wooden tables, and Dra. Rasa continued her introduction to teaching biology in the Philippines:

"When students come to PUC, most are age sixteen. They have had six years of mandatory and free primary school. The ones who come here are the lucky ones. They have also been through high school, grades seven through ten. Parents in the Philippines have to pay tuition for anything after grade six; it's about two hundred pesos [USD 23], and most just cannot do that. Our students are very motivated. Most expect to be doctors, nurses, or lab techs, and their parents, brothers, sisters, and sometimes cousins help them financially. Then these students help the next generation."

Drs. Rasa explained, "You will be teaching the Anatomy and Physiology class here, and we have decided that Ms. Perez, who has been teaching the class and the lab, will be your lab instructor. She knows where to get the supplies. She will also be attending your class as she has been wanting 'upgrading,' and she will learn from you. It has all been decided."

On the way home, Dale and I talked about the challenges we had seen and heard. We were startled that the kids' parents had to pay for high school and most couldn't afford it. The lab-instructor arrangement sounded interesting but unclear. What did "upgrading" mean to Ms. Poblano? When teachers went for "upgrading," they typically went to the States to get a degree. Did Ms. Poblano know about those plans? Did she agree? Did she have a choice?

As promised, after church that first Sabbath, our Filipino Biology faculty friends and their families brought lunch to our house. The food was incredible, and our new friends were warm and welcoming. They spoke English, except they kept slipping naturally into Tagalog or another dialect. Wanting to keep it light, I said, "Ah, I want to know, too. English, please!" They would laugh and happily go back to their excellent English. I asked for help with some of the new words so I could better fit in.

As we talked about education, someone explained, "All children begin school at age five in their local dialect; the second year, they begin to learn Tagalog, and the third year they begin English. All schooling throughout the country is meant to be in English after grade school. Still, it's easy to slip back into our own dialect or Tagalog."

◆ ◆ ◆

Dale got acquainted with the textbooks he'd use, checked out the lab equipment and supplies, and worked with the Filipino staff to learn how to find what was needed. The kids kept busy with friends; there was no school for a few weeks yet. Kimberly stayed near home with Julie and Jimmy Kneller, and Jeff explored the campus and the field between our home and the Publishing House and Food Factory.

One day, Jeff came home and announced: "I got a job at the bakery!"

"Do they know you are twelve?"

"Yep!"

"What do you do?"

"Today I picked the bugs out of the flour they use to make bread."

2020s Updates

—**Manila International Airport became Ninoy Aquino International Airport** (NAIA) in 1987, renamed after a politician who was murdered at the airport in 1983. Often the name is shortened to Manila Airport. Aquino's wife, Corazon, was president from 1986 to 1992. Before COVID, the airport was handling almost 50,000,000 passengers annually.[34]

—**The Publishing House**[35] **is still located in Caloocan City, near the previous Baesa campus; it serves the South Asia-Pacific Division of SDAs.**[36]

—**The Food Factory is now called Country Vegefoods** and is located in Silang, Cavite.[37]

—**The Philippines is one of fourteen countries in the Southern Asia-Pacific Division of the SDA Church**; the membership is 1.3 million, worshipping in more than 7,000 churches; there are 1,000 languages and dialects.[38]

---

[34] https://www.miaa.gov.ph/index.php/announcements/press-releases/naia-sets-all-time-flight-record-in-2023-passenger-volume-recovers-to-95-of-pre-pandemic
[35] http://www.adventist.asia/information/institutions/north-philippine-union-conference/philippine-publishing-house/ (Accessed February 14, 2024).
[36] http://www.adventist.asia/information/departments/services (Accessed February 14, 2024).
[37] https://www.facebook.com/people/Country-Vegefoods-Inc/1000640 (Accessed February 12, 2024).
[38] https://adventist.asia (Accessed February 12, 2024).

CHAPTER 5

Mamaya Means "By and By"

Dale

"I consider myself a good hand at carpentry, plumbing and other sorts of household repairs, but Mr. Malagit broadened my vistas."

—Dale

Early on the first morning, there was a solid knock on the front door of our new home. A diminutive older man with a broad smile and a large pipe wrench stood at our door and bowed almost imperceptibly. On his head was a frayed, broad-brimmed straw hat that had seen much sun and rain. On his face was a smile that almost made me forget how early it was.

"I feeks you water tonk, sir."*

"At this hour?"

"Yes, sir! I feeks it now."

"Sure, let's have a look at it," I said. "It is in the garage. My name is Dale."

"And my name, sir, is Mr. Malagit. My girl, she been States a'ready, sir. You know where Cee-cago?"

"Sure, the Windy City—very big. Very busy city. What does your daughter do in Chicago?"

"Oh, sir, she nurse. She bery busy, sir."

The garage was soon filled with humming, whistling, and the

scuff of worn sandals, but it would be several days before we could enjoy hot showers.

It was too early for me to be up and too late to go back to bed, so I watched Mr. Malagit work. Age had bent him, but I don't think he had ever stood taller than five feet. I estimated his weight at no more than 110 pounds, fully clothed and toting his pack of plumber's tools, which says as much about the lack of tools as about his size. I consider myself a good hand at carpentry, plumbing, and other sorts of household repairs, but Mr. Malagit broadened my vistas. From somewhere he drew a freshly cut stick and marked distances that represented spaces between the shut-off valve and the coupling, then between the coupling and the point where he imagined the first elbow would go. Then, as unexpectedly as he had appeared, he turned and said, "I be bok *mamaya*." I learned that "mamaya" means "by and by"; it was a word with which I would become much too familiar.

If we ignored the lack of hot water, the house was very nice. It provided fewer creature comforts than the rather average house we had left in Walla Walla, Washington, but it was of a caliber and luxury that only the upper middle class in Filipino society could expect. A Filipino professor had occupied it before our arrival, and he left his mark in subtle ways. For starters, the water heater had been removed, and this kindly old gent was promising to replace it for us. Hot water was simply too expensive for most Filipinos—even most college professors. A water heater could easily burn up 80 to 100 pesos (USD 10 to 14) per month in electricity, roughly 10 percent of a Filipino full professor's monthly salary at PUC in 1978.

Mr. Malagit returned as we were clearing our breakfast dishes from the table, and with him came two short pieces of pipe. Both pieces were spattered with paint of different colors and vintages; they were unquestionably veterans. The apertures had narrowed with rust and scale, but the threads were bright and new. Our installation was underway.

Additional pipes and fittings required additional trips to the shop. The measuring stick became a thing of beauty, a work of art, as the pencil of the morning gave way to the pen of the afternoon, leaving red and green inks interspersed with lead markings. Extra trips were necessary to check and recheck measurements over the days. He worked slowly and kept up a running conversation. He was a master of the patch-up job. I would meet these traits time and again in a variety of other situations, and they never ceased to offend my American value system and to deepen the sense of culture shock. The shock was intensified by the knowledge that my drive for efficiency and quality often offended the Filipino value system and was at times counterproductive.

A couple of days later, Mr. Malagit came again, shut-off valve in hand. The skin on his fingers was cracked and worn, but those fingers were expressive and fluid as he explained, "Destroyed a'ready. No more good. We need new *bahlbe* [valve]."

Getting the new valve consumed the morning that day. When the job was finally completed, Mr. Malagit stood in the kitchen with a smile that put lights in his large dark eyes.

He addressed Kay: "All done, ma'am. Now you habe hot water."

The smile grew broader and brighter.

"Wonderful!" she said, and the smiles matched. I knew she itched (literally) to dash off and bask in the luxury of the long-expected hot water, but she said, "You need something cold to drink."

"Yes, ma'am." And as they sat enjoying their cool drinks, I went to the garage to inspect the plumbing, then came back to suggest to the dear man: "Mr. Malagit, you forgot to connect the electricity."

"No worry. I tell Mr. Espiritu."

"Who is Mr. Espiritu?"

"He 'lectrician! He hook it up. He bery bery good. He do bery good job."

Turning to Kay, Mr. Malagit asked: "How many keeds, ma'am?"

"We have two kids. Jeffrey is twelve, and Kimberly is nine."

"Only two? You need habe more. You make baby in de Pilipines.

When you go home, you say, 'Dis one made in da Pilipines!'" (Much laughing.) "My daughter in States, she got two keeds. Dey both made in Amireca." (More laughing.) "Dey needs more babies, but dey got family planning a'ready."

Mr. Malagit had worked in the house for several days and was fully aware of our two very active children. His attempt at light, pleasant conversation reflected his culture's penchant for large families.

This dear man had retired several years earlier but continued to work every day in the college maintenance shop. He told us he would retire again, "mamaya" (by and by). "But right now," he said, "Dey needs me." His eleven children had all graduated from college, and he continued to pay other students' tuition. He was a delightful, gracious, cultured Filipino gentleman.

*Note: I write what I heard. Mr. Malagit's pronunciation reflects how Filipinos pronounce vowels. When he said, "I feeks your water tonk, sir," the "i" in "fix" was pronounced as our American "e," and the "a" in tank was pronounced "ah." This is how I heard it as I was trying to understand. I mean no disrespect.

CHAPTER 6

New Ways to Do Things

Karen

"The real voyage of discovery consists not in seeking new landscapes, but in having new eyes."

—Paraphrase of Merced Proust, Novelist, Critic, and Essayist

Thanks to Dra. Rasa's planning, our pleasantly green kitchen cupboards and refrigerator had been stocked just before we arrived with a few basic groceries. And the two large boxes I'd sent ahead—mostly kitchen supplies and linens—had already arrived by air freight. Our second day in-country, I arranged the kitchen and linen cupboards.

The third day in-country dawned, we had breakfast, and the day warmed up. The heat and humidity were oppressive, overwhelming. *It's so hot!* I felt flushed. I had not understood the importance of cotton clothing and so brought what I already owned: short-sleeved blouses, polyester. That had seemed practical to me. No ironing, right? Right, but no airflow either. *Hot, hot, hot—so hot, so humid!*

Midmorning, the sender of that helpful list of what to bring and not bring, Barbara Van Ornam, arrived unexpectedly. What a lovely surprise! I learned she was a longtime missionary, a nurse, who had birthed and raised five daughters on mission in Africa, had lived several years on this Baesa campus, and now lived on that mysterious "other campus" in Silang, Cavite.[39] She hadn't phoned, because she couldn't; there were *no phones*—no personal phones, no campus phones, no phones in campus offices or faculty or staff homes.

"I know this visit is a surprise," she said. "I wanted us to meet, and I'm here to take you to some markets for food and for cotton clothes. We'll get acquainted as we drive and shop."

Kimberly was occupied with the Kneller kids next door, and Jeff was exploring the campus and fields. I told them I was going with Mrs. Van Ornam and left a note for Dale so he'd know to fix lunch for himself and the kids.

Barbara drove us to a nearby sari-sari store, a small neighborhood variety store selling basic supplies—flour, oil, bread, SkyFlakes crackers, some fresh food, some canned goods, and myriad tiny plastic bags filled with crackers, chips, nuts, and candies.

She explained: "You'll need to cook with coconut oil. The only other choice is that huge square tin of lard.[40] You'll buy most of your fresh fruits and vegetables at Balintawak market, also nearby. And, yes, that banana catsup is quite good!"

We walked all the aisles, and suddenly—*How wonderful!*—something I recognized: a jar of Miracle Whip! There were even canned vegetables, and I purchased canned peas. *This isn't going to be so bad*, I thought.

"Now we're finding you some cool clothes. The place I like is Pistang Pilipino in Manila. It's a popular tourist destination, with many shops—colorful and fun with practical things at reasonable prices!"

The Pistang Pilipino (Philippine Festival) market downtown was delightful! Dozens of booths sold crafts, carvings, paintings, and baskets. I love baskets, and I purchased the first of what would become a collection. On the wall beside me as I write is a sweet painting I bought that first day, depicting the face of a tiny Filipino

---

[39] Barbara was an RN with an MA in public health, excellent background for helping others and her own family in a mission environment.
[40] It's a given that Adventists don't use lard.

child. I smile with pleasure whenever I look at it. And the market had so much clothing: high stacks of tiny dresses delicately embroidered, barongs (the men's embroidered dress shirts), and women's blouses and dresses, some in batik, all 100 percent cotton. I bought cotton blouses for Kimberly and myself, delighted by the handiwork of the Filipinas. Each time I talked to a clerk, they smiled broadly and automatically handed me items in "American size." The size was always too large, and I explained, "Ah, but I'm Filipina size!" They giggled and found me just the right size.

We bought a light-blue barong for Dale of finely woven cotton (sometimes made of kapok, fiber from a native tree). The most expensive ones were of silk or pineapple fiber, and these were see-through. Barbara explained, "The men wear a T-shirt under those." They all boasted multiple rows of machine embroidery on either side of the buttons, an embellishment considered manly and vital for the well-dressed gentleman. Dale needed one this week as Dr. Roda was going to interview him during Friday-evening Vespers.

"Barbara, thank you so much! This was a good day! One of the best things was just getting to know you—another American woman living here!" And I thought, more importantly: *She will be a good role model and a friend.*

"We'll have you come to the house for lunch soon," she said as she left to drive the thirty miles (ninety minutes) back to Silang.

That evening I prepared potatoes, some sort of protein, and heated the canned peas for supper. They looked so good on the label, but they were terrible—hard, tasteless, disgusting. We were disappointed and did not finish them. Thank goodness I had also bought fresh fruit to fill us up.

The kitchen was terrific. Still, cooking was a challenge. Fresh fruits and vegetables needed to be soaked in water with bleach, though things we could peel (papaya, carrots, potatoes) just required rinsing. The bleaching precaution affected the taste of the food. *Yuk!* We had to boil our drinking water, cautious about bacteria our bodies were not used to. It took time to make cold water available: we had to 1) boil it, 2) cool it, 3) put the boiled water in the trays in the freezer, then 4) wait for it to freeze, and 5) use ice to chill our drinking water. It was a never-ending process because—did I mention?—it was hot. The heat and humidity affected our energy, and to help balance that, we wanted and needed lots of water.

Jeff continued working a few hours a week after the Baesa campus teacher, Mrs. Thorn, arrived and school began. Mrs. Thorn was part of our church's SOS program: sustantees overseas.[41] She was an eighty-year-old retired teacher, volunteering for two years. We were reminded of the small world of being a Seventh-day Adventist: Mrs. Thorn's son John had been the principal of Rogers Elementary in College Place, Washington, where both Jeff and Kimberly began elementary school!

It was hard to know what to cook. I was occupied learning about the house, the water, the heat, what to wear, and how to be by myself most of the day after the kids started school, as well as trying to understand the customs, learn a few words of Tagalog, and successfully settle into living here for three years, maybe six.

One morning, I woke up crying.

What's wrong? I wondered. I cried awhile and reasoned that tomorrow would be better. Nothing was really wrong. *I'm just homesick. That's reasonable.* And I got over it by midday. The next day came, and I woke up crying again. And the next morning, it definitely was not okay. *No, please, I don't want to be sad.*

Every morning now, I woke up crying. I felt lost, homesick, my stomach aching, a feeling almost like fear. And it was always *hot*! I thought about my mom and regretted leaving her to deal with her cancer without me. *What's wrong with me? I'm an only child. I shouldn't have come*, I thought.

---

[41] Sustantees overseas (SOS) was the term for retired SDA employees who volunteered overseas. The current term is Adventist Volunteer Service for folks serving between one and twenty-four months for specific priority needs. https://www.adventistvolunteers.org/short-term/ (accessed February 13, 2024).

I apologized to Dale, to the kids. I was so frustrated with myself. I'd wanted this adventure. I wanted to be in the Philippines, wanted to like it. The first euphoria at everything being different and new and exciting when a person arrives in a new country is called the honeymoon period. Unfortunately, that didn't last long for me!

I talked to myself: *We are so fortunate. We have so much to make us comfortable. I have to get it together! I'll be fine.* I prayed. Morning crying continued. I tried to keep busy. Usually, by lunchtime, I was better. That pit in my stomach had dissipated. I would thank God the lousy feeling was gone and think, *So, this is what culture shock is like!*

Dale had a good idea: when his schedule permitted, after lunch, he and I would walk to the campus gate and take a jeepney into town for an hour or so. That was a huge help. We saw so many fascinating things. Still, when the next morning came, I woke up crying. *Discouraging, embarrassing, disgusting!* I had to stop this!

◆ ◆ ◆

On the second Sabbath, I chose to not wear hose or a slip under my dress (a social requirement when attending church in the US at that time). Who would know? It was just *too hot*, and it was fun to rebel a little. We sat on wooden slat benches a few rows from the front, and I stretched my bare sandaled feet out under the bench in front of us, hoping for a breeze. Church was being held under a shed roof with air wafting in from the sides.

I quietly made friends with a tiny child standing on the bench in front of us. Facing me, she smiled shyly and giggled. Then, liquid coolness. *No! Warmth.* That child had just relieved herself on my almost bare feet, while giggling and smiling at me. *Is this normal behavior for little ones here?* At least I got to go back home right then. It was hot. I've mentioned that, right? That it was hot? HOT!

I found out later that little boys were told, "Don't hold your water. If you do, you won't be able to have babies when you grow up." I'm not sure what they told little girls. And, of course, with or without underpants, there would be accidents.

— CHAPTER 7 —

Getting into It!

Dale

"If you see unfamiliar produce in the market, buy it. Even if you don't like it, you will know it."
—Ralph Kneller, High School Biology Teacher, Singapore

Ralph, our Baesa neighbor that first summer, was as Canadian as a maple leaf, but he delighted in the experience of new cultures and in thinking thoughts uncommon to more restricted folk. It was fascinating to learn from him about enjoying new cultures. He was every bit the common man's philosopher, as much at home with Shakespeare, Robert Frost, and "cell theory" as he was with automobile transmission grease and mud or the dissection of a frog.

The summer before I met him, he had taught science classes on Palau—one of those dots on the map far out in the recesses of the Pacific Ocean. In many ways, Palau is a paradise. Living in a foreign country, even briefly, Ralph got to know and enjoy that place, the people, and their culture. He told me he had mastered the fine art of climbing palm trees and came to appreciate the slippery, gelatinous flesh inside the young coconuts. He was eager to teach me about coconuts and many other things.

"Carry your camera everywhere you go," he said, "and shoot anything that interests you. Take lots of pictures, right now. After you have been here for a while, you won't see the wonder in things that become too soon common."

We explored Manila by jeepney, enjoying the newness of the place. We took our families to interesting places, like Hundred Islands National Park, where we rented bancas—very long, very narrow boats with outriggers to keep them from tipping side to side. We visited several of the more than 7,000 islands that make up the Philippine archipelago. We snorkeled in crystal-clear water that harbored a multitude of beautiful fish, coral, starfish, and more.

On one occasion, we saw a sea snake; it didn't stick around long, and we weren't eager to disturb it. The boatman said, "He bad fellow. Much poison, but he be very shy."

I found everyday Filipino scenes—markets, traffic, women and babies, older people—strange, fascinating, exciting, and captivating. I took lots of pictures, of wonders that made my new world richer and more beautiful. The novelty made me happy. Sometimes it confused me, sometimes it annoyed me, and often it made me catch my breath with admiration and wonder.

"If you see unfamiliar produce in the market, buy it!" Ralph said. "Even if you don't like it, you will know it." Another axiom Ralph developed as a guide for immersing in a culture was "Read native authors. Read trash, read the classics, but read! Literature is the essence of a people." Our families visited Filipino bookstores and bought books, went to markets, and traveled the roads through sugarcane fields and barrios. We were eager to learn and to know our new Filipino friends.

Ralph provided a truly valuable insight about the resentment expatriates felt from their Filipino colleagues. He said, "I was teaching at a small college in Canada, and over the years we hired visiting professors from the States. We really needed the information and expertise they brought us. Our school could not afford enough qualified, full-time Canadian professors to cover all the necessary subjects. We invited others to come teach for us, one class or one year at a time. We valued them. We needed them; and we resented needing them. We wished we could do it all ourselves. So, I understand the underlying resentment Filipino professors might have about needing us to teach in their college."

For me, novelty fascinated and infatuation grew. Students called me "sir"! Out in the streets, little children ran alongside me, shouting, "Hey, Joe! Where you going?" Every American male was "Joe"—a throwback to World War II and the American "GI Joes" who fought beside Filipinos to free the Philippines from Japanese occupation. Student unrest, Filipino nationalism, and American thoughtlessness have cooled the amorous respect Americans once enjoyed, but for the folks in the barrios, Americans were still admired.

It took some months, but eventually, "Hey, Joe!" started to get to me, like a constant barrage of "Hey, Cookie!" might get to the liberated woman. It was mostly an expression of friendliness, goodwill, and curiosity; seldom was there a sense of hostility or disrespect. But to me, it said, "You are foreign. You are not one of us." I was a part of a group, not an individual. I was a rich American, and they thought they knew all about me. Even Ralph was a "Joe." Roy, from the Caribbean, was also "Joe." I began to think it would be more comfortable to be ignored than to be recognized in that way, but I was never sure.

Being denied an individual personality is a perplexing phenomenon. I had a similar experience shortly after Karen and I were married. We were visiting her parents, and I consulted her family doctor about the common cold threatening to ravage our whirlwind trip to visit relatives and old friends over the Christmas holidays. The nurse entered my vital statistics on her official form and admitted me as "Karen Crandall's husband." In that moment, I gained a deeper appreciation for the feminist objection to "Cookie!" and such.

Once Doc Hendriksen had checked my throat and lungs and made the appropriate grimaces at what he saw and heard, he wrote a prescription. Then he leaned back, stretched, sighed, and said, "Can you sit and relax a bit? I need a break. I've seen too many patients today." We talked about my graduate work and his patient load.

We compared the weather I had left in California to the Michigan blizzard raging outside his office window. To Doc Hendrickson, I was an individual, and even as "Karen Crandall's husband," I had an identity no one else shared. That memory from home helped me with the "Hey Joe."

We followed Ralph's advice. We went into Manila by jeepney and to the countryside and the barrios in "the Blue Bomb," an old Holden sedan we purchased, as often as possible to see daily life in the Philippines. And we took pictures. Oh my, did we take pictures! I bought an old enlarger, created a darkroom in a large closet, and became creative with black-and-white prints. In 1978, color prints were expensive.

Ralph was right. Uncommon things, not so slowly, became common, and later I took fewer pictures. But always after, when I see those pictures, I remember the wonder, the fascination, and the strangeness that drew me to those scenes, and again they make my life richer and more beautiful.

Like Taal Volcano just a few miles from our Silang campus, which fumed a bit but did not erupt while we were there, I never became totally comfortable being "Joe."

We also read, and the reading lent meaning to everything we saw. The Filipino literary classics proved most interesting and valuable. Literature that catches and reflects the pulse of the people is the most durable, and durability defines the classics in any language or culture.

Of course, one's perceptions of another's reflections are biased by the reader's own understanding, experience, and language. Most of what I read provided immediate insight. Sometimes meaning became apparent only later . . . after new experiences.

2020s Update

Sometimes the phrase **"Hey, Joe!"** is accompanied by the "V for victory" hand gesture. According to internet entrepreneur Bob Martin,

> In the Philippines, a practice that goes back for many years, in fact since World War 2 is that the local people call foreigners "Joe." Like GI Joe. Filipinos came to know Americans as "Joe" during the war. Today, some 60 years post war, not only are Americans still called Joe (in some areas) but all foreigners are called Joe. In fact, if you are a foreigner, no matter what country you come from, you are American. You are called a "Kano" short for "Amerikano".... If they see a foreigner walking down the street, many Filipinos will shout out – "Hey Joe." For the most part it is a friendly greeting. However, sometimes it is not so friendly. Sometimes there might be a group of teens and they will smirk at you, "Hey Joe" with contempt. It is just so obvious that it is not a greeting of friendship, rather it shows resentment, even dislike. But, most commonly, it is a friendly thing.[42]

—**Holden cars were assembled in the Philippines in the 1960s and 1970s.** A 2010 Holden goes for PHP (Philippine pesos) 230,000, or USD 5,154.80.

---

[42] Bob Martin, "Live in the Philippines," Accessed February 13, 2024, https://liveinthephilippines.com/joe.

CHAPTER 8

Baesa Campus, Students, and the Classroom

Dale

"The mind is not a vessel to be filled but a fire to be ignited."
—Plutarch, Philosopher, Historian, Biographer, Essayist, and Priest

One evening, I observed someone in our backyard and rushed out to investigate just in time to see a young man scale the tall, rock-and-concrete-block wall and disappear over the top. Only then did I detect subtle grooves carved into the wall that served as footholds and notice that the glass shards embedded along the top of the wall had been broken off along the narrow span where the intruder made his exit. We were not as secure as I had thought.

For several years, the surrounding barrio had been encroaching on the Baesa campus. Tall walls topped with glass or barbed wire were common in Manila and some other cities but not in barrios like those surrounding our campus, reflecting the relative poverty there.

During daylight hours, near neighbors and persons known to the guards were generally admitted. Some of these persons helped themselves to fruit trees surrounding our house and to our very modest garden. I felt violated and was complaining to someone, probably Dra. Rasa, when I learned that this "borrowing" was something of a tradition understood and accepted by the faculty both foreign and domestic.

That information was helpful, and we found ourselves enjoying interacting with the folks we had earlier considered interlopers and thieves. Commonly, it was a mother and a couple of children. We practiced Filipino hospitality, and they were pleasant, thankful neighbors. Most of them spoke little English but understood much of what we said. We knew little of their Tagalog, but as time passed, we understood more.

When we walked through the neighboring barrio, our understanding of our neighbors' limitations increased. Narrow dirt walkways ran between rows of tiny houses. Some houses seemed only big enough for a kitchen and a bedroom. Parallel to the walkways, open trenches drained wastewater to communal septic tanks. The houses were four to six meters apart on average.

When the Baesa college campus first opened in 1932, the twenty-six-hectare (sixty-four-acre) tract of land in the Rizal province area was rural. The present lack of security and the manic pace of the world outside the wall played a large part in PUC's decision to find a more suitable property and move the campus.

In 1972, an ideal rural property of 165 hectares (408 acres) had been found for the new campus in Putting Kahoy, Silang, Cavite, forty-two kilometers (twenty-seven miles) from the current site. It was essentially free of populated borders. A small, pleasant barrio existed peacefully across a paved highway that led westward to the city of Taal and the usually inactive Taal Volcano.

Sometime before we arrived in the Philippines, the school received an attractive offer to sell the college property in Baesa to an organization planning to convert the land into a cemetery. It was ideal for a cemetery—a large piece of land in the center of a rapidly burgeoning population in Caloocan City, a suburb of Manila, the largest Philippine city. If you calculate the fees of the many possible grave sites, the company made a good buy, and PUC got a good price.

The plan was that each year, the new freshmen would start their classes in Silang, and by 1981, the entire university would move to the new campus. At that time, the old campus would be claimed by the memorial park company, and my yoyo commute would be over. The new owners had already started construction on the east side of the Baesa campus near our home.

Three days after we arrived, Dra. Rasa took me to get my driver's license. Thankfully, cars drive on the right, as they do in the States. Three times a week, I commuted about thirty-seven miles from PUC's Baesa campus to the Silang campus.

♦ ♦ ♦

The first few days before classes started were filled with activity and excitement. Organizing my courses and understanding the future was challenging, but Dra. Rasa helped me with that. She had chosen Biochemistry as one of the courses I would teach. I told her that I had taught Anatomy and Physiology (A and P) for the past nine years, and Research Methods, Genetics, Animal Behavior, and the Philosophy of Science as scheduled, but I had never taught a course on biochemistry. That topic was just not one of my strong suits, and I told her I probably wasn't her best choice.

"Well," she said, "it has been decided. You are the most qualified candidate we have for Biochemistry. Sometimes, in the Philippines, we just have to step up to what is at hand!"

I had been given a golden opportunity to learn more biochemistry. And I believe Dra. Rasa was encouraging me to not let perfect be the enemy of good. She carried a heavy academic load herself in addition to being the chair of the department and developing a biology graduate program. All the teachers taught more classes per term than I was used to.

Dra. Engracia Rasa was a respected scholar on and off our PUC campus. She received her PhD from the University of California, Santa Barbara, in 1960. At one point the Filipino governor gave her an award for her research and the discovery of a viral disease killing coconut trees in the Philippines.[43] The disease was especially rancorous on the Island of Bicol, where it killed all but 100 of their 250,000 African and buri coconut palms. Coconut is a valuable agricultural crop in the Philippines. The buri palm has large, fan-shaped leaves that are woven into fans, baskets, hats, and mats. In the Bicol dialect, the name of the virus, "cadang-cadang," is similar to "*gaddang-gaddang*," which translates to "heat-burned death."[44]

Despite the University of the Philippines at Los Baños's (UPLB) requests that she teach for them, her loyalties were with PUC and her students.

Ms. Tessie Poblano was teaching A and P before I arrived, and she was told she would have time off for upgrading. I suspect that early conversations between the administration and Ms. Poblano had not excluded the possibility that the upgrading would not take place in the US, and the exogenies of external factors (e.g., finances, administrative plans, or preferences) led to the final decision. Ms. Poblano was informed that she would "upgrade" by attending my lectures and teaching the A and P lab. That did not sit well with either of us, but a better offer was not in the offing. Surprisingly, she showed no rancor toward me, but she was not happy.

When she was teaching A and P, she had taught her own laboratory, so we discussed procedures, and I left the labs to her.

Dra. Rasa showed me the textbooks for A and P and Biochemistry. Both books were reprints of American textbooks. *Essentials of Biological Chemistry* by Fairly and Kilgore was first printed in 1963. A Philippine company gained a copyright in 1972, and I received my copy in 1978; it is still on my bookshelf. Though fifteen years old, the concepts had not changed markedly from the book I studied as a college sophomore fourteen years earlier, so I was moderately comfortable with it.

---

[43] "Cading-cading," https://en.wikipedia.org/wiki/Cadang-cadang (Accessed April 4, 2024).
[44] "Gading-Gading," https://www.csueastbay.edu/museum/virtual-museum/the-philippines/peoples/gaddang.html (Accessed April 4, 2024).

Ms. Leah Balaros, a junior biology major, had taken Biochemistry and was the lab instructor for that class. She was a good student and laboratory assistant; she knew the subject, where the equipment and supplies were kept, and how things in the Biology Department worked.

The first class I met with was Anatomy and Physiology. The students were attentive and courteous, much more so than my Walla Walla students. The PUC students sat relatively quietly when I lectured beyond the scheduled time. I was impressed with their focus and started taking advantage of what I interpreted as their eagerness to learn, giving them a few more minutes of explanations beyond class time.

One morning, perhaps a week or two after the beginning of the semester, a student stopped by my desk after a lecture and quietly said, "But, sir, we have trouble getting to our next class on time."

Were Filipino students more attentive, or were they simply reared to show more respectful behavior? I have thought about that frequently, but I'm still not sure how to sort it out. I felt only respect from the student who informed me that I was disadvantaging him and his classmates, a reprehensible act if done intentionally. He simply recognized my ignorance and informed me, and we were better friends for it.

◆ ◆ ◆

Johnny Guyo, another assistant, was very bright. His mechanical skills made him exceptionally helpful. Mechanical skills are not usually necessary in preparing laboratory exercises, but when choosing and testing specific equipment and checking the instruments' functionality, Johnny was on hand. A phrase I often heard, relative to electronic equipment, was "Destroyed a'ready!" (Translation: "It doesn't work!"). I noticed that Dra. Rasa and Ms. Poblano often asked for his help.

Don Van Ornam, PUC's business manager, and Sam Robinson, who was in charge of overseeing campus construction and the motor pool, frequently traveled to the US Naval Base Subic Bay and Clark Air Force Base (AFB) for what was called Army surplus equipment. They brought sections of two-story buildings on large trailers and set them up as temporary administration offices and classrooms on the new campus. On the Baesa campus, we received several water baths and other laboratory equipment from Army surplus.

Calling it surplus equipment might be misleading. Most of the items were available because they were out of date, worn, or broken, and we bought them because they were very cheap. To Johnny, they were treasures to fix. Good parts could be taken off one piece of equipment to replace a nonfunctional part on another, and sometimes a motor or a voltage meter from one instrument could replace a similar but damaged component on a different instrument. PUC did not have a budget like the stateside schools I was used to; improvising made educational experiences possible for less money, and Johnny was a master at repair and improvisation.

Johnny told me about the tamaraw, a small water buffalo found only on Mindoro Island, south of Luzon. Mindoro was Johnny's home, and he said he would take Jeff and me there on an adventure to find the tamaraw. That story is in the chapter titled "The Mystic Tamaraw."[45]

♦ ♦ ♦

Most students who came to our college spoke English, but some only the very basics. The history of language in the Philippines is a bit convoluted.

During the Spanish occupation (1565–1898), even though the Spanish priests were required to communicate with the Filipinos in their own dialect, Spanish words were incorporated. The oldest

---

[45] Johnny graduated with a bachelor's degree from PUC a year or two after we left the RP, and he graduated with a PhD in biology from the University of the Philippines, Los Baños. He then taught at his alma mater and worked his way to chairman of the Department of Biology there. I lost track of Johnny for years, so I am unclear about some late history. He was ill for some time and died too young.

Chinatown in the world, Binondo, established in Manila in 1594, also contributed some words. No school system was established until 1863, and the Catholic Church controlled the curriculum. Less than one-fifth of those who went to school could read and write Spanish, and far fewer spoke it correctly.[46] Much education was based on rote memorization of Bible verses.

Less than a month after Admiral Dewey led the Battle of Manila Bay in 1898, "Americans opened the first public school on Corregidor Island" and "theoretically opened up the education system to all Filipino children regardless of social position and political connection."[47] Beginning in 1898, the Americans instituted English "as the language of instruction, and a public school system was established, administered by a Department of Instruction and modeled after the US system."[48] American soldiers often volunteered to teach where the military assigned them; then 600 teachers arrived in 1901 on the USS *Thomas*—and so they were called Thomasites. The Thomasites essentially led the education system until 1935, transforming the Philippines into "the third largest English-speaking nation in the world."[49]

Throughout its history, the language of the Philippines has been influenced by interactions with Spain, the US, Malaysia, the Middle East, and Japan and diluted by words or phrases like "ball pen" and

---

[46] "Philippines - Colonialism, Revolution, Independence," Britannica https://www.britannica.com (Accessed February 14, 2024).

[47] Tupas and Lorente, "A new politics of language in the Philippines: Bilingual education and the new challenge of the mother tongues." National University of Singapore. In 1959 Tagalog was officially renamed Pilipino; then, in 1973, ethnolinguistic rivalries flared up again, and Pilipino ceased to be the national language.

[48] Nick Clark, Editor: "Practical Information: Education in the Philippines," World Education Service, World Education News & Reviews; notably, in 1925, a commission recommended that Americans also "curtail" the practice of training students in crafts and selling the products in favor of more academic instruction: "Education in the Philippines During the American Rule," K12 Academics: Slovenski Camps, Accessed February 14, 2024, https://www.k12academics.com/Education%20Worldwide/Education%20in%20the%20Philippines/education-philippines-during-american-rule.

[49] "Thomasites," Wikipedia, Accessed March 15, 2024, https://en.wikipedia.org/wiki/Thomasites.

"air con" that have no translation in the local dialect. It was always interesting to hear a Tagalog sentence interspersed with American words.

Update 2020s

—**"The Functional Literacy, Education and Mass Media Survey (FLEMMS)** shows the educational attainment of the population aged six years old and over. The survey results in 2003 and 2008 revealed an increasing trend in the proportion of the population aged six years old and over who had completed at least elementary education. From 62 percent in 2003, the proportion who have completed at least elementary education increased to 68 percent in 2008. . . . 38.7 percent of population six years old and over completed at least high school education. This figure is higher among females compared to males (41.1% vs. 36.4%)."[50]

—**A UNICEF report on Filipino education** reported in 2021 that "only 78 percent complete basic education."[51]

—According to *Rappler*: "**The Philippines ranked 77th out of 81 countries** globally in the student assessment conducted by the Organization for Economic Co-operation and Development (OECD) for 15-year-old learners."[52] This is, of course, affected by 25 percent not completing high school.

—**School may be difficult to get to.** One good example is a YouTube video recounting the stories of three children and a principal on the island of Mindoro. The children must make a two-hour hike up

---

[50] https://psa.gov.ph/content/education-women-and-men.
[51] "Education Quality and inclusive lifelong learning," Unicef, https://www.unicef.org/Philippines/education.
[52] "PH still among lowest in math, science, reading in global student assessment," *Rappler*, December 5, 2023, https://www.rappler.com/nation/for-second-time-ph-ranks-among-lowest-pisa-2022/.

and down dangerous paths to attend school; the principal rides his motorbike, and as a student he walked the same paths the children do today. The cost to ride as a passenger on a motorbike is USD 1; the children do not have the pesos to ride.[53]

---

[53] "Most Dangerous Ways to School—Philippines." https://www.youtube.com/watch?v=di_PKpeSmtY (Accessed April 7, 2024)

CHAPTER 9

Israel Was No Egghead!

Dale

"He beat the system by studying when he should have been sleeping and sleeping while I lectured."

—*Dale*

Israel slept through my Anatomy and Physiology lectures, then kept me late after the other students had departed to answer his questions. Few of the questions were related to the lecture. Someone had given him a book I had never seen before, have not seen since, and would buy if I could. It was a little book packed with wonderful facts about the human body. Israel read it religiously.

Wherever and whenever we met, Israel would raise one hand, palm out in a "Please wait" gesture. His brow wrinkling, right eye closing, and left eye turned heavenward, he was the picture of concentration, searching for the right words.

Inevitably, he began, "Sir, is it true that . . . ?" And I would know that the rest of his question related to the little book and a new wonder that neither he nor I could quite believe until we had reasoned it through and confirmed it with other sources.

His questions revolved around facts like how many cells were to be found in the human brain or how the tiny tubules coiled within the human kidney could stretch some fifty miles if removed and placed end to end.

Imagine how fine a monofilament fishline would have to be to roll fifty miles of it into two small balls the size of human kidneys and have space left for blood vessels, nerves, connective tissue, and the other stuff we might call plumbing. That line would be snapped by the smallest fishes, yet similarly tiny tubules have the task of deciding what components of our blood are in excess or are waste products of our body chemistry, toxic in some cases, and routing them to the urinary bladder while retaining useful substances and directing them back to the bloodstream.

That was the kind of stuff Israel was curious about.

All this might lead you to envision Israel as one of those skinny kids with heavy glasses and a disdain for short words and simple thoughts. But an intellectual Israel was not—a scholar, perhaps, if motivation and arduous infatuation with facts counted.

Israel was a self-supporting student, which meant if he was not in class or eating or sleeping, he was expected to be working. He beat the system by studying when he should have been sleeping and sleeping while I lectured. It was difficult to begrudge Israel's sleeping, but it did affect his exam performance. To make matters worse, his grasp of the English language was abysmal and his reading restricted to the little book of facts. He could not afford the A and P text and might not have found time to read it if he had it. By some stroke of magic or herculean efforts on his part, the name Israel Padang came to float just above "D" level in the morass of my grade book.

The simple things that Israel discovered impressed me, like the rich background of facts and ideas culture endows humans with before trucking us off to college. Perhaps that endowment has as much to do with the fit between cultural backgrounds and what is acceptable to "academia" as with the volume or even the correctness of what it contains.

One day, Israel began his postclass session with an unusually obtuse line of questions relating to the anatomy of the fairer sex.

He was uncomfortable and embarrassed: "Sir! I mean, sir! Is it true, sir, dat girls hab eggs, sir, when dey is birgin?" His dialect affected his pronunciation, and he used too many "sirs"; when uncomfortable, he compounded them.

"Oh, yes! It doesn't matter if they are a virgin or not. Girls are born with both ovaries full of tiny, undeveloped ova, or eggs. At puberty, when a girl starts her monthly cycles, one of those tiny ova will develop and grow into a mature egg each cycle. If that egg is not fertilized by a sperm and does not attach to the uterine wall to become a baby, it just passes out with the menstrual flow, and a new egg develops the next month. Girls have monthly menstrual cycles whether they are virgins or not. That's quite normal in girls and women, except pregnant ones."

"Yes, sir! Yes, sir! I know, sir, but do dey hab eggs, sir, when normal sickness come eben if dey birgin?"

"Yes."

"Well, sir, sir, then I read ob de hymen. You know de hymen, sir?"

"Yes."

"It really make de opening less, sir, and it not be stretched wide but it break and make bleeding."

"Yes." I wondered where the questions were leading.

"Cannot be! Sir, cannot be! How do eggs get out?"

"Get out of where?"

"Out ob de girl, sir! Out ob de girl what is birgin?"

"It just flows out with the menstrual flow."

"But how can it be, sir? The hymen make de opening so less? How can it be? How big is de egg, sir?"

Israel was generally coherent, but this made little sense. I tried to answer his questions and to understand how I could help *him* understand. I said, "The egg is very small. If you had it in the best light, you could see it without a microscope or magnifying glass; otherwise, you could not see it."

"You mean, sir, so small?" He squinted and gestured, thumb opposing finger to leave the smallest of gaps.

"Yes, maybe like that. About that small."

"You mean, sir, so less?"

"Yes, about that small."

"Oh! Now I know. But how can it be? Sir, I know de chicken and de bird. But girls hab eggs so small? Like dis? Really dat small? Oh, now I know how it go out. But how is hen what is so less than girl what is so bigger. I mean, it must be so . . . the hymen make the opening so less, Ah! Girls hab eggs so less. Ah! Ah!"

Israel wandered off, shaking his head, filled with a new wonder. But tomorrow would bring another question, and I wondered what it might be.

CHAPTER 10

Early Journaling: New Friends and Women Who Taught Me

Karen

My friend Linda McCloskey had suggested I keep a journal while in the Philippines. I'm glad I have these memories of the first few weeks.

May 21. Left Taipei, arrived Manila. Dra. Rasa and other faculty took us to campus, offered a welcome meal, and introduced us to the campus and our home. We moved our mattress into Jeff's room to sleep under a fan. It's hot and humid!

May 22. Dra. Rasa took Dale for his driver's license; he'll need to drive to Silang twice a week.

May 23. Barbara Van Ornam visited and took me shopping. Our poodle Pumpkin arrived at the airport; took lots of time in customs. Signs: "If no one paid a bribe, no one would ask for one."

May 24. Mrs. Gulley brought their car/now our car—a Australian Holden, an ugly bright blue!

May 25. Back to MIA to get our two air-mailed boxes; more drama in customs.

May 26. Friday. Five days in-country. Mr. Malagat was delightful and a big help! After he finished reinstalling our hot water tank, electrician Mr. Espiritu came. He told me his name was Ezekial but to please call him Ike. Such a gentle and kind young man, he offered to be my "tour guide." Today I told him I needed help finding and shopping for fresh vegetables. He drove us to his home, and we met his youngest daughter. Ike explained: "She is our second and last. We have already had family planning." Delightful to also meet his wife, Dorie, and their other child.

They live in a tin Quonset hut home near the campus. A latticework trellis supports passionfruit vines all around their tiny home. Dorie teaches math at the Philippine Union College High School; she is sweet and gracious. She gave me some suggestions on fixing the gourd, which looks like a long zucchini. Then Ike drove us to Clover Leaf Market in nearby Balintawak. What an amazing experience! It's a large shed, open on three sides. Crowded, noisy, good and bad smells—colorful, fascinating, and delightful! We bought squash, string beans, and calamansi, a tiny, citrus-like fruit, green with orange flesh, and tart! He says it's wonderful as fruit juice and perfect when squeezed inside lumpia just before each bite. I practiced asking "Magkano?" (How much?) and saying "Salamat!" (Thank you!) Magic—tummy tightness gone for now.

May 28. Sunday. One week in-country. Midmorning, Jerah and Jehzeel, darling students who are twins, brought us some raw pili nuts. "Our mother lives far North in Baguio and is a distributor for the nuts. You can eat them raw like this—and they are very delicious made into a candy." They want to come back this afternoon to show me how to make the candy.

Dra. Rasa's daughter, Ruth, came to play the organ, and we invited her to stay for lunch. She said she would take off work and drive to Silang with us tomorrow.

Busy day: The twins returned midafternoon and brought another student, Julie, and we made peanut candy. Delicious! Julie taught Kimberly to play the shell game sungkâ (SOONG-ka) on a longish narrow board with shallow bowls cut into the sides and on each end. Then Kim and I taught them all to play Uno. This day was happily full. And we learned that the pili nut is seen as a "superfood" by some.⁵⁴ Silang campus tomorrow.

Recipe: Pili Nut Candy

Boil pili nuts and remove outer skins.

Place small amount of water with sugar in skillet.

2 cups nuts to 1 cup sugar

Stir liquid continuously until sugar is dissolved.

Add pili nuts and continue stirring.

Mixture will come to solid state again, then dissolve.

Stir until golden brown; spread on foil or wax paper to cool.

May 29. Monday. Dale drove the Blue Bomb, and we picked up Ruth Rasa at 8:15 a.m. and collected mail from the Baesa campus office to take to the Silang campus. Ah, we had a beautiful, encouraging letter from Malcolm Maxwell, academic dean at WWC, telling us how hard it is to replace Dale and wondering if we would accept a "mission call" to WWC one day. The comments knotted my stomach and filled my eyes.

Ruth suggested a market that is good for shoes. Kim is so hard to fit—too big for girl's size, too small for women's. We did find some rubber sandals, which should work.

Before we left for Silang, we needed to open a checking account, and

---

⁵⁴ https://theculturetrip.com/asia/philippines/articles/pili-nuts-why-this-delicious-philippine-superfood-cant-crack-the-health-food-market/ (Accessed March 22, 2024)

Ruth helped us find Citibank—our first time in the upscale Makati area of Manila with its tall, modern buildings, many banks and other financial institutions, clean streets, and lovely landscaping. Quite impressive!

Just as we finished in the bank, the sky darkened and the wind came up. Paper was flying all around, even high into the sky—then it poured down heavy rain! We ran for the car, started the engine, and turned on the windshield wipers. The passenger-side one worked well; the driver-side wiper gave a great leap and died, facing away from its post of duty. We drove carefully, slowly, and found our way with Ruth's guidance to the Manila Sanitarium and Hospital for lunch. We all decided this was NOT the day to go to the Silang campus. Their mail would have to wait until someone else was going to Silang.

May 30. Tuesday. Nine days in-country. What to do today that's constructive and will keep me busy? After many weeks preparing to move and then traveling, now I can't fill my day productively and without homesickness. Tears again. Stomach not so bad this morning. Yeah! Dale and I both have sore throats and colds. Yuk! At various times during the morning, three young women came to interview to be our "helper." They tell us they need the job. I tried to be pleasant and also asked the right questions. I wrote down their names and said, "We'll think about it."

May 31. Wednesday. Jean Zachary, a delightful woman and a librarian now living on the Silang campus, visited us and took Kimberly and me to her dressmaker. We walked through the PUC gates, across the narrow, paved road, then down a gravel footpath between houses. Jean knocked on the door of a two-story home and introduced us to lovely Mading. What a precious woman; it was a delight to meet her, and we loved being inside her home, seeing how people really live. Like the others nearby, the gray cement-block building looked plain and primitive from the outside, but it was beautiful, comfortable, and nicely furnished with attractive rattan furniture, a console TV, and ceramic tile in the spotless kitchen. Her windows were wood-framed with translucent capiz-shell panels in place of glass. Lovely!

Mading offered to sew for us. We had brought along one of the large Simplicity pattern books from the US. She explained that we are to show her the pattern, then she will tell us how much material to purchase in the market, and she will create the designs for us. She said there are also tailors who make jeans in the design and with the labels you want: Gloria Vanderbilt, Levi, etc., "true" right down to the buttons and snaps!

Walking back to campus, we couldn't avoid seeing and smelling the gray water running in a gully alongside the walkway. The smell was offensive, the sight unforgettable—small kittens that had drowned in the gray water.

We retrieved Jean's car on campus and continued our adventures to nearby Munoz Market; it was delightful to see where to shop for food, clothing, cloth, umbrellas, plastic raincoats, shoes, restaurants, beauty shops. There were even places to get manicures and pedicures for the US equivalent of seventy-five cents. I bought a handmade, embroidered dress for Kim, raincoats for both kids, two umbrellas, and a beautiful pineapple for the US equivalent of fifteen cents. Then we went for lunch to—can you believe it?—a Shakey's Pizza Parlor for a wonderful mushroom-and-cheese pizza! Fabulous! The kids will love knowing there is an "American" restaurant to visit now and then.

We missed our turnoff and really got lost in the middle of Manila. Most folk don't use printed maps! It took two and a half hours to get home. Still, the drive was interesting. I look forward to seeing Jean again when we visit the Silang campus.

Taking stock: What do I miss? Good milk, apples and oranges (they are in some markets, but very expensive), and frozen vegetables. What do I have? Kind, helpful people. Mangoes, fresh pineapple, new fruits and vegetables I don't even know the name of yet, good crackers and cookies in neat tin boxes.

June 2. Friday. *Tonight's Vespers program featured Dr. Roda interviewing Dale, who wore, of course, his new barong. It went quite well. Dr. Roda spoke to me afterward and was very kind and understanding about my loneliness. My inner thoughts are* I can't do this for more than a year.

June 21. *A big day! Today is the one-month anniversary of our new life in the RP! I'm guessing/hoping that the most intense homesickness is over. Culture shock is an eye-opener. I sometimes feel so isolated, so shut off. It takes at least two weeks to receive mail from the US; seven to ten days from here to there. I called Mom and Dad—USD 13 for the first three minutes, three dollars a minute thereafter! I won't be doing that very often! I asked if they'd be disappointed in me if I could not stay more than one year. They were kind. And said they'd understand and that they plan to visit soon. Haven't been journaling much.*

July 10. *What a treat! Today we got a tape from WWC friends Don and Donnie Rigby—I laughed and cried! Very frustrating that we couldn't understand part of it because it was made during a party at Fisk's—lots of talking in the background, voices of friends. Delightful! And more: letters from Uncle Don and Aunt Marion, one from Mom and Dad Crandall, one from the Craws, one from Mom and Dad Clayton. A treasure trove!*

July 19. *Mail! A letter from Joe and Marilyn Galusha, WWC friends; one from my mom; and a beautiful card from Linda with a photo and the scent of strawberries (one of her favorite things). What blessings these are to me. Joe and Marilyn are caring for our piano and music stand while we are on the other side of the earth.*

July 20. *Interesting. Looking back over this journal, I note that by the second week, there were fewer entries . . . then none. I have been assimilating into the culture, into my life in the Philippines, busy with the family, and we have decided to have a helper. I stay busy and seldom get really discouraged. How delightful!*

CHAPTER 11

An Embarrassment of Riches and Fear

Karen

"We had never seen such poverty. Some experiences made me fearful."

—Karen

Most of the people we met that first month, especially those on our campus, lived comfortably—with pleasant homes and a good education—and seemed physically healthy. It took only a short time off campus, driving in town and the countryside, to see the effects of pervasive poverty and unhealthy living conditions.

We had never seen such poverty. It was evident in the housing we saw down some city alleys, along the Pasig River in Manila, in the dwellings built of cardboard, metal, and sometimes plywood like the folks whose homes leaned against our campus walls. We saw it in the gray water and sewage running in open trenches along the narrow dirt roads branching off the narrow, paved road just outside our campus gate. We saw it in the dress and behavior of the beggars—men and women—who squatted outside markets, in the young children who sold fried bananas or asked to wash the windshield of our car for a few centavos. Jeff did not like to go to town with us. "Mom," he said, "those kids should be in school."

Soon we were doing most of our shopping in the fascinating open-air markets. The closest one Ike showed me at Balintawak had perhaps forty stalls under a huge tin roof. There was a truly amazing variety of fruits and vegetables, some unfamiliar and intriguing. There were also familiar items; I was fascinated watching the woman whose job it was to peel garlic and put the cloves in plastic bags. Now, I like garlic, but I couldn't help thinking she'd never get that smell off her hands.

I worked on learning to bargain, concentrating at first on "*Magkano?*" (How much?) and "*Masyadong mahal*" (Very dear!—meaning too much/very expensive), "*Conte lang*" (Little bit only), and understanding the monetary units: eight Philippine pesos was one US dollar. It was an adventure and fun, mostly. I especially liked the tiny grocery on campus because often they had fresh bread from the campus bakery and really good, icy fudge bars, one of my favorite things since I was six, growing up in Michigan. And, of course, bargaining for the "best price" felt strange since we had more money to spend than anyone in the market, I think. Things were so inexpensive, but I was supposed to try to get them cheaper than the original asking price.

Most Filipinos did not own cars, certainly not with "slightly more than half of the population living below the poverty line."[55] Some of the middle class had vehicles, and the 2 percent of the population who were extremely wealthy (deemed to have incomes between fifteen and twenty times the poverty line)[56] and more likely to have cars also had chauffeurs. Public transportation was pleasant, easy to use, and, again, inexpensive. Jeepneys were everywhere.

That most expatriates on our campuses owned cars was one of the obvious distinctions in our level of comfort and financial security. We purchased our Australian Holden, the Blue Bomb, sight unseen from a previous missionary family. Talk about trust!

Dale and I took the written test, paid the fee, and received our

---

[55] "Poverty and Welfare," US Library of Congress, https://countrystudies.us/philippines.
[56] "Counting the Social Classes" 2022, Philippine Institute for Developmental Studies, https://www.pids.gov.ph/details.

driver's licenses. On one early trip, we drove to the airport to retrieve Pumpkin, our apricot toy poodle. It was an extravagance we had calculated would do our family more good than bad. We'd left so many animals behind, and we were told it was possible to breed her here and cover the fifty dollars her air freight cost us.[57] The contrast between our blessings and the poverty around us—the terrible housing for many, children not in school—was part of my painful culture shock and the reason the tears had come so many mornings. I grew so tired of the sadness and the sick feeling. What a relief that it did not last all day!

Our salary was nothing to write home about, but it was more than our Filipino colleagues and significantly more than most of the nationals (in-country residents). It was certainly more than we needed to live comfortably; our SDA big brother told us that one-third of our salary would go to a bank account in the US. We did get to choose where. Part of our employer's reasoning was that we would need to fit into the US economy, purchase a home, and provide good schooling for our children when we moved back.

We had planned *not* to employ a "helper," although we were told that everyone here did and we were expected to help a student by hiring her. We were middle-class American folk who weren't used to having servants, and some of the helpers we saw in faculty homes seemed overworked and underpaid.

The kids and I had been looking forward to seeing the Silang campus. Dale went there twice a week, but the rest of us had not seen it yet. As we drove slowly through our Baesa campus gates, prepared to turn right onto Balibago Road, a young man came very near my open window, a few inches from my face, stared at me, and said quietly, "Why don't you go home?"

I was still struggling with homesickness, and it was difficult to hear that and feel the disdain. The kids did not hear the comment or

---

[57] We checked out the breeding opportunities and didn't proceed with that plan. The return cost would be $200.

see my tears; I tried to put it out of my mind, only telling Dale about it later when we were alone.

We knew of a nationalistic fervor in many young folks, especially university professors and students who had bad feelings about many aspects of US–Philippine interactions past and present. Reflecting the feelings of many uninformed Americans, we told ourselves we'd "rescued" the Philippines from almost 400 years of repressive Spanish rule—not to mention our help during WWII in ridding the islands of the Japanese. A more complete look at the history reveals that while Americans saw themselves as offering "benevolent assimilation," our involvement really signified a conquest.[58]

Terrible incidents occurred during that time as Americans fought Filipinos fighting unsuccessfully to defend and direct their own country. Records show that "after the US declared war on Spain, Aguinaldo saw a possibility that the Philippines might achieve its independence; the US hoped instead that Aguinaldo would lend his troops to its effort against Spain. He returned to Manila on May 19, 1898 and declared Philippine independence on June 12."[59] The US referred to the conflict as the Philippine Insurrection or the Tagalog Insurgency. During the Philippine–American War (1899–1902), thousands of Filipinos—military and civilians—were killed, and the United States continued occupying the Philippines until 1946. Each July 12, Filipinos joyfully celebrate their Independence Day.[60]

That young man's feelings were understandable.

Some groups' dislike of Americans wasn't the only danger. I also had heard about the general unrest among university students and folks who joined militant opposition groups. On September 23, 1972, when President Marcos declared martial law, he said it was in response

---

[58] Miller, *Benevolent Assimilation*.
[59] World of 1898: International Perspectives on the Spanish American War, Emilio Aguinaldo y Famy in Library of Congress Research Guides. https://guides.loc.gov/world-of-1898/emilio-aguinaldo-famy (Accessed March 24, 2024).
[60] Michael Ray, Editor, "Philippine-American War," Britannica Online Encyclopedia, 2021, Accessed February 14, 2024, https://www.britannica.com/event/Philippine-American-War.

to various groups he thought posed a threat: the Communist Party of the Philippines (CPP) and what was called a "sectarian rebellion" by the Mindanao Independence Movement (MIM). Subsequently, human rights abuses were reported and documented by Amnesty International. An attempt was made on the life of Imelda Marcos during a live TV broadcast on December 7, 1972.

I admit I chose not to read much about those issues. I felt afraid about the current atmosphere and sad about the past inequities and the current poverty.

My fear heightened abruptly on one occasion, while riding a bus. I was sitting on the left side, near the front, seeking fresh air next to an open window when a motorcycle policeman drove near the driver's window and hit the side mirror with his nightstick. Smashed it! Why? I had no idea; it did not instill confidence in asking the police for help.

Another afternoon, Jeff and I were traveling near the center of Manila and passed some of the government buildings built by Americans from Indiana limestone in the early part of the twentieth century, even though there was beautiful marble in the Central Visayan Islands. We were surprised to see rows of police in dramatic black uniforms, holding tall, seemingly heavy, dark plastic shields in front of them and standing in formation. They seemed on alert. All traffic stopped for a short time; we waited in the relative safety of a jeepney. Thankfully, the traffic started moving, and we arrive at our walled campus safely. That evening we listened to the radio news but did not learn what the concern had been.

We heard reports of policemen shooting criminals dead in the street—not capturing, charging, and prosecuting them. Those things were often on my mind. Kimberly remembers a similar incident when I was driving in Manila: "As usual, we had the windows down because of the heat. We paused to wait our turn in traffic, and a man leaned in the window, looked at both of us, and said, 'I hate Americans.' He stepped back and was on his way. It was disturbing and sad."

On this particular day, I turned my attention to the excitement of going to the new campus, our new home, soon. The countryside would offer a significant difference in our experience.

Update 2020s

—**Poverty is prevalent**. High birth rates, low salaries, and inadequate health care all add to difficult living conditions for many. According to a Nasdaq online article:

> The Philippines' poverty rate dropped to 22.4%, or 25.24 million people, in the first half of 2023.... President Ferdinand Marcos Jr. aims to bring down the poverty rate to 9% before his six-year term ends in 2028, by investing in infrastructure and courting foreign direct investment to create jobs and boost economic growth.[61]

—**Population and Birth Control:** With a population of 112,541,844 in 2022, the country ranks thirteenth in overall population worldwide.[62] The population was just over forty-eight million in 1980. There are still strong influences from various belief systems. The Philippines is a predominantly Christian country, and most Christians are Roman Catholics, so "law is often framed around Catholic values. Alcohol and cigarettes are taxed for being 'sins.' Contraception is forbidden."[63] In 2014, a law was enacted requiring public health facilities to offer free contraception to the poor. The law is opposed by the Catholic Church, but supporters are most concerned about high poverty due to soaring population growth.

---

[61] "Philippine poverty rate in H1 2023 atg 22.4%.," (Accessed Mar 3, 2023).
[62] Honey Buenaventura, "Most and Least Effective Birth Control Methods in the Philippines," last modified September 20, 2023, https://hellodoctor.com.ph/sexual-wellness/contraception/effective-birth-control/.
[63] "Is Catholic Church's influence in Philippines fading?" BBC News, May 25, 2014, https://www.bbc.com/news/world-asia-27537943.

—**We learned, too late, important history regarding Philippine–American relations:**

> American acquisition of the Philippines in 1898 became a focal point for debate on American imperialism and the course the country was to take now that the Western frontier had been conquered. US military leaders in Manila, unequipped to understand the aspirations of the native revolutionary movement, failed to respond to Filipino overtures of accommodation and provoked a war with the revolutionary army.... [I]n the end it was the interminable and increasingly bloody guerrilla warfare that disillusioned America in its imperialist venture.[64]

—**Contemporary headlines:**

> **"US to Gain Military Access to North Philippines near Taiwan."** President Ferdinand Marcos Jr. announced that there will be an increase in the military sites to which the US will have access. The China Foreign Ministry is warning regional countries that they "should stay vigilant and ... not be used by the US side."[65]

> **"US Gets Access to 9 Military Bases in the Philippines; China Warns Manila of Being 'Dragged Into Troubled Waters'"**: "Amid mounting concern over China's increasing assertiveness in the disputed South China Sea and tension over self-ruled Taiwan, the US military managed to secure access to four additional bases in the Philippines. The United States already had access to five."[66]

---

[64] Miller, *Benevolent Assimilation*.
[65] "US to Gain Military Access to North Philippines near Taiwan," Bloomberg, March 22, 2023, https://www.bloomberg.com/news/articles/2023-03-22/us-to-gain-military-access-in-northern-philippines-near-taiwan-marcos-says?.
[66] Sakshi Tiwari, "US Gets Access to 9 Military Bases in the Philippines; China Warns Manila of Being 'Dragged Into Troubled Waters," *Our EurAsian Times*, February 4, 2023, https://www.eurasiantimes.com/edited-amid-growing-us-philippines-military-coooperation-china/ (Accessed March 7, 2024).

"East Asia realignment: Japan and the Philippines move closer."[67]

"Rights group: Duterte's legacy of violence still present under Marcos" (son of Ferdinand).[68]

"A tale of two dynasties: The Marcos-Duterte ties that bind."[69]

"Filipino journalist shot dead while live on air."[70]

"As Marcos government revives peace talks, political prisoners 'hope in moderation'": The report notes that one prison with small cells housing four to eight persons is better than another where thirty-five prisoners share a cell meant for ten.[71]

—**Maria Ressa, a Filipina-American, Princeton-educated journalist, worked for CNN and other news sources before beginning** *Rappler* **in the Philippines; it's an important online resource, offering vital accurate reporting and exposing misinformation.** She was awarded the Nobel Peace Prize in 2021, sharing it with a Russian journalist.

—**Current statistics are available in Philippines County Profile**, 2023.[72]

---

[67] Urs Schöttli, "East Asia realignment: Japan and the Philippines move closer," February 8, 2024, https://www.gisreportsonline.com/r/japan-philippines-china-south-china-sea/.
[68] Jodesz Gavilan, "Rights group: Duterte's legacy of violence still present under Marcos," *Rappler*, Dec. 10, 2023, https://www.rappler.com/philippines/human-rights-group-philrights-violent-legacy-rodrigo-duterte-still-present-marcos-jr-administration/.
[69] Bea Cupin, "A tale of two dynasties: The Marcos-Duterte ties that bind," *Rappler*, Jan 30, 2024, https://www.rappler.com/newsbreak/explainers/tale-dynasties-marcos-duterte-ties/.
[70] David Millward, "Filipino journalist shot dead while live on air," *The Telegraph*, November 5, 2023, https://www.telegraph.co.uk/world-news/2023/11/05/filipino-journalist-juan-jumalon-shot-dead-live-on-air/.
[71] Leon Buan, "As Marcos government revives peace talks, political prisoners 'hope in moderation,'" *Rappler*, January 17, 2024, https://www.rappler.com/philippines/peace-talks-political-prisoners-hope-moderation/.
[72] "Country Profile, 2023," BBC, Accessed February 14, 2024, https://www.bbc.com/news/world-asia-15521300.

──CHAPTER 12──

The Silang Campus
No Longer a Mystery

Karen

"*Life is either a daring adventure or nothing.*"
—*Helen Keller*

Our Blue Bomb carried us from the Baesa campus down Balibago Road onto Epifania de los Santos (EDSA)—a vast, ten-lane divided highway arching around the eastern edge of Metro Manila proper. It was an excellent road with well-marked overpasses and signage, filled with cars, buses, and jeepneys. We traveled for about twenty minutes and then took the Binan exit.

We saw a large textile mill and what seemed to be a small military base. And then, what a change! Off the good pavement, the road was uneven gravel with potholes—very bumpy. Sugarcane fields dotted either side of the main road before it turned and took us through fields and small barrios comprising lovely little nipa huts and other native homes.[73] Most were raised above the ground on stilts with smoldering fires below to control the mosquitos. Occasionally we spotted sari-sari stores. The children and women waved and smiled; the men shouted, "Hey, Joe!" and made the victory sign. Those friendly greetings were welcome and so different from the attitude of the young man at the Baesa campus gate.

---
[73] The nipa palm is often woven to create lovely, intricate patterns on the sides of homes, mostly those on stilts.

The road improved as we followed a winding path past beautiful coffee plantations. Occasionally, we had to drive around plastic matting on the road where coffee beans lay drying in the sun. After a little over an hour, we saw the sign for the PUC, Silang campus. We turned onto the campus road, a dirt-and-gravel mix, and wound left and right, up and down through open land. The first building we saw was modern; this was the seminary of the Far Eastern Division of SDA. Later we learned that students and faculty from seventeen countries attended those two institutions. A little further we saw several partly open-sided, shedlike buildings and road equipment of various kinds. A sign identified this location as the motor pool.

Continuing up more small hills and down dips and around a bend, we saw eight or nine men assembling a long, wooden building, assisted by a crane. We'd been told this former barracks, along with fourteen others, would become classrooms and administrative offices. Much of the equipment and many of the buildings had been cheaply purchased from or donated by the US Agency for International Development (USAID) for educational endeavors.[74]

Now there were palm trees and bushes and shrubs. A huge Quonset-shaped building on the right was the campus church. The road became much steeper, winding left and right, the "shoulders" dropping off on one side. Along one side of that ridge road stood a row of very modern homes. Dale told us these were the homes for faculty and administrative families. At the very top, the highest point on campus, a huge oil tank loomed above us. Dale explained it had been disassembled at Naval Base Subic Bay, 122 miles north of Silang, then thoroughly cleaned and reconditioned and was now the campus water tower.

"What a wonderful place to view the whole campus," I said. Jeff was the first one out of the car, heading straight toward the tank and grabbing the rungs of the attached metal ladder, then scampering to the top ahead of the rest of us! Kimberly followed him to explore and

---

[74] https://www.usaid.gov (Accessed February 15, 2024).

enjoy the view. Dale and I brought up the rear.

"Note the wonderful breeze," I said.

"They told me the temperature here is usually about fifteen degrees cooler than in Metro Manila. Behind the faculty houses along this ridge is a deep gorge with a small, fast river," Dale said.

Wanting us to know the good, the bad, and the ugly, he continued: "And there are gorgeous birds and monkeys, and snakes, including pythons, which are large but not poisonous, and 'one-steps'—small and very poisonous, so be cautious. We'll learn how to identify them. One thing to remember is they have triangular heads."

We had been invited to use Jean and Jim Zachary's home for the weekend as they were away on holiday. The floors were all of beautiful narrawood parquet, and the sofas, chairs, and side tables were of Philippine hardwood, rattan, and cane.[75] The kitchen had modern appliances, and the windows at the back of the home looked out on a lovely backyard and a drop-off.

It was a charming home, and we would have one like it in a few months.

We loved meeting the many Filipinos and overseas faculty. For several American families, this was a second or third overseas assignment; they had settled in nicely and seemed quite happy there. The campus church boasted a huge auditorium. We were invited for lunch at one faculty home and had supper with another family. We learned that the sprawling pineapple plantation we saw on the hills above the "other side of the river ravine" was owned by Imelda Marcos. The weekend was peaceful and relaxed, and the kids loved those new environs. Still, the homesickness haunted me in the mornings, even on this enjoyable trip to see where we would soon live. Most folks were kind and understanding.

---

[75] The narra tree, scientific name *Pterocarpus indicus*, has been the national tree of the Philippines since 1934. According to Wikipedia, it's also known as Philippine mahogany, Andaman redwood, Burmese rosewood, Papua New Guinea rosewood, Malay padauk, Amboyna wood, narra and asana, Pashu padauk, and angsana. It is primarily used for high-grade furniture, plywood for light construction, lumber, and keys for marimbas!

2020s Update

—**EDSA**, the 23.8-kilometer (14.5-mile) highway creating a semicircle skirting the east side of Metro Manila, was named for Epifanio de los Santos y Cristóbal, a historian, jurist, artist, literary critic, and scholar. In 2015, 330,000 vehicles traversed the highway each day. You can watch Jeremy Renner make his way between Magallanes and Taft Avenues in *Bourne Legacy*. EDSA is honored as the site of an important bloodless "exorcism": There was to be a coup, but Marcos learned of it, so rebel leaders held a press conference to announce the rebellion against Marcos. They then called on Archbishop Jaime Cardinal Sin (yes, that's his real name) for help, and he appealed by radio for support for the rebels. The first to arrive on the scene were priests and nuns, then citizens of the republic, and Marcos's dictatorship was toppled.[76]

—**Taal Volcano's** first known eruption was in 1572, estimated then to have been 18,000 feet, and eruptions in 2020 and 2022 have covered large areas with ash, damaging some nearby crops and properties. The elevation presently is 311 meters. Philippine online news source *Rappler* reports twenty-four active volcanoes and says Taal is "one of the world's lowest and deadliest volcanos."[77] It is "one of sixteen volcanoes recognized by the International Association of Volcanology and Chemistry of the Earth's Interior (IAVCE)."[78]

---

[76] "29 things about EDSA You May or May Not Know," https://coconuts.co/manila/features/29-things-about-edsa-you-may-or-may-not-know.
[77] Pauline Macaraeg, "TIMELINE: Taal Volcano eruptions since 1572," *Rappler*, January 13, 2020, https://www.rappler.com/newsbreak/iq/249127-timeline-taal-volcano-eruptions.
[78] "What Is Taal Volcano?" Philippine News, February 14, 2020, https://philnews.ph/2020/02/14/what-is-taal-volcano-about-the-volcano-in-the-philippines.

CHAPTER 13

Becky, Extraordinary Helper and Friend

Karen

"Ma'am, the helper does all the work."

—Becky

Before arriving in the Philippines, it seemed to us that having servants would validate the "rich American" image we wanted to avoid. However, once we were there, everyone we met—Filipinos and overseas workers—assured us that *all* the professors and most of the staff had helpers, sometimes more than one. And the term "helper" did seem more palatable than "servant."

Most of the helpers on campus were students, and we were *expected* to help them by hiring them. Most could not go to college if they didn't earn tuition or room and board, and many preferred to work in a home rather than in the Food Factory, cafeteria, or on the grounds or custodial staff. We didn't want to jettison our ideals, but gradually, our thinking changed. Almost daily, students came to our door asking to work for us. In our third week, still considering the pluses and minuses, we took their names and were leaning toward finding just the right arrangement when Becky knocked on our door. She was tiny and soft spoken yet quietly confident.

"Ma'am, I'm Becky Bea, and I would like to work for you. Is that possible?"

I invited her in and asked Dale to come meet her. We sat together in the sala, and she introduced herself, explaining that she was from the Bicol Region in Southern Luzon, she had eleven brothers and sisters, and her father could pay for her college tuition but not room and board. She wished to work full-time for room and board.

"I will do all the work: I will cook, clean all, polish floors, wash clothes, and shop."

"That sounds wonderful. It seems good for you as well as for us."

It sounded perfect because I was still fighting homesickness and lack of energy due to the heat and humidity. I also did not know how to prepare Filipino food and wanted to learn. Dale and I looked at each other. We liked her immediately and were warming to the idea of her being our helper. But we wanted there to be guidelines.

"Salamat, Becky. We think we'd like to have a good partnership with you, so it's important that you understand that our children will make their own beds, pick up their clothes, and they will wash the dishes once a day."

I wanted that to be clear, because I had friends in college who had been raised by helpers, amahs, or servants, and as young adults they didn't possess some very basic life skills—like emptying the trash regularly.

"Oh, no, ma'am. I will do."

"No, Becky, they will do. It's good for them."

"But the helper does all the work."

"Perhaps, and salamat, but not in our home."

It seemed hard for her to believe we would require our children to do those chores. She expected to do all the work for the use of our helper's room and meals with us. We walked her out to the room she would use. We had originally been embarrassed to find we had a "helper's room" in our house, but now it was a blessing. It was small, but it had a nice bed, dresser, large window, and its own CR (comfort room/bathroom). Becky was delighted with everything about that room.

"Ma'am, sir, I have never had a room of my own. It is very nice."

We decided to hire Becky. No kidding! What a blessing for us, and essential for her, because she could not continue classes without a job. We told her we wanted to hire her, but she could only work half-time, and we would give her seventy pesos per month. She was stunned.

"No, ma'am, sir, I don't need that. Just my room and board is so much."

"Yes, Becky, we want to pay you."

We found she had never been paid cash for her work. Her ₱70 a month would cost us $10. We felt embarrassed not to pay more; however, we had been told by other overseas workers it was the "top rate" and that it would eventually cause problems among the Filipinos, expatriates, and their helpers if we paid more.

"I can begin now; *maraming* salamat,"[79] Becky said, and she moved in that day.

Becky was a wonderful worker and a pleasure to have in our home. She had a quiet and happy nature, worked efficiently, and was an excellent cook. She became a special friend to our children and to us, and she helped us learn more about the culture in many ways—going shopping with us, teaching us how to barter, bartering for us, telling us stories, and sharing Filipino beliefs and traditions.

One day, she and I were exploring Divisoria Market, one of the oldest and largest markets in Manila.[80] It was embarrassing for both Becky and me when one of the merchants asked Becky if she would go with us when we returned to the US. We both just smiled.

Soon I was venturing out in jeepneys by myself to explore Divisoria and other markets. "Where is your companion?" was a common greeting when I walked by myself, reflecting the expectation of companionship, *pakikisama* (having a good personal relationship with others). I was surprised the first time Becky took my hand as she guided me across an intersection, though I'd seen other women—and men—walking hand

---

[79] Tagalog for "Very many thanks."
[80] Early non-Christian Chinese merchants were not allowed to do business inside the original Intramuros commercial area, so they focused on an area near the Pasig River. It is now called by some the "mother of all markets" in Manila, http://abroadcast.com/bargain-abroad/divisoria-market-manila-philippines.

in hand or arm in arm. It was an expected closeness and for safety, not sexual in any way. Likely some were romantically involved, but no one would know because the hand-holding was so common.

Friends on campus said, "Oh, you mustn't go to Divisoria by yourself." But I'd learned how to be wise and safe—wearing no watch, no jewelry, and holding my small, flat purse waist high against my body with my wrist through the loop on its corner—and never had problems. I went wherever I wanted via jeepney and eventually drove on my own, learning to get my bumper ahead of others to manage the fact that there were no working intersection lights.

One afternoon, we were eating on our beautiful, enclosed porch, and a piece of silverware fell on the tile floor.

"Wait," Becky said quickly. "Look before you pick it up. Is it fork or spoon? If a silverware is dropped, it means a visitor is coming." She giggled shyly. "If a fork, a man is coming; if a spoon, a woman." She was obviously embarrassed but still loved telling us the superstitions.

Cooking and shopping go hand in hand, and Becky was a huge help with both. I learned that almost every entrée begins by sautéing garlic and onions, and I learned to make pancit and lumpia. Shopping and eating became fun. There were so many wonderful new foods, fruits especially. Most of them my family had never seen: dark-red, purple, or brown mangosteens; rambutan, about the size of a hen's egg with hair (*rambut*) on the outside; and santol, starfruit, *tambis*, and jackfruit, the largest tree-borne fruit in the world. The giant durian elicited comments from "wonderful" to "awful" because of its strong odor—putrid to some. We learned that some airlines won't let passengers bring durian on board because of the smell. My favorite new fruit was atis (sugar apple), looking like a small hand grenade with its greenish skin covered in half-inch mounds filled with hard seeds worth getting past for the exquisite taste inside.[81]

---

[81] Atis fruit, also known as sweet sop or sugar apple (*Anona squamosal L.*), from Central America and the Caribbean, was introduced to the RP by the Spanish. The tree bears fruit three times a year. The seeds are poisonous to eat but are used as an herbal medicine.

Becky and I shared meal prep. There was almost always rice in the fridge, and one evening after dinner, I made rice pudding: white rice, sometimes a well-beaten egg, brown sugar, cinnamon, and a pinch of nutmeg, all covered with milk, dotted with butter, and baked. Yum! After our regular meal, I took a bowl of the warm, just-out-of-the-oven rice to Becky in her room. She graciously thanked me. Later that evening, when I went to the garage to check the laundry, the bowl was sitting on the floor outside Becky's room, still almost full. I knocked on her door.

"Becky, is something wrong with the rice?"

She said awkwardly, "I'm sorry to waste, but it is so sweet!" Her face showed her distaste. "I never had rice like that. Just too sweet. We never make it like that."

She explained that sometimes for a treat, she reheated rice, added savory flavorings, and put it all in sticky buns.

"Let's try that soon," I said, hoping for the best.

Later, we made sticky buns together. Becky loved them. I emphatically did not.

We loved watching Becky polish the floors. The job required a coconut husk that had been cut in half to expose the fibers on the flat side, Johnson's Floor Wax, and "Becky's dance." Imagine this: first she washed the floors, then took off her shoes, put her right foot on the rounded part of the coconut husk, spread some wax on the floor, and, starting at one corner of the room and pushing with the other foot, she pushed and glided and created a lovely sort of dance forward, then back, and forward again, moving left to right so the fibers polished the floor to a high gloss. It was good exercise, too. She insisted on polishing the terrazzo floors of our Baesa campus home. I wasn't sure it was necessary, but I let her choose how to spend her time caring for us.

Becky helped my understanding, experience, and attitude about life in the Philippines. Not all stories about helpers were pleasant. Some families provided only room and board and no other payment, leaving the helper with little to no cash to purchase items for themselves, family, or friends or to move forward with other life plans.

Leaving the Philippines for work as nannies, housekeepers, or on the high seas brings its own challenges.[82] Many Filipino men and women contracted with individuals or companies, often for two years or more. If they had children, family members in the Philippines cared for them while they were gone. Usually, the remuneration was several times the Filipino wages at home, and many folks felt it was worth the separation and helped increase the quality of life for their family at home.[83]

Overseas Filipino workers (OFW) have been "significantly contributing to the Philippine economy" since the mid-1980s.[84] In 2017, as much as 11 percent of the economy came from OFWs sending moneys home.[85] With the Philippines identified as "one of the world's top sending nations of migrant workers," some call OFWs the "backbone of the Philippine economy."[86] Sometimes two helpers are hired so they won't be lonely.

Some contracts are fair and well managed for both parties, while others are definitely not. There are many types of abuses, including physical, emotional, and sexual abuse; employers in other countries withholding the guest worker's passport; and employers

---

[82] https://www.nationalgeographic.com/magazine/article/guest-worker (Accessed February 15, 2024).
[83] Rachel Aviv, "The Cost of Caring," *The New Yorker*, April 11, 2016.
[84] Raymundo J. Talento. "Measurement of the Migrant Workers in the Philippine System of National Accounts (PSNA) 2004 https://unstats.un.org/unsd/tradeserv/TSG%200 (Accessed February 15, 2024).
[85] The Philippine Statistics Authority (PSA) reported in 2017 that there was "an estimated 2,339 million OFWs" and they "were considered economic heroes of the country because of their significant contribution to the growth" of the economy, $34 billion in 2018. Overseas Filipino workers (OFWs) include permanent residents and short-term contractual workers. Compareremit.com/money-transfer-guide/contribution-of-the-ofw-to-the-philippines-economy (Accessed February 15, 2024).
[86] Story by Support@Yehey.com; September 24, 2022 https://www.com/en-us/money/markets/ofws-the-backbone-of-the-Philippines (Accessed February 2024).

not providing adequate housing or food.[87] Similar to employers in the Philippines, some give their helpers only one day off every two weeks, and some provide only room and board, no cash.

Our experience with helpers was positive. I regret I didn't simply sit and talk with Becky more often, asking more about her family or offering to drive her home to visit and meet them. I could have learned so much more. She was a precious friend.[88]

Update 2020s

—OFWs have faced new challenges in the last ten years. The Department of Foreign Affairs identified the top causes of death for that period. COVID-19 caused an estimated 800 to 900 deaths, often *without* support from their employers. The actual number is unknown because the information may not be reported correctly or at all. Other causes: vehicular accidents, natural or medical causes, and murder or foul play. There have also been 3,371 criminal cases opened against Filipinos (mostly in Malaysia). Several Filipino government agencies are working to stay aware of OFW issues and provide a safety net.[89] One young woman in the United Arab Emirates defended herself with the knife her employer used to attempt to rape her. The employer died, and she was sentenced to death. That charge was dropped; however, she was sentenced to five years for stealing a phone and is serving her term for that crime. This is only one aspect of issues that arise from interracial relationships and cultural

---

[87] We met a middle-aged Filipina outside the RP who had worked for a physician's family for twelve years. She said her job was "doing everything": cleaning, cooking, laundry, shopping, etc. She received only room and board, no monetary payment, and she worked six days a week and had not been able to go home to the Philippines in all that time.

[88] Becky is now a wife, mother, grandmother, and librarian; we communicate via text and phone.

[89] Michelle Abad. "COVID-19 top cause of death among Filipinos abroad in last 10 years—DFA." *Rappler*, Mar 2, 2023, https://www.rappler.com/nation/overseas-filipinos/dfa-report-house-hearing-top-cause-death-filipinos-abroad-2013-2023/.

differences in behavior and expectations.⁹⁰

—The Philippines's first hospital offering free care to OFWs and their dependents opened in May 2022. Rodrigo Duterte, then president, described this service as "the government's way of thanking OFWs for their 'valuable contribution to the country's socio-economic progress and for their critical role in upholding the Filipino identity in the global community.'"⁹¹

—OFW teachers are being hired for school in the US.⁹² School calendars and grading systems are similar in the US and the RP; that's one reason this move is practical for US schools, and they have hired more than 1,0000 teachers in the past few years. OFW teachers report finding students disrespectful and classroom management a challenge.⁹³

—Varied Jobs for OFWs: For many years, medical professionals have been leaving the RP to work internationally and are seen as gentle and attentive caregivers. Another category not so well known is work on the "high seas"—in the military, on tankers, cargo ships (400,000 workers), and cruise ships (325,000 workers).⁹⁴

—The quick turnaround (usually a two-year contract), especially in the Middle East, means that obtaining resident status is difficult or impossible. Labor-market disruptions (e.g., COVID, job placement

---

⁹⁰ Ana P. Santos. "[DASH of SAS] Lessons about intersections of migrant life, sexuality, inter-racial relationships." *Rappler*, December 17, 2023, https://www.rappler.com/voices/thought-leaders/dash-of-sas-lessons-about-intersections-migrant-life-sexuality-inter-racial-relationships/.
⁹¹ Michelle Abad. "What you should know about the OFW Hospital." Rappler, Dec. 20, 2023.
⁹² www.bing.com/videos/search?q=this+week+filipina+school+teachers+in+us; School in Nevada hires more Filipino Special Education teachers, annual salary at Php 2.1M - The Summit Express
⁹³ Eli Saslow, "An American Education." https://www.washingtonpost.com/nation/2022/10/02/ (Accessed April 7, 2024).
⁹⁴ 2021 Overseas Filipino Workers (Final Results) | Philippine Statistics Authority (psa.gov.ph); Filipino Seafarers Find Their Future – and Lives - Adrift - VERA Files.

companies going out of business) are tragic for workers, leaving them to fend for themselves.

—**Being seen as "part of the family" can be a blessing and a curse.** Some domestic workers in the Philippines live with their family—either an older sibling, cousin, or other relative—and sometimes are not paid at all, their employers believing that room and board and other privileges as a family member mean there is no need for cash. Of course, the workers cannot move ahead in their lives if they have no actual monetary income.[95]

—**An article from late 2023, "OFW who refused to leave employer during Hamas attack brought home," reveals how close some OFWs feel to their employers.** This particular employer was elderly, and her caretaker protected her the best she could as gunmen fired into their bomb shelter, dying in the process. Many helpers feel that they are "family already."[96]

—**The phenomenon of immigrant women working as nannies** is candidly and touchingly described by Rachel Aviv in a *New Yorker* article titled "The Cost of Caring."[97]

—**Early Filipino American history is beautifully shown in an animated presentation titled "A Filipino American Story (Since 1587),"** created by NextDayBetter and the AARP AAPI Community for Filipino American History Month and found on their website and YouTube.[98]

---

[95] "For Filipino domestic workers, being 'part of the family' can be a blessing and a curse," Quartz, Accessed February 14, 2024, https://qz.com/1005108/for-filipino-domestic-workers-being-part-of-the-family.
[96] Michelle Abad, "Remains of OFW who refused to leave employer during Hamas attack brought home," *Rappler*, Nov. 3, 2023.
[97] Rachel Aviv, "The Cost of Caring: The lives of the immigrant women who tend to the needs of others," *The New Yorker*, April 11, 2016.
[98] "A Filipino American Story Since 1587" https://www.facebook.com/NextDayBetter (Accessed April 7, 2024).

CHAPTER 14

Education Challenges and Insights

Dale

"One of the most cohesive factors in choosing a course of study is family ties."

—Dale

Biology was a big department at PUC; however, there was little appreciation for field biology or the process of science. I was surprised to find that many students, even those coming from rural barrios, did not distinguish between a mouse and a shrew. I told them about the shrews living in our new home, and they insisted that they were mice; they had never seen and knew nothing of shrews. And yet we had shrews cohabiting with our family and living in the organ, right there on campus.

The shrew family consisted of a mother and five or six half-grown young. We watched them move silently around the living room in the evenings, forming a train-like procession, babies following in single file behind the mother, often with the nose of each one touching the tail or the rear end of its leader. They moved with a stereotypic saunter and in a predictable path around the perimeter of the living room, looking for roaches, beetles, geckos, and whatever passed as shrew food.

The teacher who had recently lived in our house had sold his electric organ, but it remained there for weeks until the owners claimed it. I examined the organ for damage, fearing that the shrews were chewing wires or some other vital component, as mice do. I found no damage, but I did find a sizable pile of dog or cat food pellets. I surmised that the former resident owned a small dog or a cat as most of the pellets did not match what we were feeding Apricot. The shrews did not seem to be eating the dog food, but it must have resembled food closely enough to elicit the hoarding behaviors.

Mice have chisel-shaped teeth and are omnivorous, chewing most anything, seemingly for the sheer delight of the chewing. They and their rat cousins sometimes chew the insulation from electrical wiring, causing short circuits, sparks, and house fires. Not so with our shrews. Shrews have sharply pointed teeth and largely prey on insects, invertebrates, and other tiny organisms. They were pleasant, compatible, and entertaining houseguests.

Konrad Lorenz, a 1973 Nobel Prize laureate, tells in his 1952 book, *King Solomon's Ring*, of his experience with water shrews—a different species than our Filipino shrews, but showing some of the same nearsighted behaviors and following the same path on repeated evening excursions around his house.[99] Their path tended to follow walls, as was true for our shrews.

Lorenz placed two stones in their path, which produced confusion at first, but they soon learned to jump on top of the stone and proceed on their journey. After a few days, he removed the stones. When Lorenz's shrews came to the spot that the stone had occupied, they jumped and landed in a confused muddle on the bare floor and spent some time exploring with their fellows before moving on. The shrews learned that the stone was not there and moved confidently on the following evening! I had plans to test our shrews in a similar manner, but the organ's new owner appeared unexpectedly, claimed the shrew's home, and the shrews must have moved on, because we never saw them again.

But back to my students not knowing the difference between a

---

[99] Konrad Z. Lorenz, *King Solomon's Ring* (New York, NY: Apollo Editions, 1952).

mouse and a shrew. I also discovered that if asked for the name of a bird we spotted, Filipinos would typically say they didn't know. But if I asked for the Filipino name of the bird, they knew it. It is easy to miscalculate what is understood cross-culturally.

Biology is necessary for the much-desired careers in medicine, nursing, and other paramedical professions. A professional biologist would make a significantly lower salary and have less prestige than a physician or nurse, and diplomas in those areas make emigration to the States easier. And in the States, they will have even higher prestige and, more importantly, a higher salary.

My students focused on learning the facts needed to reach their professional goals. Filipino students excel at memorization and panic with analysis. Memorization has a long history in education in the Philippines. Some of the first textbooks students used, especially in the Spanish mission schools of the eighteenth century, were religious devotionals and catechisms. Students were required to recite portions of these texts verbatim, even though they often did not understand the meaning of the Spanish words.[100]

I thought I had a fair understanding of and sensitivity to race relations, but here I also had to deal with tribal differences with which I was not familiar. I organized my A and P students into equal-sized groups. In the second week, I realized a group that had been small to start with had lost a member. I asked the girl why she had moved to another group.

She replied, "But, sir! I cannot learn in that group."

I asked, "Why is that so?"

She said: "Well, sir! You see, sir! They are Visayan, and I am a Tagalog."

This was something I knew too little about to argue. I chose

---

[100] Gaspar Astete, *Catecismo de la Doctrina Cristiana*, was one such document required to be used in primary schools under a royal decree, December 20, 1863. See Blair and Robertson's *The Philippine Islands*, Vol. XLVI, p. 98; 1912. Census of the Philippine Islands (Washington, 1905), p. 485; Jose Rizal, *The Social Cancer*. 1886. Translated from Spanish *Noli me Tangere* by Charles E. Derbyshire. (Manila) McCullough Printing Company. Printed in the Philippines, 1956 (renewal), 103–104.

to save the student–teacher relationship and let her stay where she would be less distracted. I still ponder that decision.

One of the most cohesive factors in choosing a course of study was family ties. It is rare for a student to pay their way through college all by themselves or even with the help of their immediate family. The parents and extended family often sacrifice to help a student reach their goals, and the student pays a price: the extended Filipino family has a voice in deciding what a student will take as a major and what they will do after graduation.

It is also expected that the student can and should return the favor. This may involve helping their parents become more comfortable financially; it may mean helping an extended family member get through school and into a productive and lucrative occupation; and sometimes more. Being maximally productive often involves going to the United States or another foreign country. One fond hope is that they will live in the States, be successful, and share their advantages with family back home.

The plan is often modified if the student is a female and a male relative needs monetary help. This is seen as a reason for the woman to stop attending school, get a job, and help the often-younger male financially. Girls may also be encouraged not to marry—and might be seen as not "salable," even with a degree—because they are often older when they finish their degree. One young woman facing these decisions shared this with me: "We are expected to help our brothers because they will have the responsibilities of a family."

Frequently, all classes were "suspended" in the Metro Manila area (including our campuses) by the Ministry of Education. The reason: flooded conditions and washed-out bridges made it difficult for some students to get to class. Flooding was an issue in Baesa but not for our students at the higher-elevation campus in Silang. But if we did not follow those directions, both campuses would be in violation of the law. So, sometimes there were no classes and no labs for a week, which played havoc with the academic schedule.

In the past, a significant portion of the human skeletal material needed for A and P laboratories had been supplied by the students from relative's graves! The remains were traditionally well cared for and buried by the family.

One student brought the complete skeleton of his older brother. He kept close tabs on where and how the bones were treated. Later he became an A and P lab instructor. When he graduated, he asked Dra. Rasa if he could return his brother's bones to his village cemetery. He knew precisely where each bone was. These materials were precious gifts seen as sacrifices from the students and their families; some were returned to their families when requested.

However, as precious as they were, bones were often handled carelessly. All the styloid processes at the outer edges and other delicate projections were broken off the skulls. The bones had marks all over them because when the instructors designed the lab tests, they sometimes took a felt-tip pen and indicated the part to be identified with a large smear of red or black ink. They tapped on bones with pens and pencils to bring attention to the object of study, and the bones were sometimes tossed carelessly back into the storage boxes. I lectured about respect for life at all levels—especially in the case of human materials—and the need to handle lab specimens carefully. Eventually, it seemed a little less damage was occurring.

Equipment and supplies were a challenge. It wasn't easy to find or keep on hand the supplies that seemed essential to me. For example, there was no lens paper on campus, and I cringed as I saw students running to get out of the rain while carrying a well-worn—but precious and expensive—microscope.

Teaching on the Baesa campus on Mondays, Wednesdays, and Fridays and driving two hours each way to the Silang campus on Tuesdays and Thursdays gave me limited opportunity to prepare for my classes. Then there were occasional faculty meetings on the Silang campus. One particular memory involves a serious conflict; folks were at an impasse, things were growing rather heated, and the meeting ended without a decision. A Filipino colleague approached me apart from the others.

"You don't understand this at all, do you?"

I admitted that I surely did not.

"It's tribal," he explained. "With different people groups in the Philippines, it's important to each that they have a voice in the leadership. If we make a decision today, it will go one way. If we wait to make the decision 'til we are all on the other campus, it will go 'our' way. But! You must not discuss this with anyone. I just thought you should understand."

And I thanked him for that crucial insight and caution.

2020s Update

—**The three major island groups** are Luzon, Visayas, and Mindanao, each with distinct customs, languages, and characteristics; **the major dialects** are Tagalog, Bisaya, Hiligaynon, Ilocano, and Waray. The current count of dialects is 170 to 200, according to various sources.

CHAPTER 15

Being Needed Makes All the Difference

Karen

"You can only go halfway into the darkest forest; then you are coming out the other side."

—Chinese Proverb

We settled into our new routine: Dale taught classes on both campuses, and Jeff and Kimberly kept busy in their one-room school six hours a day. After school, Kimberly was with friends or with Becky, and Jeff worked in the bakery and explored the fields beyond our home. My morning homesickness and tears continued most mornings. *Discouraging!* I tried to be positive. I walked, I prayed, I took jeepney rides with Dale and by myself, and I surely appreciated Becky's help.

One beautiful day, Jim Zachary—Jean's husband and a professor from the seminary on the Silang campus—knocked on my front door.

"Karen, I need your help. Could you come to my office in Manila two days a week? I hear you are a good secretary. Please, I have a huge new project and need your help."

His new project sounded fascinating: 100,000 Bibles for Metro Manila! The plan was that Faith for Today, a stateside SDA evangelistic group, would send Bibles to be distributed to leaders in community/barangay groups who would study the Bible together, led by volunteers. The culmination would be a huge crusade in Metro Manila. I reasoned that the kids would be in school most of the day, and Becky could manage the house and the kids very well while I was gone.

I needed to be busy, to feel useful, and didn't have to think long about his request. I accepted. What a challenge! Dale was thrilled for me. We talked to faculty and students about the best way to get to the center of Manila; I wasn't ready to drive in that traffic yet!

The first few workdays, I rode PUC's minivan with the nurses going to work at the Manila Sanitarium. Talking with the nurses was informative and fascinating, and it felt good to make more friends. Jim's office was on the second floor of the North Philippine Union Mission offices across the street from the sanitarium.[101] The other secretaries in the office, all Filipinas, were welcoming and gracious and a delight to work beside. I worked two days a week, and it felt amazing to get up early and have a real focus for the day.

Soon I learned to go the twelve miles by myself, taking two jeepney rides going and coming back—paying five US cents for each jeepney ride. The trip took at least an hour each way. I was learning to fit in, and what I saw on those rides increased my understanding and comfort with the culture. I thanked Jim many times for that opportunity.

In the first few days on the job, I learned I needed to wear the uniform of the other office secretaries. Very briefly, the idea surprised me; then I realized, *Well, that will help me fit in*. I purchased the designated nylon knit material at the market, and on a day off, I walked to the home of my seamstress, Mading. A few days later, my uniform—a blouse and skirt—was finished. The other women at work were elated to see me wearing their uniform; and now I looked the part and looked forward to those days at work, typing, listening, and learning common phrases needed for my work and for traveling alone in Manila.

---

[101] Established in 1941 and repaired by Dr. Richli after a naval torpedo was detonated in the elevator shaft as it was being built, it was a revered part of the medical system in Manila. Now the Adventist Medical Center Manila.

Frequently, while working on my nice IBM electric typewriter, there was a "pop" and a flicker, and the lights in my office dimmed; some in other areas went out completely. Then I heard the chorus of women at their desks saying, almost in unison, "Oops, brownout!" Work stopped, the nail files came out, and friendly chatter began. Well, you couldn't see to work. The windows were in the men's offices, while the women's desks were in a central corridor. In a few minutes, sometimes as long as two hours, the lights came back on, and work resumed. Sometimes surgeries were disrupted at the sanitarium across the street, but I learned they had a few generators for really urgent activities and that the brownouts happened irregularly and often.

I remember fondly one particular day at work: as I walked down the stairs from my office to the lobby, heading across the street to the San cafeteria for lunch, I realized: *I am not homesick; I have not been homesick for three mornings.* What a blessing! I was going to be all right. I never felt the tight stomach and fearful feelings again. Such a relief! I needed to learn the Tagalog word for "Wonderful!"[102]

So now, with a pleasant home, a wonderful husband with a job he found fascinating and challenging, children well cared for and learning a whole new way of enjoying the world, a car in our garage that worked at least part of the time, an excellent helper, a job I truly enjoyed, and many new friends, life was good. Everything was in order. I felt an "embarrassment of riches." And no Filipino ever made me feel they resented my blessings.

It took feeling needed, helping with a fascinating project, and focusing outside myself to settle in. And, oh, yes, I was getting a salary.

Far Eastern Division of SDA:
Memo: Action has been taken to approve your employment on 3/8ths of a fractional budget effective on July 1, 1978. It is our understanding that you will be working as a secretary in

---

[102] It's *kamangha-mangha*.

the Seminary and will also be hostess on the Baesa Compound. You will be paid on a flat rate basis and therefore, it is not necessary for you to submit a monthly report; however, we would appreciate receiving notification when you take vacation or when you go on furlough with your husband.

CHAPTER 16

No Cats for Cat Lab

Karen

"Filipinos are masters of improvisation and creativity born of necessity, the mother of invention."

—Dale, My A and P Professor

When the more dramatic reactions of my culture shock settled down and I could concentrate, I registered for the A and P course on the Baesa campus. While a social work major at WWC, one of my requirements was an A and P course; the professors knew the information would help me better understand and assist clients.

I found the course material fascinating—and the professor, Dale, was helpful and close at hand. He was a good teacher; I loved that he called our textbook "an owner's manual." Sometimes, preparing for tests, I'd lie in bed at night, silently going over body systems in my mind: *I take some lovely mango into my mouth, chew, and my teeth and tongue and saliva break it down; then it travels down the esophagus to the stomach, where enzymes begin their work; then it goes through the renal arteries to the nephron where the kidneys extract it from the blood and . . .*

Tessie Poblano, the Filipina professor who previously taught the A and P class, was our lab instructor and knew where to get lab equipment, reagents, models, and specimens. However, there were no cats for Cat Lab. At the end of a busy lab period, Tessie announced, matter-of-factly: "Cat Lab begins next week; it's important that you find your cat and bring it to lab. We will euthanize it and prepare it for dissection."

Did I hear correctly? I tried to process her instructions. What did they require of me personally? Of course, I told my instructor and partner; he found it fascinating, humorous, and challenging. We realized the school had no money, perhaps no source, for lab animals. He accepted the challenge for us both and assured me we'd figure it out before the next lab.

The next weekend, we drove to the Silang campus, and I described my dilemma to friends there. One friend said, "Ah, we have a cat we don't want. You can take her!"

"No, thank you, but *I don't want your cat*" was my immediate and firm response.

We had a lovely weekend, but someone put their unwanted cat in our car as we left Silang. The kids loved the idea of another pet. Little did they know. We housed the doomed cat in our garage and cared for it for a whole week, and I tried to prepare myself, Jeff, and Kimberly for what was to come.

Then I said to myself and Dale: "What was I thinking? I am not going to kill that cat! How can we even explain it to the kids?"

On the day of the afternoon Cat Lab, Dale came home for lunch and found me standing in the kitchen by the screen door to the garage, tears streaming down my face, watching the cat eat what would be her last meal.

"I'm not going to kill that cat!" I said. "What were we thinking?"

"I'll help you," Dale said. "It won't hurt her. We'll put her in a bell jar, and she will simply go to sleep."

"You are not hearing me," I said emphatically. "I've been feeding that cat for a whole week. I am *not* killing that cat."

After lunch, my class instructor/husband left the garage with the cat. I did not go to lab that day. When he came home, he told me that he indeed had taken the cat to the lab, put her under a bell jar with an ether overdose, and the cat had become a specimen. My specimen.

The next week, Cat Lab was held outdoors under the trees so the pungent smell of formaldehyde and other chemicals and decay was not overpowering. The other three A and P students in my group shared in the dissection of my cat on a table under the trees, and I, offering to create the notes for all of us, watched at a distance. I unwittingly and unwillingly had made a significant contribution to Cat Lab: my cat was pregnant, so we had babies, too. Great! A bit nauseous, I made the lab notes for our team and did not touch her or her babies. When folks asked me later if my instructor husband had given me an A, I replied: "I *earned* an A."

In spite of it all, or maybe because of the drama, I value the information I gleaned from that A and P class, the instructors, my lab mates, and the situation. Because of the coursework and the cultural experience, I would be better able to understand and assist my clients and their families in my work as a medical social worker—my goal at that point. I would finish my schooling when we got back to the States.

Filipinos feel differently about cats, dogs, and other house pets than I'm used to. Many Americans feel their family is incomplete without a pet, maybe several. I'd already noticed that most Filipinos I met did not have house pets. For one thing, animals with a pedigree are expensive to buy and require costly veterinary care and inoculations. Some Filipino families own watchdogs, which are taught to bark and frighten people away from homes, chicken pens, and businesses. Many folks learn to fear cats and dogs: those they see in the streets are unkept, scratching and rooting for food in garbage piles and filthy gutters. Folks knew the animals had likely not been inoculated and might carry diseases like rabies. Children learn not to get near them.

While chatting with a coworker who had small children, I asked if she would like me to have friends in the States send the *Our Little Friend* and *Primary Treasure* story papers given to children every week in SDA church, and I'd share them with her and other mothers.[103]

"Oh, no, salamat po." (Thank you [with respect].) "I don't read those to my kids. I've had those papers before, and I didn't like the stories. They talked about cats and dogs and other animals as pets. I do not believe children should be close to animals like that; it's dangerous. I would never let my children have those kinds of pets. I really think the stories are not true."

Fascinated, I thought it would help to share our experience with her: "Dale and I always have had pets—cats, dogs, horses, chickens. We love them, and the children love and play with them, and they live in our homes with us. We take them to the veterinarians for their shots so they are healthy and safe. I do understand that we all have to be careful of animals on the streets who are not cared for and may have disease or are mean."

Yet another reason why Filipinos have negative feelings about dogs, cats, and rats is that a wide variety of animals are used as street food.[104] In some areas, dog meat is eaten for special occasions, historically when preparing for war; and it's believed eating the meat helps produce body heat needed in the cooler temperatures in areas like Baguio, the summer capital where President Marcos had a summer palace. Some items, like civet cat coffee, or *kopi luwak*, are costly.[105]

Many families keep chickens or ducks for their meat and eggs. Specialty duck eggs are used for a famous treat called balut, which may fascinate or seem revolting. The eggs of Pateros ducks, also known as *itik* ducks, are incubated for eighteen days, then the shell is cracked, and the contents are eaten. They are high in protein and

---

[103] These children's papers are published by Pacific Press; OLF since 1890; PT since 1947.
[104] "Star meat" was a term used for rats, "S-T-A-R" being "R-A-T-S" spelled backward. These were not rats found in city streets but rather hunted in the fields and brought to market.
[105] "Civet Coffee-Why the World's Favorite Coffee is Kopi Luwak." https://purekopiluwak.com/civet-coffee/ (accessed Feb/ 15. 2024.

thought to be good for energy and recovering from too much alcohol, and some believe they are an aphrodisiac. This practice also exists in Laos, Cambodia, and Vietnam, having been introduced long ago by seafaring Chinese. It's common to hear street merchants chanting in a singsong manner: "Ba-luu-uu-uuuuut."

We limited our street food to "just-out-of-the-hot-oil" fried bananas and bottled drinks. And we had our own unusual pet, a civet cat, described in chapter 32, "Civet Cats, Owls, and Other Critters."

2020s Update

—**Street Food:** a current list of street food may be of interest.[106]

—**Pets:** In 2020, families in the Philippines owned almost twelve million pet dogs, according to the Philippine Canine Club's records; likely many more were not listed in this prestigious club's records. An article describes the valuable traits children learn caring for pets (e.g., empathy, responsibility, identifying and managing their own emotions) and urges adopting pets and ensuring they have food, shelter, and care (not sure if that includes veterinary visits).

---

[106] https://www.chefspencil.com/popular-filipino-street-foods/ (Accessed February 15, 2024)

CHAPTER 17

Jeepneys: Carnivals on Wheels

Karen

"The ingenuity of the Filipino took the basic jeep and made it into practical and later glitzy-looking transportation reasonable enough for almost everyone."

—*Karen*

It was wise and kind of Dale to distract me when I was homesick, taking me by jeepney to interesting places and helping me focus on my sociological and anthropological interests. We would "get down" (the appropriate term for getting off a jeepney), walk a bit, perhaps do a little shopping, buy a basket or two or some other ethnic artifact—or fried banana on a stick—and then head back to the campus, getting more in touch with our new country and city by the most popular means of public transportation. On those jeepney rides, we sat side by side and knee to knee (think "jeep-knees"), traveling with Filipinos, seeing what they saw, going where they went, and shopping with them. It helped us feel more a part of normal life in Manila.

Jeepneys are such a blessing. For very few pesos you can go almost anywhere in the city—or throughout the whole country, for that matter—at any time of day. You need to take a ferry between islands, and then there will be a jeepney at the ferry dock on the other shore, waiting to take you anywhere you wanted on that next island. I enjoyed taking them to work in Manila, two rides each way, five cents each ride, over an hour to go twelve miles.

I remember an article in *National Geographic* called "Jeepneys: A Carnival on Wheels," but I can't find the source of that declaration. According to another source, "the use of *borloloys* [unnecessary, superfluous, fashion accessories] ... are typical in the urban-suburban areas and most provinces. There ... are regional preferences for certain accessories."[107] The jeepneys I saw were indeed colorful: lots of shiny trim, tin, or brightly painted metal on the body with multicolored decorations. Some had tiny lights outlining the windows; almost all had tassels, mirrors, religious icons, and hand-crocheted panels hanging in at least the front window, stating something like JESUS LOVES ME or GOD BLESS or GOD IS LOVE. Often, flashy plastic decals or air-brushed art displayed sexy maidens and comments along the side or back. Music typically blared from speakers, and many jeepneys had multiple horns for decoration and noise. Horses were also a popular decoration. No two jeepneys were alike!

The American military sold or left many World War II Willys Jeeps and miles of metal track dubbed GI Track—metal fourteen inches wide, typically in sections of eight to ten feet.[108] Now it is often used for driveways and the tops of walls or to create walls in homes and businesses. The ingenuity of the Filipino took the basic jeep and made it into practical and later glitzy-looking transportation reasonable enough for almost everyone. Most Filipinos can't afford their own car or truck or jeep, and most folk do just fine with the

---

[107] Godofredo U. Stuart, Jr., "Jeepney," www.stuartxchange.org/Jeepney.html (Accessed February 16, 2024).

[108] The Willys MB US Army Jeep (formerly the US Army Truck, quarter-ton, 4x4) and the Ford GPW were manufactured from 1941 to 1945. These small four-wheel drive utility vehicles are considered the iconic World War II Jeep. Over the years, the World War II Jeep later evolved into the "CJ" civilian Jeep; https://en.wikipedia.org/wiki/Jeepney (Accessed February 16, 2024); GI Track was government-issued galvanized iron track sections, not gastrointestinal tract.

masa (mass) transportation provided by jeepneys.[109]

The jeepneys are often handmade, with "angular and boxy construction, gas-guzzling and weighty with its 20 plus sheets of 15- to 18-gauge stainless steel or galvanized sheets, [their] guts usually surplus Japanese diesel engines," and they are "severely lacking in safety features and unadaptable to universal safety and seat-belt regulations."[110] There are basic requirements for drivers; they need to have "specialized licenses, regular routes, and reasonably fixed fares."[111]

In the front seat is the driver and two or more passengers. The back portion has seats running front to back and against the windows. Some are meant to hold ten, some twelve, and some fourteen passengers. That doesn't mean that's all they hold. We once counted twenty-nine people, most with packages, some holding chickens, and one iguana on a twelve-passenger jeepney.

Visitors from America sometimes asked, "Isn't it dangerous to ride the jeepneys?" They'd heard tales of robberies. Perhaps it happened; we never experienced that ourselves or knew of any person who had. But we were always leery of being the first and only passenger because according to the stories, occasionally two people would board with friendly smiles and less-than-friendly intentions. As you sit with your camera or camera bag on the seat beside you, one person might sit across from you, interact with you, perhaps drop something on the floor. When you reach down to help retrieve the item for them, the other person might relieve you of your camera or bag, then get off—not physically hurting anyone.

We urged our friends to use jeepneys and warned them not to get on alone and not to put an expensive camera beside them on the

---

[109] In 2010, President Rodrigo Duterte announced he planned to have all jeepneys over fifteen years old taken off the streets; drivers are fighting the plan. www.npr.org/sections/parallels/2018/03/07/591140541/a-push-to-modernize-philippine-transport-threatens-the-beloved-jeepney (Accessed February 16, 2024).

[110] Godofredo U. Stuart Jr., "The Jeepney was once called the "Undisputed King of the Road," http://www.stuartxchange.org/Jeepney.html (Accessed April 7, 2024).

[111] From an article about the history of the Philippine jeepney at www.tourisminthephilippines.com/transport.

seat in plain sight!

Riders are advised to note and use the overhead handrails to keep steady; and holding a handkerchief over the nose is a great help to shut out fumes from outside. Almost everyone, including Filipinos, does that. Otherwise: "It's good to ride; follow practical guidelines and enjoy!" we told visitors. We didn't worry about traveling by jeepney. We loved it!

To some, jeepneys are the "undisputed king of the road."[112] I challenge that descriptor. Any bus will take the right-of-way. Once, we were traveling in the far-left lane on EDSA—the ten-lane highway around Manila—and a massive bus came alongside us in the lane to our right; the driver honked once and moved into our lane and into us, smashing into our right front fender.[113]

We had been told not to talk to anyone at an accident, as the Americans were always blamed. However, we sought compensation, and dealing with the bus company took hours the day of the accident. After many phone calls and visits to the offices, we were told that the driver no longer worked for them, so they were not liable. I was afraid of traveling anywhere near a bus. I often observed them travel up and over the median curbs to get where they wanted to go.

Jeepney Traveling Instructions[114]

Riding jeepneys is always fascinating and educational. Several factors make the trip easier. As with all communication, it's most helpful to use open-ended questions (e.g., "How" or "When" or "Where"), not yes/no questions, and to speak slowly, smile, and say, "Salamat" (Thank you!). Wear your camera bag or backpack on the front.

---

[112] Today some jeepneys are seen as a "tarnished icon, its survival threatened from many fronts—bullied by government regulations, victimized by rising costs and the competition of cheaper alternatives," http://www.stuartxchange.org/Jeepney.html.
[113] Epifanio de los Santos Avenue.
[114] These guidelines are based on a booklet I created for visitors while working at the Far Eastern Division Seminary.

I. Traveling by jeepney: finding the right one and getting on.

   A. Don't ask: "Is this where I get the jeepney to Central Market?" If you ask like this, the response will almost always be "Yes!" Filipinos want to be kind and agree—especially if they don't understand the question.
   B. Do ask: "Where do I get the jeepney to Central Market?" or "Please show me which is the right one to Central Market."
   C. Respond with "Salamat!" (Thank you), pronounced "sah-LA-maht."
   D. Watch the person who gave you the information; they will likely indicate when you are near the right place to get on the jeepney.

II. Traveling by jeepney: getting off (the term Filipinos use is "getting down").

   A. Don't ask: "Is this where I get down for Central Market?"
   B. Ask: "Where do I 'get down' for Central Market?" Speak slowly, smile, and wait for a response.
   C. Respond with "Salamat!" (Thank you), pronounced "sah-LA-maht."
   D. Watch the person who gave you the information; they will likely indicate when you are near the right place to disembark/get down/get off!
   E. You can use your peso coin or your knuckle to tap the roof, signaling to the driver when you wish to "get down."

2020s Update

—Jeepney Modernization: A weeklong national strike of jeepney owners and operators was planned in March 2023. Jeepney organizations talked with palace officials, a compromise was reached, and the strike only lasted two days. The disruption was minimized during the strike as some students and adult workers were able to work from home.

There are many reasons for concern. Some organizers wanted to phase out the jeepney; others noted that many are old and need to be replaced. New models, of course, are more expensive. "Luckily," according to J. C. Punongbayan of *Rappler*, "some jeepney manufacturers have already prototyped modern jeepneys, and have actually gotten the nod of government itself. The challenge now is how to scale up the production of relatively cheap modern jeepneys."[115] There have been some positive effects; the government is offering to subsidize the modern jeepneys. Where will that money come from?

—**Buses:** Reports from an American living in the Philippines debunk the "old, rickety, falling-apart" expectation of some travelers. There is a lot of competition, and many folks opt for bus rides.[116]

---

[115] "PUVs in the Philippines (rappler.com)" https://www.rappler.com/topic/public-utility-vehicles-in-the-Philippines.
[116] "How to Ride the Bus in the Philippines - Live in the Philippines" https//liveinthephilippines.com/how – to – ride-the-bus-in-the-philippines (Accessed March 7, 2024).

—— CHAPTER 18 ——

A Visit from My American Family

Karen

"I don't know how you do this!"
—Dad Crandall

Jeff, Kimberly, Dale, and I had a joyful reunion with my mom and dad a few months after we arrived.[117] We met them at the airport with our Blue Bomb, taking them on the same route as our first drive back to the campus—Roxas Boulevard along Manila Bay, showing them the Cultural Center, Rizal Park, the Manila Hotel where MacArthur lived during WWII, then winding through noisy, crowded city streets and pointing out jeepneys, tricycles, and buses and the carts with baskets and clothes, then down Balibago Road and through the gate to our campus with the guards at the ready.

My understanding parents were well aware of my battle with homesickness and relieved that I was past the worst of it. When we arrived at our house, Jeff retrieved Mom's crutches from the car for her and then walked ahead, up the three steps, kindly opening the door to our lovely home. Mom walked cautiously up three steps and stopped for a moment on our tiny cement porch.

"Grandma, look up!" he said.

Too late, I realized why: he wanted to impress Grandpa and Grandma with our geckos, which, attracted by the porch light, were

---

[117] Larry and Naomi Crandall (Karen's parents from Battle Creek, Michigan).

skittering above us on the underside of the porch cover. My mom hated lizards, geckos, snakes—anything in any distant part of their families, even. I worried. Unnecessarily, it turns out. Being a good sport, she made an appropriate comment about the geckos.

"I'll just go inside, away from them."

She didn't know they were on the walls and ceilings inside, too.

We entered the sala with the cool, terrazzo floors, ceiling fans, rattan furniture, and lovely floor-to-ceiling windows. They both loved it all! Jeff's room became their guest room. The first weekend, we drove them out to the Silang campus—our future home—and noted the coffee plantations, sugarcane fields, pineapple and coconut plantations, and the barrios and the interesting variety of homes. We drove the whole campus, showing them our future home; then we headed through the gate to see the amazing Taal Lake and the smoking volcano in the middle and then along Tagaytay Ridge, visiting the markets selling fruits, vegetables, and flowers.

A few days into their stay, my dad developed a bad cold—likely from the many weather changes he'd experienced recently. They had left snowy Michigan and flown China Airlines to enjoy a few days en route in Hawaii, Tokyo, and Taipei, following our suggested itinerary until they arrived in the Philippines. The heat and humidity were new to them. We'd acclimatized a bit.

My dad's cold made him miserable. I knocked on the door one morning and went in to see how he was. He had stripped down to as little as he thought was decent and was sitting on the edge of Jeff's bed, sniffling, wiping his red eyes, blowing his nose. He looked up at me and groaned: "I don't know how you do this!"

My parents were happy to be there, but things were getting to them. They were dismayed to see men, women, and children living in cardboard and tin shacks along the Pasig River and learned that 25 percent of the six million residents in Metro Manila were "squatters."[118] We also showed them many lovely things in Manila,

---

[118] US Library of Congress Country Studies, http://www.countrystudies.us/Philippines/34.htm (Accessed February 16, 2024).

but where there were nicer homes, there were also cement-block walls topped with broken glass or barbed wire to discourage robbery We also saw the reality of street-side cafés and stores serving folks with their rolled-up metal doors open to the heat and dirt. It was hot in our no-air-con car, windows open; and we saw the flies around the shops serving food and drove past a homeless man, ragged, dirty, and leaning against a statue in the center of a roundabout.

For thirty years my dad had been the director of public works and city engineer of Battle Creek, Michigan. He had been responsible for the safe management of water, streets, and sewers; things were almost always in good order in the successful Cereal City. Dad learned that much of the sewage in Manila emptied untreated into Manila Bay. It was too much for him. The drive through Manila depressed him.

"I don't know why people aren't just dying on the streets!" he said sadly.

"Well, some are," I replied.

For a change of pace, we drove north to Baguio, the summer capital, which is more temperate. The Marcos family have their holiday palace there. We stayed in a pleasant and simple cabin owned by the North Philippine Union of SDAs. Walking in the marketplace, buying food and crafts, and watching folks create carvings, baskets, and batik were all fascinating. We saw many artisans working outside their homes in the countryside and women squatting at the riverside to make reed baskets.

Visiting the Easter Weaving School was a real high point. Imagine many women sitting flat on the floor, feet straight in front of them, with straps around their lower backs to keep the tension on the frame of a long loom starting at chest level and continuing about fifteen feet at a forty-five-degree angle into the air. The width of the woven cloth they created was about twelve inches, and eventually most was cut to precise lengths for napkins, placemats, bookmarks, purses, and more. Those artisans are well known for their lovely colors, patterns, and quality work; we purchased beautiful items I'll use forever, and they inspired Kimberly to create her own beautiful backstrap loom later. We purchased several of these items to give as gifts to folks back home.

Another day in Manila, we enjoyed a meal in a charming restaurant on the third level of one of the two beautiful modern shopping centers. I remember my mom's quiet courage as she left the restaurant, walking ahead of me to the top of the escalator. I tried to get ahead of or beside her, but she got there first, extended the rubber-cupped ends of her crutches "securely" onto the moving steps, and walked on. I still get a frightened feeling in my stomach when I remember that, but she did just fine and was happy to show me how independent she was, knowing I was having a hard time being away while she managed her cancer complications and treatments.

Mom and I shopped in an air market and bought material; the next day, we walked down that tiny lane to Mading's home. My mom loved all of that. She had a couple of things tailored for herself, including a beautiful caftan, dark brown with white embroidery, still hanging in my closet. We purchased a barong for my dad so he could wear it when he showed his slides and told his friends back home about his adventures here.

It was a joy to share our new life with them, and it was easier for them to picture it from then on. I wrote letters to them every Thursday, made carbon copies, and still have my set to read and treasure. While describing Filipino culture to my parents, I realized that each of us was acculturating—becoming not just tolerant but understanding, valuing differences and adjusting our behavior. Becoming bicultural. This was encouraging and exciting.

Carol, Dale's sister, frequently wrote us about her family, her home, her horses, and missing us. We wanted her to visit, and she wanted to come, but it wasn't likely because she had four children and horses to care for. We encouraged Dale's brothers, Wayne and Gary, and their spouses to visit. It seemed otherworldly to them, and they could not easily spend the time. Traveling to the other side of the world is a big deal.

Thankfully, Dale's parents would be visiting in a few months, and friends and colleagues from WWC had planned visits for work and pleasure.

Update 2020s

—**Visiting the Philippines on YouTube:** It's possible to see the markets and other sites we visited via YouTube videos of Baesa, the Easter Weaving Room, Taal Volcano, Balintawak, etc. Things look too modern to us now, but there are still reminders of how we saw them forty years ago!

—**Easter Weaving Room** was established in 1909 under the direction of Deaconess Anne Hargreaves. It has modernized, of course, now using many mechanized spinning and weaving aids. You can see the weavers and equipment at the website Go Baguio![119]

—**Cell phones, computers, iPads, FaceTime, Messenger, Zoom!** All these things now help families and friends stay in touch, do business, keep records, find necessary services, learn about government regulations, and ultimately not feel so isolated when families are on opposite sides of the earth![120] We had none of them.

—**There are many more shopping malls in Metro Manila.** One source lists over 1,100 shopping malls; there were two large malls in 1980.[121]

---

[119] Easter Weaving Room | Easter School Baguio City | Go Baguio! www.gobaguio.com/easter-weaving-room.html (Accessed February 16, 2024).
[120] Now some guidebooks include "useful apps" to make life easier, e.g., *Culture Smart! Philippines: The essential guide to Customs and Cultural.* Graham and Yvonne Colin-Jones and Jorge Mojarro (Authors); Kuperard: Turkey; 2nd Ed 2021.
[121] Shopping malls in Metro Manila 2020s: https://rentechdigital.com/smartscraper/business-report-details/philippines/metro-manila/shopping-malls (Accessed April 4, 2024)

CHAPTER 19

Polillo Island Graduation

Dale

"That man is richest whose pleasures are cheapest."
—Henry David Thoreau

Guards unlocked the PUC gate with the sunrise, and two students and I stepped from the Baesa campus into the narrow, rapidly filling street, boarded a jeepney, and headed for the heart of Manila. Twelve miles, one transfer, and one hour later, we boarded the bus that carried passengers and cargo over the Sierra Madre mountains to the small seaport of Infanta. A mix of cardboard boxes and woven plastic rice sacks filled the aisle of the battered vehicle; an old treadle sewing machine perched precariously on top of it all. I decided it would be wise not to sit near that pile.

We were leaving Luzon, the largest island in the Philippine archipelago, to visit tiny Polillo Island, the largest of the twenty-seven Polillo islands off the northeast coast of Luzon, in the Philippine Sea. It was not so far away—twenty-five kilometers (sixteen miles) east; however, getting there took a long time. The graduating class of Polillo Island Academy (PIA), a Christian high school, had invited me to speak at their ceremonies. My companions, Edith and Esther, were going to sing at the graduation. Edith had graduated from PIA the year before.

We traveled east toward the coast. The road was unpaved and flat for a time, then wound upward dramatically; sometimes I had a better view over the edge than I wanted. The bus stopped, and the driver announced there would be time to eat at the small open-air café while the engine cooled. Passengers untied cloths enclosing banana leaves in which rice and dried fish or vegetables had been carefully wrapped. A small girl passed through the bus selling *siopao,* a bread-like bun filled with onions and other vegetables or meats. One side of her face was greatly distended and coated with a bright-blue paste.

"What does she have on her face?" I quietly asked my companions.

Esther answered, "She has a swelling. What do you say in English? Ah—"

"Mumps?"

"Yes, yes, mumps!"

"Yes, I know, but the blue stuff: what is that?"

"Oh, that is medicine."

"Do you know what kind of medicine? What is it called?"

"Yes, it is blue bar."

"What is blue bar?"

"You buy blue bar in the market. It is used for laundry. You know, to wash clothes."

I recognized the color now as that of the harsh laundry soap with pumice and bleaching action.

"Is there anything mixed with it?" I asked. "Anything but the blue bar?"

"No, just blue bar. When I had that swelling, my *lola* [grandmother] put it on my face. It is the usual medicine."

"Does it work? I mean, does it make the swelling go down or make you feel better?"

"I don't know, but it is a usual medicine. My lola thinks it is good. Maybe it is a superstition."

I declined the siopao, and my face felt strange below my tongue. I knew that was foolish. I wondered what the people of this mountain village might think of the "germ theory." I walked over to the nearby café. Flies marched freely over the cooked rice and fried chicken, and the man dishing it up placed a finger to the side of his nose and blew onto the ground. This practice is cleaner, it is thought, than blowing into a handkerchief or tissue and carrying it around in your pocket. The café had lost its attractiveness.

The road had been torturous, but after the café stop, it grew steadily worse. The driver crossed to the other lane when the lane we were traveling in slumped off toward the valley below. At another point, a stream, now dry, had cut so deeply across the road in flood time that the bus hung suspended momentarily on its back bumper as the front wheels climbed too steeply from the streambed; that bank slumped away under the weight of the bus, and we proceeded to climb the farther, gentler bank. As the road turned downward, we spotted ocean beaches far below through the trees, and I began to relax and talk.

When we reached the smoother, paved road, the passengers unwrapped scarves, towels, kerchiefs, hankies, and assorted clothing from around their faces and shook the dust out the windows. I decided to wear something on my head for the trip home.

The bus stopped in the quaint seaside village of Infanta, and we boarded a small, weathered, wooden ferry. The tropical sun warmed the planks of the deck, and the sea air was cool against the skin. She was a matronly old tub but a luxury compared to the bus. My companions sang softly the songs they would sing for the graduation; the road and the bus seemed far behind. Our destination, Infanta, sat fifteen miles (twenty kilometers) into the Pacific.[122]

The water lay still, unruffled by the air, until the boat's movement stirred the surface and created a gentle breeze that ran fingers through our hair. The road had been hot and dusty, the ruts deep and jarring, but the boat was everything the bus had not been. Two kilometers offshore, a flock of doves passed close overhead, and I wondered at their being so far from land. Not so far, really, but I expected doves to stay near shore.

---

[122] Pollilo, Quezon. Wikipedia. http://en.wikipedia.org/wiki/Polillo,Quezon (Accessed February 16, 2024).

The surface shattered beyond the bow, and flying fish skittered across the mirror stretching before us. Fins moved with the rapid rhythm of wings, and the first several strokes beat upon the surface. Rings of ripples formed where the fin-tips touched, then widened to meet with others. The fish were free of the surface after five to ten meters, and there seemed no limit to their gliding. Some skipped upon touching down, but most simply dipped their heads and disappeared with the slightest disturbance. A large, less graceful fish broke the surface and splashed its way clear of the bow.

Map of Quezon Province with Polillo highlighted.[123]

Polillo Island had been but a name and a promise of mild adventure. Now she rose as a dark wrinkle on the horizon. A coral garden passed below us, and I wondered if it could be explored without scuba gear. Crystal-clear water made depth estimates difficult.

---

[123] Ibid.

As we neared the island in the early evening, we spotted a few bright bulbs toward the center of town, lit with a generator. Candles burned in most windows. Somewhere in the night, a guitar twanged, and a man sang softly. An old car knelt on a front rim near a stuccoed sari-sari store. It was the lone reminder of the vehicles rampaging the roads we had left behind. Boys lounged against a post in front of the store, chuckling and shoving gently. Heads slowly turned as the girls passed—not so different from towns and boys and girls anywhere.

The next morning, I slipped from the house before sunrise to examine the details last evening's light had hinted at. The town was awake now. In many small dirt and grass patches between dwellings, women were sweeping with stiff brooms fashioned from the shafts of palm fronds. Other yards had already been swept clean of leaves and assorted debris that had accumulated the day before.

One woman was having difficulty setting fire to a small pile of rubbish. Similar piles blazed or smoldered in adjacent yards. The dirt areas were clean and tidy.

A small boy passed, carrying a large basket. In husky, accented tones, he partly sang, partly chanted, "*Haat pan de sol*," offering hot bread—or, literally, "hot bread of the sun/of the morning."

The woman straightened from her still unkindled fire and motioned with an underhanded wrist flip as though drawing something to herself, a common hand signal to invite someone closer. If the palm is up with fingers curling toward oneself, the gesture is considered crude and rude (the way you would call a dog). The boy veered toward her, singing his song once more in sharper, more clipped phrases to continue calling attention to his wares; then, in murmuring tones, he began negotiating this morning's price.

Alberto Perez—teacher, senior class sponsor, and my official host—found me as the sun rose through the palms. He lived with the Azuala family. We had eaten with them the night before. My companions for the trip, Edith and Esther, had been spirited off to stay with friends, and I stayed in the grandest house in town. In typical Filipino tradition, the residents of Polillo were offering their very best hospitality.

"I am sad you have been alone," Alberto apologized. "Your breakfast is waiting in your room, if you like it now."

In the corner of the room, a small table was filled with food, juices, and a pitcher with a hot drink.

"Have you eaten?" I asked.

"I will eat later."

"Why don't you eat with me? There is plenty."

"I will eat at my place."

I expected he would go eat, but he did not. He sat and I ate.

"Would you help me with some of this food, Alberto? It is very good."

"Maybe my landlady is waiting for me."

I expected he would leave now, but he did not.

"You must help me. I can't eat all this, and my host will think I did not like his food."

"Okay," Alberto said, "I will help you."

"Here is an extra plate and spoon and fork. It looks like the Azualas expected you to eat here, with me."

"Maybe," Alberto said.

Maybe indeed! I had almost given up.

In Filipino culture, accepting an invitation to eat the first time you are asked is rude. Filipino hospitality demands that before one eats, he must invite those about him to share his meal. Courtesy and culture demand that a guest refuse the initial invitation and perhaps several subsequent ones, until he is convinced that his would-be host is truly intent upon his guest eating. The host—and I, a stranger, was yet the host—must extend more than courtesy demands; and Alberto, the guest, must be well mannered. It is an honor for a host to feed his guest, even if the host remains hungry. *What was I thinking?*

We finished eating and went out into the narrow street.

Heat shimmered as we entered a quaint old church. It was the

Sabbath day, and church services began early as usual so they could conclude before the midday heat. Ladies used palm-leaf fans to cool themselves and those nearby. This graduation weekend, the program involved many people—students, faculty, and musicians. My assignment was to address the seniors with words of wisdom that would carry them through life.

As part of my remarks, I read, "Two roads diverged in a yellow wood, and I, I took the one less traveled by, and that has made all the difference."[124] I marveled at the students' accomplishments and wondered about the choices they would make. This was a special day, and the speeches and celebration lasted well past noon.

At dinner the evening before, Mrs. Azuala had invited Alberto and me to lunch. The memory of her table, filled with delicacies, made the services feel even longer. I was hungry. As we left the church, a Filipina spoke to us in the lovely, fluid tones of the local dialect.

Alberto interpreted: "Mrs. Unsay has invited us to have lunch at her place."

"But Mrs. Azuala—"

"Mrs. Azuala knows. But perhaps, Mrs. Unsay says, we could eat at her house also?"

"But what about Mrs. Azuala?"

"Oh, we will eat at the Azualas' house first. Then we will eat at the Unsays' house."

"It will take too long if we eat at the Azualas'. We will be late."

"They want to wait for us."

"Where is her house; is it close by?"

"Not so near. It is out in Barrio Tanza."

As we walked further, we saw a boy pass on horseback, sitting astride a sack of rice. Music was still drifting from the church. The pianist had left and been replaced by small girls playing one-finger melodies. The adults created coveys as they spilled into the street.

---

[124] Robert Frost, *The Road Not Taken: Selected Poems.* (New York: Gramercy. 1992).

Friends and relatives separated by duties and distances of the week were immersed in catching up. Those who did move away seemed drawn to a single house. A man passed with a gas cylinder on a cart and entered the house.

"That must be the oxygen," Alberto said. "The lola is very sick. Her heart is very bad. She is a very old woman. Maybe we can go first to see the lola; do you think?"

"Maybe we should start toward the Azualas'. They are expecting us for lunch."

"Maybe we can go first to see the lola, do you think?" Alberto urged. "The lola's family will be honored."

"But after dinner at the Azualas', we're to go to Mrs. Unsay's place in Barrio Tanza. Won't we be too late?"

"Never mind, it is just okay," Alberto assured me.

The richly patinaed wooden steps of the lola's house recounted years of bare feet passing. Our shoes went into the amalgam of footwear—boots, shoes, thongs, flip-flops, and slippers—of well-wishers already here to see the lola, and we climbed to the raised first floor. A curtain of heavy, coarse cloth hung over the doorway to another room, and pinned to it was a cardboard sign: NO VISITING - SILENCE PLEASE. Visitors sat about the large room, speaking in hushed tones and wearing solemn faces.

"Maybe she will die," one visitor said, clucking with her tongue.

"Maybe we should pray," said another.

"Yes" was the reply from many.

Alberto and I were welcomed; folk indicated we should sit on the couch. Soon he said to me, "Would you like to go in now?"

Despite the bold sign prohibiting visiting or talking, there had been a steady ebb and flow through the draped doorway.

"Perhaps it would tire her," I whispered to Alberto.

Was it simply the Polillo style of Filipino cookery, or was it Mrs. Azuala's unique cooking or the pungent garlic and onion odors drifting from the kitchen below that made me so antsy? Appetite and impatience grew.

"Maybe you would like to go in to visit her before we go to eat?"

"Oh, maybe not, Alberto. She wouldn't know me. We would tire her. You go if you like."

Polillo was a place of hospitality, and her people knew no hurrying. The slow drone of a fly summed it up, and the scent of a flowering tree added soft accent. In my heart, I loved it, but in my head I was thinking about how hungry I was and how Mrs. Azuala and the folk in Barrio Tanza were waiting for us. *Why are we bothering this poor, sick lola and her family—especially me, a total stranger?*

Alberto said: "Maybe it is okay for us to go in now."

What?! I thought. *Has he not heard anything I've said? Ah well.*

I gave in. At least it would get us on the road sometime soon. We waited at the curtain as a small boy and his mother came out; then we slipped past the barrier and into the sickroom. There seemed to be people everywhere, but all was quiet, and peace suffused the room. Smiles and nods turned our way.

The sick woman lay on a slightly padded, wooden-slatted bed. She faced a large, open window, her back to the doorway. An attendant bent and stroked her hair, spoke softly, and motioned in our direction. We had been introduced, but no one spoke. It was not expected. The atmosphere in the room spoke of peace, and it would have been a sacrilege to disturb it. It was enough to visit; more was not expected.

Alberto breathed the words "Her son" and indicated a young man sitting on the bed near her head. The man held her hand and stroked it lightly. A woman identified as a sister gently waved a woven palm-leaf fan over her head. "Another sister," Alberto whispered, indicating the one smoothing powdered talc over the sick woman's back and shoulders. Another woman sat near the foot of the bed, her hand resting upon an ankle and caressing it. Each one reached out. Each was touching and saying without words, "We are here, we love you, we care."

What a contrast this was to the false cheer of sickrooms I had known. Peace, dignity, compassion, and quiet were our companions.

There was no pretense. It was a pleasant place to be, but others were waiting, and so, I suspected, were my hostesses, Mrs. Azuala and Mrs. Unsay.

As we entered the street, Alberto said, "It is good that we came. The family is honored."

I believed him and wished it could always be so easy to please people. Henry David Thoreau had it right: "That man is richest whose pleasures are cheapest."

The lunch at Mrs. Azuala's home was fabulous. We were late, and it was all right, and we had a delightful time. Our hostess's savory art made it impossible to eat "a little less" in preparation for our second dinner invitation.

2020s Update

—**The Polillo islands in Quezon comprise one of the key biodiversity areas (KBA) identified as priority sites for conservation in the Philippines**. They are home to globally important species, including the Gray's monitor lizard (*Varanus olivaceus*), the Philippine cockatoo (*Cacatua haematuropygia*), the Philippine warty pig (*Sus philippensis*), and the Philippine rusa (Hampson et al. 2000).[125]

—**Early History:** Trade relations between the natives of the Polillo islands and Chinese merchants existed long before the Spanish conquerors came to the archipelago. Trade involved a mix of Malay, Hindu, Chinese, and Tagalog peoples.

—**History, 1942:** Japanese Imperial forces landed in Polillo in 1942, during WWII. In 1945, the Commonwealth troops of the 5th and 52nd Infantry Divisions landed in Polillo and routed the Japanese.

---

[125] Villanueva, Leajim A., et al. "Addressing Fragmentation within a Key Biodiversity Area: Options for a Strengthened Community-Based Intervention in Polillo Islands" https://serpp.pids.gov.ph/publication/public/view?slug=addressing-fragmentation-within-a-key-biodiversity-area-options- (Accessed February 16, 2024).

CHAPTER 20

A Working Holiday

Dale

"Imelda Park! Imelda Park!" my adolescent diving buddy exclaimed; which translated to "With these goggles, everything is so beautiful!"

Alberto's estimate of the distance to Barrio Tanza was accurate; it was indeed "not so near." Because of the distance and the oppressive heat, we signaled for a tricycle, a pedal-powered bicycle fitted with a third wheel and a bench seat behind the peddler.

Our driver was a young man of seventeen or eighteen, and he worked hard. The road narrowed and roughened. Pedaling became more difficult, and on the downhill grades, the boy's left foot came off the pedal and pressed atop the tread of the front wheel to slow our wild descent. He was hardened to his task. Muscles rippled as arms pulled the handlebars and thighs pressed downward. Yet talking to us did not seem to make him short of breath.

That arm is strange, I thought. His arm had clearly been broken and poorly set, or not set at all. The ends had mended together nevertheless, and it was strong; his efforts on hills proved that. Both bones of the forearm must have been broken to have healed so oddly. It's difficult to set both bones. Even in hospitals, they sometimes have to set one of the bones as best they can, give it a few days to mend, and then rebreak what is poorly aligned and adjust it. Sometimes they operate and pin the bones together.

Obviously, both the radius and ulna had broken; that would mean four broken ends inside a fleshy mass that doesn't let you handle the pieces easily, directly. The muscles attached to the elbow and wrist would contract in pain and force the broken ends past one another. *Now I am the A and P teacher, going through each problem*, I thought wryly. *But how did it happen?*

In my mind, I saw a young boy fall from a tall coconut palm. I was his father. He was crying; there was so much pain. The dad was thinking, *Bones are poking through the skin. I need to fix it*. He stretched the forearm and pressed with fingers through the tender flesh. The jagged ends of the bones met and ground together, the ends balancing on one another. *Success. Sweet success. Now just get the tips of the ulna past the radius and press it so it lines up.*

The boy flinched, cried, and the ends of the first bone separated. Trauma-sore muscles were jabbed by the ragged ends. "Son, I'm so sorry."

In my mind, I tried again. This time the ends of the other bone came together. *Now, if the big bone will come around right.* The boy was exhausted. This time he did not flinch. Perhaps he did not feel it anymore. Tugging again—*Almost!* The bones separated again. The boy cried out. What could a father do? He wished there were a doctor on his island. This beautiful place where boys were not bothered with city evils.

It would be small comfort to know that such a break would be difficult even for a trained physician.

"Is there a doctor, Alberto?"

"What? What doctor?"

"Any doctor." *I'll not call attention to our driver's arm.* "Is there a doctor for the lady we saw today?"

"No. I mean, there is a doctor who comes sometimes from Manila," Alberto explained. "But, no, there is no doctor here. I hope she will be okay. She is a kind lady."

"Some of the students from here want to be doctors," I reminded Alberto. "Perhaps you will have one someday soon."

"Perhaps. This is not a good place for a doctor. People have little money."

"Will the doctor be coming from Manila to see this lady?"

"No, but they say her son will come tomorrow. They have wired him already, sir."

"Must he come so far?"

"California. He is a doctor in California."

Stunning!

At our second lunch, we kept each serving as small as we were allowed to. Mrs. Unsay was also a good cook and a delight to visit with. It would have been even more enjoyable on an empty stomach. The last course included *halo-halo*, a dessert that differs depending on who prepares it. Halo-halo literally means a mixture of everything. In Tanza, a municipality in Cavite, it was made from young, gelatinous coconut spooned fresh from the shell in thick ribbons, mixed with sweetened beans, tiny cubes of gelatin in a variety of colors and flavors, sago, sweet kaong (palm fruits), and unidentifiable inclusions with one feature in common: everything was intensely sweet. The concoction was liberally doused with warm, sweet, canned condensed milk.

Halo-halo is a real delicacy, a festive food. However, my overburdened digestion rebelled in revulsion.

"You hab halo-halo or it be gone," advised the small son of our hostess.

"Mamaya," I said. (By and by.)

"Look, sir, very delicious," said a small girl, holding up a cup of the concoction for my inspection. "See, sir, it has kaong, macapuno, raisins, everything. Good. You like it, sir?"

"Yes," I said. It was the smallest serving I had seen. It would likely be the smallest serving I could get away with. "Yes." I extended my hand. "Maybe I am ready now."

I thought I could get some of it down, and I did. *Oh my, what is this? Certainly not halo-halo.* It had to be pancit—that delightful main course dish of rice noodles sautéed with onions and garlic and the vegetables on hand—coated with the thick, syrupy sauce of halo-halo. *Oh no.* I realized this was the halo-halo the little girl had dished up for herself! She had used the bowl from her main course of pancit. The serving was mercifully small because she had already eaten part of it. That was also why she ran off to the other room to get a clean spoon for me.

Across the room, the small girl whispered to a friend, casting furtive glances my way. She was embarrassed. I would pretend I did not know. *Why didn't I follow Alberto's example from the morning and refuse at least once?*

Americans are too aggressive or assertive, or maybe Filipinos are too . . . what? I don't know. All I know is that I stood at the crossroads of our cultures and took a wrong turn; but the journey was worth it.

During our time at the Unsays', a group of boys, perhaps fourteen to sixteen years old, recounted a diving adventure. They described large fish and argued about who had caught what. This experience took me back to my little village of Killmaster, Michigan, and the group of boys I used to fish with growing up.

"Is there good diving off Polillo?" I asked, remembering the coral garden the day before.

"Oh, sir! It is wonderful! Do you dive?"

"Yes, whenever I can."

"We are going tomorrow. Can you come with us?"

That might work! I had nothing to do the next day, and we were not boarding the boat to the mainland until midafternoon. I checked with Alberto to be sure I was not scheduled or expected to do anything the next day.

"What time do we leave?" I asked the boys.

"Early, sir. When you like?"

Well, early was just right with me. Fortunately, I had packed my snorkel, mask, and flippers. The rest of the day dragged on as I eagerly anticipated the joys of the coming morning. There were formal celebrations in several homes that evening, and, again, Alberto and I were invited and attended them all—as did, it seemed, everyone else. The wonderfully social sharing side of Polillo was embraced by every neighbor, friend, relative, and parent. This was their wealth, and they were lavish with it. The several homes, food, people, and events meld together in memory. It was a late night.

I got up early the next morning, and Alberto was there almost immediately to help with another generous breakfast. As quickly as convenient and fashionably polite, I exited the house and entered the street to a covey of waiting boys. The yards and paths were cleanly swept, and a few fires consumed the last of leaves, paper, and other debris.

Passing quickly to the beach, we found a group of two- or three-person dugout canoes, or bancas, pulled high on the sand. Each craft had one or two small outriggers attached parallel to the sides for stability. The outriggers were bamboo poles about four inches in diameter and eight to ten feet long, held a meter or more from the side of the banca by lighter bamboo shafts near the bow and stern, making it essentially untippable so that climbing in and out was safe and easy. We dragged five of the bancas to the water and set off.

The fish, coral, and other creatures passing beneath our bancas were beautiful, but the boys seemed only interested in paddling. Suddenly we were over a reef. It was like switching to high definition. Fish, coral, mollusks in beautiful shells, sponges, and graceful waving algae surrounded us, and the boys were abandoning ship! We tied the bancas together and anchored the whole flotilla. The water was six to twelve feet deep.

At that depth, the reds and yellows were bright. Water filters out the longer, warmer wavelengths and turns deeper coral more somber, bluish tones. Very deep water filters out so much light that plants dependent on photosynthesis are severely limited and drop out of the biosystem. Many animals still sport beautiful red and yellow pigments, but their warmer beauty is not perceived below fifty feet and is significantly diminished at twenty-five. I had just solved my question about diving the coral garden we passed over yesterday. Judging from the colors, that had been in at least twenty, maybe thirty feet of water, great for scuba; but this, six to twelve feet, was perfect for snorkeling.

It was wonderful to be a boy again. The others wore goggles of a sort I remembered from an old *National Geographic*. The lenses were small ovals. Two wooden facepieces fit watertight in their eye sockets and were held together with a small loop of monofilament fishing line. They were secured with a wide, black rubber band around the back of the head. I was fascinated! The rubber band had been cut from an old inner tube, and they had carved the facepieces. The glass lenses were chipped from broken window panes and the edges rubbed smooth on beach stones. Glue or pitch from a local tree held the lenses securely in carefully crafted grooves.

If possible, they were even more interested in *my* mask. It was store bought, made of molded latex with, of course, a matching strap and a tempered-glass lens about six inches in diameter. It cost probably $35—cheap, as far as US dive-shop masks go. I was keen to see how their masks worked and had no trouble making a swap. Remarkably, the little wooden mask did well. I was larger than its owner, but the curvature of its sides fit the shape of my face, and the salt water did not rush in as expected. They were not perfect, but then neither are the store-bought ones.

The surface water exploded, and a boy wearing my goggles gesticulated wildly and yelled. It was not clear what the problem was. *Is he choking on water? Has he seen a shark?* No! He was saying "Park," not "Shark," and the others were laughing and punching his arm or slapping the back of his head and pushing him under the water, all soft, gentle punishments that said, "We love you, bro, but you worried us."

He had been screaming, "Imelda Park! Imelda Park!"—which translated to "It is so beautiful with these goggles. It makes me think I am in Imelda Park."

Imelda Marcos, wife of President Ferdinand Marcos, had a big heart and a closet full of shoes. She is known for her efforts to beautify the Philippines by developing a number of beautiful, extravagant parks designed to pique her citizens' pride and satisfy her own love of beauty. After all, she had been crowned beauty queen of the Philippines a few years before marrying Ferdinand.

But I digress! The point is, this boy was wildly elated by the sharp, wide-angle view provided by the store-bought goggles and so compared it to the beauty icon he most related to. The reef exceeded the beauty of the parks. The dive was incredible, the colors indescribable. I swam the rest of the morning and into the afternoon with one or another of the boys' goggles as they tested mine. It was a wonderful experience. In the end, I gave my goggles to the first boy, and he gave me his. I have them today and would not trade them for anything. The memories make the handcrafted pair most precious.

2020s Update

—Filipino physicians in the US are likely part of the Association of Philippine Physicians in America (APPA), established in 1972.[126] Included on the website are guidelines for Filipino physicians who want to practice in the US. In 2022, the total number of all physicians in patient care in the US was 1,073,616.[127] And 19.1 percent were Asian.[128]

—Filipino Physicians in the Philippines: in 2020, there were just over 28,000 Filipino physicians practicing in the Philippines; in 2016 there were just over 39,000.

---

[126] The Association of Filipino American Physicians (APPA), https://www.theappa.org (Accessed February 16, 2024).
[127] U.S. physicians - statistics & facts | Statista https://www.stastista.com/topics/1224/physicians/#topicOverview (Accessed February 16, 2024).
[128] Physician Demographics and Statistics in the US https://www.zippia.com/physician-jobs/demographics (accessed February 16, 2024).

―――CHAPTER 21―――

Time to Move to the Side of a Volcano

Karen

"A tree that is unbending is easily broken."
—Lao Tzu, Chinese Philosopher

Ten months into our Philippine odyssey, when most of Dale's work was on the new campus, we packed our belongings again and left our lovely Baesa campus home. We were sad that eventually most of those campus buildings would be destroyed. The Eternal Gardens Memorial corporation, which had purchased the entire campus, continued its literally groundbreaking work, turning the property into a huge cemetery.

We did look forward to having the whole university and seminary located on the beautiful site in the Cavite province, situated about halfway up what was left of Mount Taal. The original cone is still active and steaming in the middle of Taal Lake.[129] The lake itself is only three meters above sea level. The road along the north side of Tagaytay Ridge, which surrounds Taal Lake, offers a spectacular view over the lake, past Taal City, and to the South China Sea. That area is a focal point for visitors to Luzon. We often enjoyed the drive from the campus, 6.9 miles past pineapple fields and coffee plantations, to shop at the fresh fruit and vegetable markets on the ridge; we also

---

[129] ABS-CBN News reports 302 volcanic quakes in twenty-four hours at Taal Volcano, 3/27/2021. Eruptions occurred in June of 2020. http://www.phivolcs.dost.gov.ph (Accessed February 16, 2024).

took visitors for banca rides to the still-walkable area of the volcano.

Palms, pines, tropical grasses, vines, and flowers covered the hilly campus. Guava, banana, and papaya trees were being cultivated. There were noisy birds, lizards, beetles, ants, and many other fascinating creatures. Yet it was wonderfully quiet—and cooler than Metro Manila by about fifteen degrees. What had been jungle was systematically being turned into manicured grounds surrounding classroom buildings and dormitories, some previously military barracks obtained through USAID, and new ones with prefabricated walls creating multistory apartments for married students and home for faculty and administrators.

No regular faculty home was available, so we temporarily lived in what was to become the dean's apartment on the second floor of the new girls' dormitory, not yet occupied by college students. I'd been reading Thomas Merton and Lao Tzu and was learning the value of being flexible, like bamboo—and we made a comfortable home there. On our feature wall in the sala we hung an eight-foot, round, woven, multicolored rug, grouping our burgeoning basket collection below it. We ate on our new dark-brown narrawood plates set on a brown, red, and gold batik tablecloth we'd purchased from a Thai student; fabric was used for currency to help some students with school bills. Sometimes we used the placemats we'd purchased at the Easter Weaving School in Baguio. The stairway outside our main door was three meters wide and descended to the empty lobby of the dorm. It was quiet, as nobody else was there yet, and we were safe, with guards patrolling outside.

The kids were busy in school, Dale was teaching and doing research, and I was working part-time at the seminary. After a few weeks, we were asked to move to the apartment of the American elementary teacher, who offered it to us while she was on furlough.[130] Living in her apartment and using her dishes, chairs, and beds felt strange. She would be back in three months, and by then our permanent home should be ready for us. Most of our belongings were in storage. The one-room expatriate elementary school was on our right, and another family's apartment was on the other side. It worked well, and I was happy.

Finally, the day came to move into our home across the wide lawn from the teacher's apartment. Hibiscus plants of many varieties and hues adorned the yards, and tropical plants surrounded our home. This being the highest point on campus, there were welcome breezes. It was a beautiful place.

Our home was nice: a ranch style, but quite different from those in Walla Walla. Burglar bars protected each window, but bright-pink bougainvillea vines softened the look a bit, beautiful from inside and out. The home was made of gray stucco, and behind our home was more lawn, which dropped precipitously into a deep canyon. There were tall grasses, then trees, and a small river too far down to hear from our place. We could hear it and monkeys in the nearby trees when we visited our friends farther along the winding ridge road back to the main campus.

The best part of the housing in Silang was that all faculty and administrators had exactly the same size and design: lovely narrawood parquet floors, a very nice kitchen, sala, dining room, three bedrooms, and two baths. Notably, this was the only campus we saw in the Far East where the American and national faculties had the same housing. Finally, *that* part of being an American was not embarrassing. On our sister campus in Hong Kong, Americans lived

---

[130] Furlough time has changed over the years of SDA mission; the value is multifaceted: 1) rest and holiday; 2) visiting family; 3) taking advanced courses; 4) restocking; and 5) providing time for the children to experience their home culture, as it's expected they will return there one day. While we were in the RP, the Far Eastern Division offered a three-month furlough every three years; currently the policy is three years in the mission field and one year at home. https://www.ministry127.com/missions/the-purpose-of-missionary-furlough (Accessed February 16, 2024).

in rambling brick ranch homes with views of the sea far below, while the national teachers lived in two-story cement-block apartment buildings in the center of the campus.

As at the other campus, many of the Filipino faculty chose not to have a water heater. They considered it healthier. In addition, most of them used small refrigerators and gas hot plates instead of the full-size refrigerators and stove/ovens that overseas workers had. Each of those choices reduced the electric bill. Their salaries were less than ours. That wage difference was embarrassing.

We had the essence of a United Nations General Assembly on campus. Students, faculty, and staff at times represented at least seventeen countries; the majority were Asian countries but also included were Australia, Finland, Russia, Trinidad, and the Caribbean. Many of the children created their own private language, a mix of English, Tagalog, and Indonesian/Malay.

Children absorbed the new culture quickly: Leila, from the Caribbean, took her three-year-old, Shari, to visit one of the American neighbors. Leila knocked on the door, and Shari said, "Mommy, nobody's home."

Leila continued to knock, and each time, Shari said, "Mommy, nobody's home."

No one came to the door; no one was home.

Leila asked Shari, "How did you know no one is home, sweetie?"

"No shoes."

Most everyone we knew—even the Americans—took off their shoes at any front door and left them on a mat outside, so there was usually a colorful pile of mostly sandals or flip-flops. Tiny Shari understood the implications. No shoes meant no one was home. Some folk use slippers inside, but we learned the cool floors felt good against bare feet.[131]

Jeffrey, grade seven, and Kimberly, grade four, were in the "American school" with the ten other expatriate kids. The big kids

---

[131] We continue to take off our shoes at front doors.

helped the little kids, and the little kids learned far in advance of their years. Those were some of the positives; but there were important negatives, especially for Jeff. He was disappointed and frustrated that there were no sports, no music lessons (he loved music), and not one expatriate boy his age. Those were key facts we hadn't asked about.

Kimberly enjoyed the students, especially the Van Ornam twins, who were her age. A second classroom was for the international and Filipino students. Soon the two schools participated in activities together, which helped the American kids learn more about the holidays and histories of the countries represented there.

Plans moved ahead to establish the graduate program in biology. Dale stayed busy with classes, graduate students, and committee meetings. His research on circadian rhythms stalled because he needed reliable twenty-four-hour electronic monitoring for the fruit flies whose light cycle he was studying; so he had time to read more books about the Philippines, sometimes by the light of the beautiful, tall gas lantern from Ohio gifted to us by Heather, his WWC graduate student.

I walked about half a mile to the Far Eastern Division Seminary building two to three days a week for my work assisting Professors John Jones and Ray Holmes with letters, schedules, and manuscripts. And I developed a guidebook for new students and faculty. John was the son of Lucille and Carl Jones, two WWC teachers who had shared their experiences on Baesa campus with us before we journeyed to the Philippines. He asked me to help plan and manage the graduations for the seminary, which was an ongoing task. There were graduations every quarter so that as soon as coursework was completed, the students could return to their regular jobs in Indonesia, Hong Kong, Korea, Japan, Finland, Singapore, Thailand, Malaysia, and other points east. Graduations were joyous, meaningful, and colorful times for students, their families, and the seminary faculty and staff. We asked the family members to wear their national costume, and the graduates carried full-size flags from their home countries for the ceremonies.

I really enjoyed being a part of the seminary, and I could also sit in on several of the seminary classes taught by friends and colleagues, professors trained at Harvard, Vanderbilt, and Andrews University. The focal point above the chapel's raised platform was a map of the world, which Leslie Harding, dean of the seminary, created using wood veneers of various colors and patterns—and he arranged the design so that the Philippines would be in the center. Everyone loved that.

When we moved to the new campus, Becky's classes were still on the Baesa campus. We paid for her dormitory room and her meals in the cafeteria there. She visited us as often as possible, mostly on weekends and during school holidays. Because there were no phones on either campus, we usually did not know when she was coming.

Some Fridays, after classes, Becky rode a series of at least three jeepneys to the gate of the Silang campus. It took her about three hours. Then she walked from the gate, following the winding dirt road through the campus and up the hill to the ridge where the faculty homes were. She cleaned or baked, quietly fitting into our schedule and doing whatever needed to be done. She accompanied us on many trips into the countryside. The highlight for her was Baguio in the mountains to the north. She had never been there or to some of the other places she visited with us. Becky was truly an important part of our family.

There was no helper's room in our Silang campus home. No problem; when Becky visited, she shared Kimberly's room, which had twin beds. It felt good to have her more integrated, but she told me it felt strange to her at first. Often, when we were chatting with friends or relaxing in the evening, perhaps playing games in the sala, I'd hear the telltale creak of the ironing board or the rustle of baking pans.

"No, Becky, don't work now. Come play Uno with us."

"No, ma'am, salamat po, but I want to do this." And she ironed or baked, thanking us in that way for paying her room and board. Our home in Silang had even newer appliances than in Baesa, and she loved to bake. Kimberly often worked with her, and Becky would say,

"Do I hear a little mouse in my kitchen?" They had fun together.[132]

We hired other student helpers to work part-time. One Filipina also worked for an Indian family, and we benefited from her new skill at making chapatti—my favorite Indian bread. And once or twice a week, Quivin (pronounced "Kevin"), a delightful character and an excellent gardener, worked in our yard, planting and keeping our flower beds beautifully trimmed and weeded.[133] He knew the names and habits of many plants that were unfamiliar to us.

One afternoon, he knocked at the back door and asked: "Ma'am, do you have a bank?"

My automatic response to the unexpected question was to repeat it: "Do we have a bank? Well, no."

"Ah, ma'am, I just want to make a deposit." A grin, a twinkle in the eye. *Ah.* Light dawned in my dim mind, and I invited him in to use the CR (comfort room).

---

[132] It truly was a delight to have Becky in our home as a part of our family; she was a very good example to our children of cheerful, quiet responsibility.
[133] Several folks in the US provided gifts to the "Worthy Student Fund" to help Quivin with his expenses.

──── CHAPTER 22 ────

Expatriates and Culture Shock

Dale and Karen

"Culture is the total way of life of a people, learned and integrated."
—*Gottfried Oosterwal, Cultural Anthropologist, Director of Missions Institute, Andrews University*

The slow, steady flow onto our campus of fresh faculty and student expatriates from the United States, Australia, Trinidad, Finland, and multiple Asian countries brought a fascinating variety of joys and frustrations as we adjusted to the Filipino culture and its peoples.[134] Most of us were working at enjoying becoming bicultural—learning about the local customs, values, and behaviors, incorporating some and accommodating others while retaining our cultural norms. The goal was acculturation, not assimilation. It was complicated.

The non-Filipino faculty and administrative expatriates and their families totaled thirty-two Americans, four Canadians, three Jamaicans, and two Finns and represented a wide range of ages, interests, and occupations: we were university professors, librarians, nurses, a business manager/overseas advisor, and a construction supervisor with our families. Karen worked at the Far Eastern Division Seminary as an administrative assistant. Four of the women worked from their homes.

---

[134] An expatriate is someone who leaves their home country to live and work in another country. In 1978, we were called "overseas workers" by the Filipinos and our American SDA administrators.

During our first ten months on the Baesa campus, there were two families of four and a senior-aged volunteer elementary teacher. When we moved to the Silang campus, there were twelve students in the eight-grade elementary school with two American teachers. Five American children attended high school at a small private boarding school in Singapore for ten months of the year, returning to campus during Christmas breaks and the summers.

Some folks had brought furniture. We purchased sturdy and beautiful sala sets created from sturdy Filipino rattan, cane, and wicker, planning to take them home with us. Many of us enjoyed displaying woven rugs, baskets, and carvings, and Dale started a collection of artfully crafted fish traps and bait holders. One family wanted to remain as American as possible, covering their wood parquet floors with thick carpets and displaying a wall-to-wall, floor-to-ceiling photo mural of the northern Michigan woods.

Don Van Ornam, our business manager, and Sam Robinson, our construction supervisor, working with the US State Department and USAID, were able to bring items to our campus that were no longer needed by nearby American installations: US Naval Base Subic Bay and Clark Air Base. Also, each expatriate faculty and business family was gifted a gorgeous teak dining room table, chairs, and hutches when the American embassy closed there. All of us were given microwave ovens as part of this process.

Dale and I said, "No, thank you. We don't need that."

Don patiently explained: "We have one for each family, and it has to be in your house. Maybe the next family will enjoy it."

We let them put the abominable thing out of sight on top of the electric dryer in the garage. I did not want our Filipino visitors to see yet another expensive thing that would separate us from them, advertising our ability to have the latest available devices. Already, when visitors came through the front door of the Americans' homes, their line of sight went to the humungous electric refrigerator. One eccentric and free-spirited couple, Denise and Larry Herr, deciding they didn't even want to use the washer and dryer installed in all American homes, chose to stomp their clothes in their bathtub and hang them out on clotheslines to dry. Excellent exercise, too.

Our family loved the markets! Some expatriates found them disorganized, dirty, and frustrating; some sent their helpers to shop local whenever they could. We often heard "No wonder things take longer to get done; you can see that they sleep most of the time" or "Well, it's hard to get help in the markets. They're sleeping in the back."

We shared what we loved about the markets and would explain, "Most of the folk we see in the markets when we shop midday have been there since 4 or 5 a.m. to set up their stall—when it's cool. So it's reasonable that they take naps during the day. Some vendors sleep overnight in their stall. Some live there full-time!"

We loved the smells of fresh garlic, mangoes, atis, durian, lychee, and the craftsmanship of the embroidered or batiked clothes. Going into the meat areas was fascinating, dare I say challenging, with cows' tails hanging nose level and the pervasive smell of fresh meat, including whole hogs, fish, squid, chickens, and "100-year-old" eggs; this Chinese-influenced delicacy (pronounced "da-LEK-a-see") usually involved coating the chicken, duck, or quail eggs in a muddy paste made of lime, ash, salt, and water, then keeping them covered or wrapped for some time (not 100 years), often buried in the earth or in an earthenware jar. They are said to be an "acquired taste."[135]

As interesting as the things being sold were, Kimberly and I found the unpleasant smells overpowering. Once, in Quiapo Market, I could not hold my breath long enough on my way to the vegetables and had to inhale deeply as I walked through the meat section. I can still almost bring back the odor.

Dale made friends with the sellers at Balintawak Market near Baesa. He took photos and then returned to the market and gifted

---

[135]"Century Eggs-Chinese Delicacy" https://disgustingfoodmuseum.com/century-eggs, "Culinary Lore: Food Science, History and much More!" https://culinarylore.com/specialty-foods:what- are-hundred-year-old-eggs (Accessed February 17, 2024).

the printed pictures to the sellers. It was a delight to him and them—precious to those who had never owned a photo of themselves or their children.

Some things bothered one person and left another unaffected; however, the traffic got to everyone sooner or later. Dale stood on a Manila corner one day with a Filipino friend, who said, "Manila traffic never bothered me until I returned from graduate school in the States."

We had spent two years in Southern California and recalled the horrendous LA traffic, but the rules of the road helped there. It would take a logician's analysis to describe the difference, but to the casual observer, LA traffic moved more quickly and orderly from points "A" to "B" than in the Philippines; there were fewer horn blasts, and it was safer to cross the street. We learned the main rule, even in crowded Manila, was that whoever got their fender ahead of another had the right-of-way. Lots of horns honked, but we seldom saw angry behavior or heard ugly altercations. We could both maneuver on rugged country roads and in the heart of the city. Folks did look strangely at Karen driving the Blue Bomb in Manila; Americans, especially women, usually had chauffeurs and were sitting in the back seat.

Throughout the country, the ever-ringing chorus of "Hey, Joe" echoed from curious children, sari-sari store clerks, and from the windows of nipa huts. To some, this represented warmth bordering on affection, and to others an impersonal insult.

Several expatriate families enjoyed one special Fourth of July weekend in a resort on the coast of Batangas on southern Luzon. We learned tinikling,[136] the national dance, which involves jumping between bamboo poles laid horizontally on the ground. We sang John Denver songs while sitting on the beach around a campfire, like "Take Me Home, Country Roads" and "Grandma's Feather Bed," and we also sang patriotic American songs. Often when traveling with Kimberly

---

[136] "Culture Trip. Tinikling: The National Dance of the Philippines with Bamboo Poles" http://theculturetrip.com/asia/philippines/articles/tinikling (Accessed February 17, 2024).

and her new friends, Carla and Janelle Jones, I sang those songs with them—to the distraction of the driver. Secretly, he loved it all, too.

Some of us regularly enjoyed making music together, with piano, guitar, lute, recorder, and a reportedly 400-year-old harp, a Spanish one John Jones had purchased in Baguio and renovated to appear as close to the original as possible. Precious, beautiful memories. The Joneses had a small nipa hut built down the hill behind their house, near a huge tree where noisy and curious moneys lived. From there we could hear the fast-moving little river far below. Some of us read and played music there as often as possible; some used it for early-morning meditation.

A common form of entertainment for some of the forty expatriates on our campus was to sit and exchange fresh frustrations served up by this new experience. For example: we were on a college campus, and the only available phone was sixty-eight miles (42.3 kilometers) away in Manila. Because of road conditions and traffic, it was a one-and-a-half-hour drive, if there was no problem with our car. Roads rivaled the Craters of the Moon National Park and made senile wrecks of even vigorous young cars, while we had an old, resuscitated Holden. It seemed everything took longer—going to town, shopping, and making financial transactions, whether at the bank in Manila or with the unofficial money exchange in the barrio.

While some complained that the campus guards invaded their privacy, others complained about the lack of security. If one person was unhappy with the living conditions, another felt that salary differences and assigned housing placed us so far above the living standard of the Filipino teachers that a breach was created in relationships. We all wanted to get along; mostly we did. We wanted to be as positive as we could for our own peace of mind.

There was always an "overseas faculty Christmas party." One of the highlights was finding and wrapping a ten-peso gift (USD 1.25) that could be appreciated by either men or women. To begin, each of us chose a number, and then the leader would pick numbers from a container and read them out. The person matching that number would take a gift from the pile or "steal" from another player.

The gift we brought was not chosen by a second player once the first person opened it. It was *Doctor to the Barrios*, a book in a series by Filipino physician Juan Favier.[137] We honestly thought the others would like to learn more about Filipinos. Ah, well, best-laid plans. One of our American colleagues said: "Well, we know who brought *that* one, don't we?" And there were groans.

All of the campus folk knew which food the Americans brought to church potlucks or parties because we used our prized narrawood dishes purchased in the Philippines. Tupperware was another giveaway.

American professors and administrators, tourists, friends, and families frequently visited. A "hostess" was identified to make it all work smoothly. On-campus families took turns hosting them, and we met many interesting people; frankly, this duty sometimes felt tiresome. Occasionally we heard this childish exchange:

"We're having four overseas guests for dinner tonight."

"I hope they're tasty."

Some of us were out of our comfort zones for the first time. The two of us had never lived outside the US. We all learned from our Filipino and international students and colleagues. Some had lived in other faraway places and were more adaptive. As the Van Ornams had been in Africa for many years, their five daughters were born there, and they were adept at adjusting. They often made American-tasting vegetarian entrées, substituting local products. Adventists urge eating healthy, with the "Garden of Eden diet" of fruits, nuts, and grains as a part of meal planning, trying to remain healthy in mind, body, and spirit.[138]

---

[137] Juan M. Flavier, *Doctor to the Barrios: Experiences with the Philippine Rural Reconstruction Movement.* 1970. New Day Publishers: Quezon City, Republic of the Philippines.

[138] Figures vary between 30 to 50 percent regarding how many SDAs are vegetarians. Some are vegan; some are lacto-ovo vegetarian. The original diet in Genesis is seen as the healthiest: fruits, nuts, and grains.

Finnish American seminary professor C. Raymond Holmes wrote about his experiences on the Silang campus, calling his book *Boiled Rice and Gluten* (both of which he emphatically did not like). That was how he described the Adventist Filipino diet. That, of course, is not accurate, though Filipinos do have lots of rice—there are thirteen kinds. They often make a viand (the main dish) of sautéed vegetables and fish, chicken, pork, or some other protein in a tasty sauce. Ray's book was self-published and had a lot of loving humor and also honest frustration about his cross-cultural experiences.[139] He did love teaching his multicultural students.

Our Filipino neighbors usually had fruit trees and gardens of vegetables and flowers. We once complimented a neighbor on his large and healthy banana tree.

"We are amazed at the size and number of bananas on your tree."

"It's the *yur-een*," our neighbor offered.

Stumped, we asked: "What is *yur-een*?"

"*Yur-een*," he said. "You know, night water."

Well, of course.

Many of us learned enough Tagalog to greet and thank folk and to barter for food and handicrafts. John Jones had been a missionary kid on the Baesa campus in the 1940s when he was an adolescent, and his parents were missionaries; he still remembered much of the Tagalog he'd learned from his Filipino friends. And, as mentioned before, some of the kids on campus created a combination of English, Tagalog, and Indonesian whose meaning most of their parents did not understand.

Some of us loved to explore the countryside, barrios, cathedrals and chapels, fields and beaches, historical sites, the outdoor markets, and the two glitzy indoor malls. Imelda Marcos created a glamorous cultural center at the edge of Manila Bay, and many of us attended the ballet and other cultural events there. One fantastic show was *The Nutcracker*; the dancers wore eighteenth-century Filipino clothing,

---

[139] C. Raymond Holmes, *Boiled Rice and Gluten*; self-published, 1972.

featuring the beautiful terno dress with its "butterfly" sleeves popularized by Imelda Marcos and worn since at least 1910.[140]

Four of us traveled to the villages known for Easter celebrations, which we found touching and dramatic. Other Americans, some of them very conservative Christians who believed Catholic ritual to be ostentatious, were repelled and did not want to hear or see anything about those events combining animistic and Christian beliefs and rituals Karen details in chapter 27, "Easter Celebrations: People Look for Answers."[141]

We also shared our different expatriate cultures and interests among us. One American graduate student had lived as a young bride in India. Her husband worked as an advisor in a nonprofit development organization off campus. Another American family of self-employed Mennonite missioners lived near us. They were a photojournalist team writing for in-flight magazines. Their articles always included information about social concerns within the countries they photographed and wrote about. They taught us their prayer before meals—a Shaker tune, "Simple Gifts": "'Tis a gift to be simple, it's a gift to be free." We often used it for our meal prayer.[142] Soon all the expatriates were singing that song.

It's accurate to define culture as "the total way of life of a people, learned and integrated," as Gottfried Oosterwal does.[143] However, that means there is no way to wholly assimilate into a new cultural environment. Early in our experience, Karen wanted so badly to

---

[140] "Fun Facts: Who invented the Philippine Terno?" *Rappler*, Jan. 27, 2017 (Accessed February 18, 2024) https://www.rappler.com/newsbreak/iq/terno-history-maxine-medina-imelda-marcos.

[141] Animism is the belief that objects, places, and creatures all possess a distinct spiritual essence. Animists believe in good and evil spirits (anitos) which can do favors and inflict harm. https://en.wikipedia.org/wiki/Animism.

[142] Composed in 1848 by Elder Joseph Brackett. www.alfredshakermuseum.com/history/simple-gifts, then arranged by Aaron Copeland and set in his suite "Appalachian Spring" Appalachian Spring | Modern Dance, American Ballet & Copland | Britannica (Accessed February 18, 2024).

[143] Dr. Oosterwal founded the Institute for World Missions, offering five-week training sessions for families going on foreign service appointments and has written extensively on mission.

understand, enjoy, and fit in. But for a time she was so very sad and homesick.[144] Eventually she came to think of things as simply different and became more accepting and joyful. We would have learned valuable lessons about culture shock had we attended the training offered to us before we left.

After studying on our own, we learned that culture shock is a kind of grief. Big change often results in some degree of grief. When one experiences the loss of a job, the death of a loved one, or moving to a new home, job, city, or country, one may react with sadness, anger, fear, and physical and emotional upset before working toward adjustment and then usually acceptance of the new situation. The adjustments are not smooth at first; there are often highs and lows before learning to manage and not just survive but thrive in the new situation.

We have a sculpture created from very darkly stained wood. Imagine a person seated on the ground, legs crossed and knees drawn up so they almost touch the bent head. The arms are wrapped around the legs, and the hands completely hide the face. It's a common sculpture in the markets and named *The Ugliest Man in the World*. To Karen, it expressed how she often felt during the first three months: "Please go away. Don't talk to me. I want to pretend I'm not here." She titled the piece "Culture Shock."

As our colleagues returned to their homelands, we received letters detailing "reverse culture shock." Things back home moved too fast, people were too materialistic, so many people were obese, many were indifferent or rude, technology blasted them in the face and pocketbook, and inflation and civic improvements turned old haunts into strange new places.

We had joys and regrets, loving the travel and the work, the friends and the understandings that have helped us become more well-rounded citizens of the world. We wish we'd chosen to spend more personal time with Filipinos, creating regular get-togethers to learn about the country, its history, its customs. Karen's later

---

[144] See chapter 4, "An Embarrassment of Riches," and chapter 7, "Early Journaling."

sociological training was instigated partly due to witnessing all the things people do to be happy and healthy, adapting to their history, culture, and environment. She wishes she'd created Filipino–American discussions, which could have helped everyone involved.

Update 2020s

—**Blue Zone Adventists:** *National Geographic* fellow Dan Buettner wrote about five "blue zones" where folks live longer than expected of the general population. Interestingly, Loma Linda, an Adventist hub, is the only community in the US identified as a blue zone.[145] According to an ABC article, "Buettner found the residents live 'as much as a decade longer than the rest of us' due to their vegetarian diet, regular exercise, and abstinence from alcohol and cigarettes."[146] The animal ethics involved are secondary but appreciated. Other studies have described lower rates of cancer and cardiovascular disease.[147]

—**Health in body, mind, and spirit** is an admirable goal; each culture has its way of making that happen. Only about 30 percent of SDAs are vegetarians or lacto-ovo-vegetarians. Many Filipino Adventists called chicken, a Filipino staple, the "flying vegetable of the Philippines."

---

[145] Alexa Mikhail. April 2, 2023. "A look inside America's only blue zone city—home to some of the world's longest-living people." https://fortune.com/well//2023/04/02/longevity-tips-loma-linda-california-blue-zone-cit6y (Accessed February 18, 2024)
[146] "Seventh-day Adventists advocate a vegetarian diet — but it's not because of animal ethics" - ABC News
[147] "This American diet could add 10 years to your life." www.nationalgeographic.com/magazine/article (Accessed February 18, 2024)

CHAPTER 23

A Time for Everything

Karen

"There is a time for everything, and a season for every activity under the heavens."

—Solomon, Ecclesiastics 3:1

Expatriates were required to go on a two-week holiday once a year, off campus and "out of country" if possible. Holiday pay was available only if we complied. We appreciated that requirement, and for our first holiday we chose Hong Kong. The funds covered the cost of the flight for all four of us, and we stayed at South China Union College, a sister college where they provided a small brick two-bedroom home to us for fifteen dollars per night![148] It was an amazing holiday. We took public transportation, used the airport brochures for self-guided walks, bought rice-pattern china pieces and kitchen pottery, and rode the Star Ferry, double-decker buses, trains, and taxis—each an adventure. On our holiday the following year, we took a circle tour offered by Thai Airlines, spending five days each in Bangkok and Singapore, again with pleasant accommodations in SDA institutions in each place.

When it was time for the kids' teacher, Ms. Hemme, to go on holiday, she asked me a favor: "You know, it's my job to be sure we have a bouquet at the front of the church each Sabbath. Will you take care of that for me for the two weeks I'm gone?"

---
[148] Renamed Hong Kong Adventist College in 1981.

Now, I did want to please her, and she knew that I'd taken an *ikebana* (Japanese flower arranging) class from Makiko, the wife of one of our Japanese students. I hesitated, and she said, "I'll show you exactly how to do it." I agreed.

We walked to the center of the lawn between our two homes, and she showed me which blossoms she thought I should use to create the appropriate "spray" for the church: three portions of a papyrus-type plant for the basic framework, several sprigs of sweet-smelling white sampaguita (the national flower), and hibiscus. The color choices could be mine.

I'd learned that hibiscus was lovely during the day but would wilt by nightfall. Then I was told how to "fool" the flowers: if they were picked midday and put in the refrigerator, they would stay fresh for display into the evening.

Ms. H taught me yet another trick.

"Timing is everything," Ms. H said, "It is important that these smaller white ones be picked as buds on the morning of the service. They are perfect because they are white and they fill in anything else—and they will open right on time at 8:45 a.m." That was hard to believe, but it wasn't pleasant questioning Ms. H, so I didn't. She left on holiday, confident she had prepared me to do the job correctly.

Early on that first Sabbath, I carefully picked the appropriate plants and arranged them in the large vase she had provided As instructed, tucked in at evenly spaced locations were the tiny white hibiscus buds. I placed the completed "spray" at the front of the church, and just before 8:30 a.m., Dale and I arrived for the song service.[149] I leaned over to share the secret of the white buds with a girlfriend. We both grinned, decidedly *not* believers in the appointed timing of the specially chosen buds. We enjoyed the song service—and waited. We bowed our heads in prayer and surreptitiously watched. The program proceeded, and those hibiscus buds opened

---

[149] Services began early because the heat and humidity gained momentum throughout the day.

at 8:45 a.m., *right on time*! Muffled sounds accompanied our wide eyes and vanishing disbelief. Ms. H did know the appointed time, even while on vacation.

———CHAPTER 24———

"Can't We Stop This Killing?"

Dale

"Sometimes hunting isn't about the hunt at all."

—*Outback*[150]

Genteel Ms. Janet Miller sat at her book-laden desk and pounded a white-knuckled fist on an austere, gilt-lettered volume. "Can't we do something to stop this killing? I can't sleep at night. They respect nothing and nobody!"

Janet Miller was the Far Eastern Division Seminary librarian. She could use words to calm storms among people and make it feel like the sun was shining; but this day, she was the storm. Workmen hired to construct the many new buildings rising on our campus had riled her. They were shooting the colorful songbirds we enjoyed, using slingshots and air-powered pellet guns. Those workers lived in the buildings they were constructing, and many had nowhere else to go. They were transient, moving from job to job, and the time and costs of public transportation eliminated the option of commuting beyond the blackened pots steaming over open fires in the rubble surrounding the construction.

"They are starting to shoot down by the river. The campus has been designated a wildlife preserve, but it doesn't seem to matter to

---

[150] https://www.teepublic.com/t-shirt/3013014-sometimes-hunting-isnt-about-hunting-at-all (Accessed March 24, 2024).

them. Can't we *do* something?"

"We can try," I said. I had tried a year earlier with hunters on the old campus and was willing to try again, though this time I felt much less enthusiasm for the task.

It was November, and winter birds were migrating through the Philippines. The arrival of the migrant shrikes and other species signals hunting season for many Filipinos. Some hunt for sport and some for food. Ms. Miller was new to our campus and community. She had arrived about the same time as the shrikes, and for her the pugnacious little birds were part and parcel of the clotheslines and bushes about her small apartment.

The absence of the harsh *keek-keek-keek-keek* call of the shrikes as they moved south was as noticeable to birdwatchers as their arrival. Ms. Miller was a confirmed birdwatcher. Now the absence of the shrikes and a favorite stork-billed kingfisher coincided with the presence of the construction workers. Their slingshots and air rifles also confirmed her suspicion that the birds had all been killed or chased off the hill. I suspect the workers got the kingfisher and several of the shrikes, but the urge to continue their journey to Negros and others of the 7,000-plus islands had mercifully urged them to continue their migration.

Shrikes are aggressive little devils. They have no compassion for other birds in their feeding territories; they make screaming dive-bomb attacks and are especially intolerant of other brown shrikes, eventually sorting out individual feeding territories. I had fallen in love with those raucous shrikes and the other birds before watching them being shot out of the trees near our house. But first let me tell you how the love affair developed.

In August or early September of our first year, while living on the Baesa campus, we purchased two little finches from a street vendor in Manila. One was bright red and the other bright green. They were beautiful little birds. Even the tiny cage was delightfully made of bamboo. I couldn't believe the bargain I had struck.

We wanted to surprise our children, so for a few hours, we hid the birds and their cage balanced on the edge of the sink in our bathroom. The satisfaction of our clever purchase faded when the birds began bathing in the fruit-jar lid we filled with their drinking water. Red and green stains were splattered around the cage, in the sink, on the wall, and over everything in splash range. Beneath the red and green dye, we found drab little brown finches, a common species in the rice fields. Obviously, they had been dyed; we wondered what that might have done to their tiny eyes and ear holes.

The little brown birds were introduced to the children, who removed them from their tiny bamboo cage and released them in our large, screened-in, roofed veranda. There were floor-to-ceiling screens with burglar bars bolted, to secure the house. Those finches seldom left the burglar bars, where they enjoyed the breezes and were sheltered from the sometimes torrential rains and predators. Their droppings fell inconspicuously among the ferns and palms in a flower bed below the bars. Our dining table was in the center; when they flew, they flew mostly around the edges, and we enjoyed their antics at every meal.

In early November, a brown shrike claimed a long, sweeping, naked limb in the large mango tree outside our veranda. It was his private perch and battle station. The two small finches behind the screen were a constant source of irritation to him. His attacks, aborted by the screen, and his changes in dive-bomber strategies were hilarious to watch. A few brown shrikes winter in Manila rather than traveling farther south, but I believe this one had decided that those two little finches were leaving before he did. Then a local nimrod with his air rifle ended the shrike's campaign.

The shrike and the finches were my birds. Well, I saw them as my birds. They lived and fed on my rented property, and I would not tolerate this poaching! A gentle approach seemed to work well at first. I simply asked the hunters to find somewhere else to hunt and was met with: "I'm sorry, sir! Sorry, sorry, sir!" or "Sorry, I do not want to offend you." It was soon apparent that the acquiescence held little regret, and the "Sorry" was more displacement behavior than apology. It was simply a Filipino expression for avoiding confrontation, so I found myself confronting the same poachers time and time again with the same frustrating results.

Early one Sunday morning, I confronted Nestor Arguelies, a recurrent poacher. He didn't say, "I'm sorry."

He said, "How long have you lived here?"

"About seven months, I guess."

"I lived here thirty-one years," he said, and I judged that to be his age. "Do you work for the college?"

"Yes." Didn't everyone know this was college property? Surely this fellow knew the neighborhood.

"Where do you work?" I asked.

"My father was a teacher here, but he is retired now. Is this your house?"

"Yes."

"I mean, do you own it?" Nestor asked. And he continued asking questions of me: Did I know Dr. Roda, president of the college and his friend? Did I know Pastor Arragonte, president of the North Philippine Union and chairman of my college board? He knew the answers to his questions as well as I, and although his approach annoyed me, he was teaching me lessons about Filipino values. He had hunted this land before I came. He didn't say so, but if I didn't like it, I should leave, not he. His nonfrontal attack stood in contrast to my own, and that, too, held a lesson. Priority superseded legality, and what a neighbor asked of your property was not to be denied; that is Filipino hospitality. Foreigners and strangers are usually indulged to a fault, but there are limits.

He implied that the animals and the fruits and vegetables in my garden were to be used, not wasted by disuse. Yes, many "strangers" took the fruits from our trees, too. Pretty birds are for children's fantasies. Men cannot afford such triviality. My strange behavior raised questions about motives. Did I trust him, and did I fear the loss of the material treasures Americans hoard in their houses? He and I knew what was meant, and I was the better for having met Nestor Arguelles. Our interactions were crucial to my understanding his culture and his viewpoint.

Ms. Miller's feelings were what I'd experienced a year ago, and she needed to hear and try to understand Nestor Arguelles and his gentle "Filipino ways."

"Can't we put up signs prohibiting this hunting?" she asked.

"I suppose we could," I said, "but that would be about as effective as me coming into your kitchen and saying 'Leave those little cockroaches alone! They are God's creatures, and He loves them!' What is more, those songbirds are meat for the worker's table."

"Perhaps you're right," Ms. Miller said sadly, "but don't they understand that birds eat insects that destroy crops, and if they would leave the birds alone, their crops would yield more food for the table than the birds do?"

"But the birds are the food they want on their table today. They see so many birds and fruits available all over campus, and they need the food. That meal is more important to them right now." I wanted her to understand their perspective.

"These people just don't look to the future."

She was right, but the "storm" was subsiding. For Ms. Miller, a resignation was developing toward what was and would continue to be. I had not changed her values as Nestor had not changed mine, nor I his. But there was understanding, the temporary acceptance that allowed us to get on with life and with each other.

Update 2020s

—**Bird Trade:** Bird trade in Southeast Asia is a huge, illegal trade.[151]

—**TRAFFIC is a British wildlife monitoring network whose long-term vision is "world living in harmony with nature."** They recently reported that 312 birds and mammals were found in our home in Pasay City. Some are considered delicacies—and aphrodisiacs. Birds are valued for their song, their beauty, and on some restaurant menus.[152]

---

[151] https://www.wildlifealliance.org/southeast-asias-thriving-illegal-bird-trade (Accessed April 2, 2024).
[152] "Demand For Pets Endangers Southeast Asia's Birds," Radio Free Asia, https://www.rfa.org/English/commentaries/asia-birds-07312018171743 (Accessed February 18, 2024).

―――CHAPTER 25―――

Differences Are More Interesting

Dale

"The truth of my experience is that we are all a lot more alike than we are different."

—*Anne Lamott, Author*[153]

I was teaching field zoology, and while I understood the theories and principles applicable to stateside species, most Philippine plants and animals were strangers to me. Very few wildlife guides were available, none in the library, and I was playing catch-up.

The Silang campus is located on fallow, abandoned farmland sporting areas of brush and trees. Bordering the south property line is a deep gorge cradling a narrow river that rages over large rocks in the rainy season and meanders lazily or exists as disconnected pools through the dry season. The campus is a haven for wildlife, and I set out to make new acquaintances on a beautiful afternoon with blue skies, soft clouds, and gentle breezes that softened the sun's sharp rays.

I discovered a large black-and-yellow garden spider had woven a beautiful web in a small bush. She looked similar to the garden spiders in my rose bushes back in Walla Walla and seemed to me an old friend, like Charlotte, the famous spider in E. B. White's children's novel and the movie *Charlotte's Webb*. Garden spiders are common

---

[153] Anne Lamott quote, https//w.acquotes.com/quote/1086596 (Accessed February 18, 2024).

around the world and are also called orb weavers, and their webs are architectural marvels.

Orb weavers spin strong, straight strands of silk radiating from a central point like spokes of a bicycle wheel. Then, starting at the hub, they lay a continuous sticky strand of silk over the spoke-like superstructure in an ever-expanding spiral, creating a circular orbit around the center, hence the name orb weaver. The sticky, circular strands trap flying insects and other creatures that wander onto the web. When prey is captured, the spider rushes in and spins a silk cage around the prey to secure it. Oil on the spider's body prevents it from sticking to its own web.

What a beautiful spider! What a beautiful web! Fortunately, I had my camera, but the wind had gotten stronger and was moving the bush so radically that I expected a blurry picture. *No problem!* I steadied the bush with my knee, keeping my hands free to take the picture; but the spider disappeared. I freed the bush and let it move. She returned. No matter how subtly I tried to steady the bush, she always detected the disturbance and fled. I did not get a picture. She could distinguish the erratic shifting of the wind-tossed bush from my artificial reduction in movement and sensed a danger. What a marvelous adaptation of a very simple nervous system.

The orb spider was a lucky find. I was already acquainted with them, but I didn't know the name of this Filipino cousin. I made a mental map of the surroundings so I could locate the bush, and the web, and hoped we would meet again when students came along.

While occupied by the spider, I heard a rooster crow. *Strange*, I thought. *Who has chickens out here?* There were no houses nearby. Eventually I spotted the rooster scratching about for seeds and insects in a small clearing. He was stunning, with a large, bright-red comb, red eye rings nearly covering his face, and equally bright-red wattles at the throat. The neck and upper body sported long, silky, metallic golden feathers. His breast, wings, and back were brilliant, reddish auburn. The rest of the body was black. The tail was held high and dramatically arched and shimmered with iridescent blue-green-purple highlights in the bright sunlight filtering through the trees. Gorgeous!

In time, a hen emerged from the bushes. Lacking the rooster's bright, showy plumage, she was a beautiful mix of golden tan about the head and neck, shading into brown over the back, with black lines on the feathers. Her wings were darker brown with a nearly black tail. What a beauty!

Somewhere in the midst of my observations, I realized these were junglefowl, not someone's chickens. Junglefowl are wild birds native to India, Malaysia, the Philippines, and Indonesia. Mitochondrial DNA studies suggest that the many breeds of chickens today originated from the domestication of junglefowl over 7,000 years ago.

The afternoon was passing, and it was time to seek other venues and new adventures. I searched for tracks, scat, and other signs of animals inhabiting the wilder areas. As if on cue, I spotted tracks. They were fresh and led directly down the unused roadcut. What I was seeing were cow tracks. These tracks were not uncommon, but this was an uncommon place for them. I was not near the usual pasture, the barn, or the milk shed.

I had seen evidence of cow tracks and cow pies in the lawns by the women's dormitory and sometimes by the classroom buildings. Those tracks were easily explained, and we were learning to expect them in the most unexpected places. The two boys who herded the cows were fun-loving teenagers who took every opportunity they could create to bring the Wild West to the Far East. Sometimes their horsemanship did as much to scatter the cows as it did to control them.

The boys often drove the cows to pasture by a path leading up and down the steep banks of the ravine behind the ladies' dormitory. The ravine route was one of the longer paths to the pasture, and the steep banks surely sapped the cows' energy and sent milk production plummeting. It was the closest path to that dormitory, however, and provided the best opportunity for displaying equestrian skills, bared chests, and work-hardened bodies to the girls. So, it became the path of choice for the cowboys.

But why were there cow tracks on the unused roadcut I was following? Likely, the cowboys had simply lost control of a couple of milk cows. The area was too wild and remote to provide an audience, and it was not en route to the pasture. But the tracks did not appear to be wandering. The cows who made them were moving at a brisk pace. If the boys had driven them, there should also have been horse tracks, but the only other tracks were occasional sandal prints.

Wildlife and field exploration for my class forgotten, I bent my energies to deciphering the mystery of the cows. There had been two, possibly three, moving steadily, not stopping to munch the grasses growing into the roadway. The road ended abruptly at a dry creek bed where the wet season had eroded a deep ditch. The cows' hooves had pulled topsoil and grass from the opposite bank into the creek bed. The cows' tracks beyond that were hopelessly lost in the deep, rich grasses bent left and right and pressed to the ground by recent storms and by the workers cutting bamboo that grew there. I had lost the trail.

I sat on the creek bank and pondered the case of the cows. But then I saw a small, brown, fantailed flycatcher circling and rising high above the grassy field. I was guessing it was a flycatcher; I didn't know the Philippine birds, and he was moving too quickly to offer details. Sharp, plaintive, staccato calls punctuated the bird's flight as he rose above a dense clump of cogon grass. Call and wingbeat were synchronized; each call signaled an upward step in the tightly spiraling path the bird traced high into the early evening sky. Up, up the bird continued until it was but a speck, and then, folding its wings, the beautiful little creature plummeted earthward, banking sharply to miss the grass tips by the barest of margins. Without so much as a pause, the next spiral began. The force of each downward wingbeat was remarkable. The bird seemed to leap two or three steps up an invisible, winding staircase. The pattern was not unlike the mating displays of male hummingbirds, nighthawks, and other birds I knew back home.

I recalled the morning I woke at Wallula Junction in Washington State near the confluence of the Columbia and Snake Rivers. I had been live-trapping pocket mice, and I rolled out a sleeping bag sometime after midnight to enjoy the stars and desert night sounds rather than depending on caffeine and "late-night radio"—more John Denver—to get me safely back over the mountains to the marine biological station on Puget Sound where I was spending the summer.

At first light I woke to what sounded like gunfire, and it was near. As the stupor of sleep receded, I spotted a nighthawk climbing into the sky before plummeting toward me with folded wings. When I feared it would strike the ground (or me), its wings snapped open, and it swept once more heavenward. More courtship displays. The snap of wings as they filled with air was like the pop of the sail as a boat turns about, catching the breeze that will once more drive it on its way.

The little Philippine fantail was probably one-fourth as long and had a wingspan a sixth or less of the common nighthawk's wings; consequently, the sound the nighthawk made at the bottom of its dive was louder and sharper. The fantails' courtship produced more of a gentle, buzzing pop.

As the golden twilight deepened, the delightful little bird ended his display and entered the clump of cogon grass that seemed his focus. It was a new species to me, a "lifer" (birder jargon for "first time seen"), and I was pleased. I needed to find a field guide to know his name. I concluded (or wished to believe) that the cogon grass clump was his home and that the lover he had been courting so arduously awaited him there.

The sky melted from gold to red, then violet, and I turned homeward. Field zoology crowded my mind; for now, I would leave it to the cowboys to worry about the cows.

The organisms I found were new to me, and I already knew a lot about them because I knew their kin. I was happy for that, but what I did not know seemed more interesting, more exciting. Becoming acquainted with Philippine wildlife was not unlike the adventure of experiencing Filipino culture and new friends; their value systems, their joys and sorrows, their lifestyles, and how they coped with life's problems revealed interesting differences.

People are more alike than different, but the differences are more interesting. There is more adventure in the unknown.

―――CHAPTER 26―――

Beauty Is What Works

Dale

"From my Filipino colleagues, I perceived, always a gentle, tangential approach. There never was a 'frontal attack' such as I made."

—Dale

Ralph Perrin, a doctoral candidate from Loma Linda University (LLU) in Southern California, came to teach at PUC as part of the affiliation between the two universities that made the fledgling public health program at PUC possible.

The consortium was decidedly unbalanced: Hedrick Edwards was the dean of the graduate Public Health Program at PUC; he was currently at LLU for upgrading. The PUC Biology, Chemistry, and Nursing faculties taught classes in the program. The students were registered as PUC students, and LLU provided specialized classes. Each had different goals and interests. The PUC faculty were resident, while the LLU faculty were transient. Expertise was the purview of LLU, and the logistics were in the hands of the PUC faculty. It was a complicated and frustrating situation.

The evening before the monthly Graduate Council meeting, Ralph was concerned: "I won't be here when the next class starts," he said, "but I probably should make some arrangements for transportation, since Hedrick won't be back in time. I'm just afraid if I don't do it now before I leave, no one will, and the students have to use public transportation—and that takes money and more travel time."

Ralph had been on campus less than two months but had suffered several encounters that left him amazed and wiser. The standard administrative responses to many problems seemed to be "Ignore the problem, and it will go away" or "If you can ignore the problem, there is no problem." For levity I quipped, "You have already been here too long, Ralph."

"Well," Ralph continued, "I don't know if I am supposed to be a member of the Graduate Council or not. I go to meetings because there are problems in the Public Health Program that must be solved; but this one really isn't my problem since the class doesn't start until several weeks after I leave."

"If you don't handle it, Ralph, who will? Me?" I asked. "Besides, it will be more effective coming from you, since you are the designated dean currently."

Ralph smiled. The idea of a graduate student being the dean of a school of public health was, well, absurd, and yet he knew I had not said it entirely in jest. Dr. Hedrick Edwards had been running a "one-man show" at PUC, with periodic infusions from Loma Linda, for the past three years, but right now Hedrick was on furlough, and he would not return until well after Ralph completed the course he was teaching and resumed his graduate studies back in California. Ralph was teaching three intensive, half-semester courses.

Our Graduate Council agenda was boldly printed on the chalkboard as we entered the PUC president's office and settled comfortably around a large US Army surplus conference table. The agenda was uninspiring. One item was a request for approval of a field trip taken a few weeks earlier. All field trips must be approved. In jest we discussed canceling the field trip and speculated on the consequences if we failed to approve it. The field trip item was the best part of the agenda.

When we finished the agenda items, Ralph expressed his concern about transportation to Manila. When he returned to LLU, the public health students at PUC would attend a short course taught at the Manila Hospital and Sanitarium, some ninety-six kilometers from campus. It could take at least two hours to go that distance. When Ralph left, the students would be without a mentor and, if his apprehensions were realized, without transportation as well. Most students and many professors did not own vehicles.

One committee member said: "We should be able to wait until Dr. Edwards returns to make a decision."

Another countered, "Well, they shouldn't mind going public until then."

Going public meant riding the capricious jeepneys and buses. It meant starting early and arriving late. And for the students, it would mean unexpected expenses.

"Will students be able to report their expenses?" someone asked.

"Well, students who are sponsored may be reimbursed later," another responded.

Sponsored students are those who 1) have found a "wealthy" friend or 2) are sent by their employers—organizations to which they have rendered the appropriate amount of service or to whom they will be indebted for years to come—to "upgrade" their qualifications. Such students are often able to report all necessary educational expenses. Of course, they have to pay them first and wait for reimbursement.

The rest of the message was clear. Self-supporting students would get no help with transportation expenses.

"How many self-supporting students are involved?"

"Maybe two or three *na lang* [only]," we were told. However, we knew there were many, many more.

"Could we not cover the expense of transportation for those students?"

"No! No! We would cause trouble. Sponsors of the other students would not want to pay if we did that."

At this point, I was inspired: "Why can't we supply a van, charge the students all the same, but make a special grant in the amount of transportation costs to the nonsponsored students?"

The idea became a motion, which passed, and the meeting adjourned. I was the proud author of the special assistance legislation, but I was uncomfortable about the aggressive tactics used to bring it off. Had it been necessary to foment guilt over our failure to develop an adequate course program on campus? Did I have to point out that the students were paying for administrative inadequacy? Perhaps. It had seemed the central issue. And it had been effective and efficient, hadn't it?

From my Filipino colleagues, I always perceived a gentler, more tangential approach. There never was a "frontal attack" like I had made.

Weeks passed. I was enjoying a rare quiet evening at home, with no committee to attend, hot mint tea in my cup, and my favorite music on the turntable; nothing was going to interrupt this.

"In the background John Denver was reminding me it was good to be home.

The plastic disk whirled, and I unwound. Sweet memories! My heart was back in Walla Walla. My mare nickered from her paddock. The mint crowding between the bricks of our front walkway smelled so sweetly when crushed underfoot, filling my nostrils. Never mind that the hint of mint now came from my teacup. Another lovely odor wafted in from the kitchen, and I hesitated somewhere between the mare's beckoning and a steaming slice of Karen's rich, dark bread in the present. Then the rest of the song kept me remembering things about home and roads and trucks grinding.

"Dale, Dale! Are you there?"

"Uh, yes. What?"

"Wasn't the graduate school going to cover travel expenses for the unsponsored students?"

"Yes," I said, brought back to current reality.

"Well, they aren't."

"They what?!"

"We shouldn't have told him, Lynn," Karen said quietly.

Lynn was one of the self-supporting students. She and Karen had been in the kitchen, chatting, waiting for the bread to finish baking. Now Lynn stood in the dining room, the informal boundary between the sala and the kitchen.

"That's right," Lynn explained. "Damocles says Mr. Buzon says they have no money."

"Well, how are you getting to Manila? The classes have started, haven't they?"

"We rented Polmaro's jeepney. It holds all but three of us and is much cheaper than the van the college offered us."

"How did the students accept that?"

"Oh, they just smiled and paid. Only two of us really made any fuss, but then, we aren't Filipino. Of course, we are the ones who could better afford to pay. That's the embarrassing thing."

"But then, we aren't Filipino" was rich in meaning. It said culture shapes behavior, and it said much more. It spoke of a hot, humid climate where ambitions ebb with perspiration, a climate where mild exertion can melt one down. It was a statement that spoke of hundreds of years of foreign domination and of the somewhat benevolent dictatorship that was nonconducive to self-expression.

"Well, Lynn, the next Grad Council is just a couple of days off. Let me see what can be done there."

Graduate Council provided another uninspiring agenda. The only item that gave promise read TRANSPORTATION PROBLEM. Then the trouble began.

"Well, we can't be blamed. Dr. Edwards left without making arrangements."

"Well, it was Dr. Salamonte who was supposed to make arrangements for this class. Shouldn't that have included transportation?"

"We made arrangements in last month's Graduate Council. Why are we talking about arrangements now?"

"Oh, yes! We voted to provide a van and subsidize nonsponsored students, but that won't work. Mr. Buzon says there is no money for that."

"No money! No money where?"

"No money for graduate student transportation."

"Of course there is money. How is it that Mr. Buzon gets to decide how the graduate school spends its money? He is an accountant. He tells us what the balances are and where the money has been spent. Does he also make value judgments about the Graduate Council's value judgments, about how its funds are spent?"

"But we cannot be blamed for the lack of transportation."

"Dr. Edwards is not here, and he is in charge of the Public Health Program."

"Well, didn't we fly Dr. Salamonte all the way from the States to coordinate the program? Specifically, this course in Manila? That should have included transportation."

"But he has returned to California already."

"We cannot be blamed that arrangements were not made. The students will just have to pay. It is not our fault."

"Wait! Wait! Let's stop talking about blame and fault and talk about responsibility." I pressed hard and demanded no compromising answers. Evasiveness challenged a sense of principle. Submissiveness gave way, as it must, to aggression, but I had not learned the lesson.

Once again we were united. Principle was involved, and this august body was foursquare behind principle. Dr. Damocles would go to Mr. Buzon and liberate the funds. The special assistance legislation had been resurrected; all was well with the world.

Graduate Council was dismissed in time for the faculty meeting, which ran through the lunch hour. The Academic Standards Committee had a time conflict with the Biology Club Executive Committee. I discovered that I could be more productive with several meetings scheduled for the same time. That left an entire evening free.

I would devote this evening to *Equus*, the slick journal on horses and horsemanship. I dusted the rocker and settled in, spotting an interesting article title, "Conformation: Athletic and Aesthetic."[154] It began with a discussion of airplanes:

> It is a little-known bit of historical trivia that when Wilbur and Orville Wright sketched out their preliminary designs for the first working flying machine, the device was represented as a magnificent piece of art work, something like a rococo summerhouse, but even more along the lines of the Taj Mahal.
>
> "Well," said Wilbur, while reviewing it, "it looks nice, but it'll never fly."
>
> "Whaddaya mean?" demanded Orville, who had put in the fine baroque curlicues.
>
> "See, what we need," explained Wilbur, grabbing a bit of chalk and a brown paper bag, "is something more like this" and he roughed out what later became the prototype launched at Kitty Hawk.
>
> "Well, I think it's the silliest looking dam' thing I've ever seen," replied Orville, "but it's too cold in here to stand around arguing, so let's get started."

And you know the rest of the story. Actually, that bit of historical trivia is so little known that the article's author might be the only one who knew it, but it served to make his ultimate point: beauty is not only what is pleasing; beauty is what works. And that was the lead-in to this article about horses!

"Don't tell him now"—quiet whispering from the kitchen.

"Uh! Don't tell me what?"

"These cookies are really good!"

"What? Come on, Lynn. What aren't you going to tell me?"

"Okay, so, we took public to the San again, twice."

---

[154] Hamilton, Samantha, "Conformation: Athletic and Aesthetic." *Equus*, no. 30 (April 1980), 22-28, 78-79.

"You what? That was all settled. The entire Graduate Council agreed. The student representative to the Grad Council must have told you that. Dr. Damocles said he would simply tell Mr. Buzon that we have the money."

"Oh, that's not the problem."

"Well, what is the problem?" I asked, incredulous.

"Marcello has been sick."

"What does that have to do with anything?"

"Marcello drives the van."

"But don't we have someone else who can drive the van?"

"I'm sorry, Dale. Why don't you just give it up? All the students have."

It was true, and that was as disturbing as the lack of transportation. This passivity was anathema to my Western mind. We were permitting the indignities I perceived in the faculty and the administration to be dumped on the students.

The problems involving transportation were part of the pattern. This pattern was apparent in the studied slowness with which a thesis advisor could read and return drafts. It was seen in the servitude extracted by some from domestic help. One of my students had missed the first week and a half of lectures in Zoology to help the faculty member with whom she lived move into a new house. The power of position and authority created a virtual class system, as it does most everywhere, I've learned. It simply plays out in different ways.

The faculty and administrators had themselves known similar treatment short years earlier; a person who has been dominated pays back in kind when they achieve a more dominant position. This seems a trait common to all peoples, though not every person.

Why does education not effect a change? I saw reason and logic (powers of philosophy) denounce and deride the system; and I saw culture (powers of the society) win out. Were the judgments from my value system as sound as they seemed to me? How could I know? Both systems have been around a long time. They both seem to work. Maybe *Equus* was right. Maybe I was and still am hung up on aesthetics. But maybe not. Perspective is difficult to maintain when reference points move.

◆ ◆ ◆

Postscript:

One night weeks later, Lynn was at our house again. She had sent me the "last final copy" of the Constitution of the Graduate Student Association some days earlier for another reading before the final typing. We worked on it a long time and looked at it again tonight, and there was nothing to add.

She turned toward the door, then hesitated and said, "Do you have the minutes of the August Grad Council?"

I did not. I suspected they were not yet typed.

"I thought they were out," she continued. "Somebody told me that the minutes acknowledged they would reimburse us for travel expenses. The president told me, 'No. It says subsidize, and they will only go 50 percent.'"

The president's comments were interesting. He had not yet read the minutes and was not in the meeting where they were generated. He had been on a trip to the States. I predicted that the minutes would read "subsidize" when I finally received them.

"What was the word used in the meeting? Was it 'reimburse' or was it 'subsidize'?" Lynn pressed. She had committed herself.

"I can't reach back that far and be sure of the exact wording, Lynn. It's been over a month. But I do remember the intent of the motion. I made it. The intent was to cover the expenses, and I suspect that was the wording; and I am sure all the members understood that as I had made a very pointed speech before stating the motion."

"I have to get to those minutes, you know," Lynn explained. "I only have a few weeks before I'm finished here. The money is not so important, but this thing has become a principle with me."

Lynn had not forgotten. She is an all-American woman, and somehow the cerebral nature of the advice she had given to me ("Just give it up!") had not sat well with her world.

———CHAPTER 27———

Easter Celebrations
People Look for Answers

Karen

"Fear of the unknown, of illness, of the future, and of mysterious forces leads people to look for answers, and they find them in their belief systems."

—*I. V. Mallari*[155]

The RP is a majority Christian nation with 4 percent of the world's Christians; about 80 percent are Roman Catholic.[156] Many Christian Filipinos celebrate the Easter holidays with festivals, parades, and community and family gatherings. One of the biggest Christian celebration events we witnessed involved flagellants. They combine their animistic belief, with its focus on and fear of good and evil spirits, with Spanish Roman Catholicism, with its emphasis on rules and confession and penances and worship of the Virgin Mary and the Christ Child, *Santo Niño*, who became the Suffering Servant.[157]

---

[155] I. V. Mallari, *Vanishing Dawn*. (Manila: Philippine Education Company, 1954, Pp. 81-82)

[156] Eoghan Hughes, "The 10 Most Christian Countries" https://www.therichest.com/the-biggest-/the-10-most-christian-countries (Accessed February 19, 2024)

[157] Flagellants, originally from *flagellare*, to whip. Background information about when and where this behavior is practiced is found here: https://www.catholic.com/encyclopedia/flagellants (Accessed February 19, 2024); McKensie Perkins, "What is Animism" Updated on April 15, 2019. www.learnreligions.com/what-is-animism-4588366 (Accessed February 19, 2024).

An emphasis on the Santo Niño developed in the 1500s when the Spanish arrived with a message reflecting the focus on the family, especially the mothers, already emphasized in Filipino culture. I remember a delightful Christmas Eve service in a tiny Catholic church on Tagaytay Ridge. The soft-spoken, corpulent Irish priest tenderly held the small, plaster Santo Niño for each worshipper to kiss—wiping the baby's head with a soft cloth between each kiss. The representative doll was then placed in a manger at the front of the sanctuary.

Many people are drawn to dramatic observances, especially during Easter weekend. In festivals for honoring saints throughout the year, the men usually lead in public activities, sometimes carrying a replica of a saint through the streets.

One Easter weekend, Dale and I accompanied friends John and Pat Jones to the town of Navotas, a few miles north of Manila on the northeastern shore of Manila Bay.[158] We wanted to worship, observe, and try to understand. John, a New Testament scholar in the seminary, and Pat, a nursing professor at PUC, had lived in the Far East many years and had studied the many different ways folk worshipped.

Walking into the town, we heard Scripture being broadcast on overhead speakers for the whole community to hear. We found the small chapel where women were taking turns reading the portions describing the events of Passion Week.

With those words creating a sacred atmosphere, we became part of a crowd entranced by colorfully costumed amateur actors parading through town in a religious pantomime (*Senákulo*) of the events of Easter. Those dressed as Roman soldiers were dragging an actor portraying Christ, who supported a cross resting against his shoulder. The fierce-looking "soldiers" stopped many times to pantomime beating Christ. Actors playing the disciples and the three Marys followed, weeping. Hundreds of people lined the narrow streets, jeering or cheering.

---

[158] A fishing port, unloading about 800 tons of fish annually.

The culmination of this walking Passion Play involved Christ being tied to a cross in a mock crucifixion. It was very touching. We learned that the crucifixion is even more dramatic in a few other towns; some men and women are actually nailed to crosses. A few have done that for several years in a row. I was not interested in witnessing those activities; we did appreciate seeing the activities in Navotas.

The voices reading Scripture followed us as we strolled to a field where perhaps forty tight-bodied, bare-chested young men stood side by side, swinging flails over first one shoulder, then the other. The flails were made of intertwined cords with a bamboo rod at the end of each cord. They swung the flails back and forth over their shoulders, hitting their backs until the skin became bright red as the blood rose just under the surface from the force. John told us that the number of rods, each about six inches long, reflected how many years each man had promised to participate in this ritual. Many would be back next year, and the next. We closely examined one of the flails, which contained sixteen of these reeds, indicating that the wielder had promised to perform this ritual each Easter for sixteen years.

In the field beyond the men were two large rectangular containment ponds for raising fish. Soon the men formed a line and marched single file around the edge of the ponds. Their reflections in the water were dramatic and sobering. They had covered their faces with a square of white gauze or other lightweight material, worn to ensure anonymity and reflect the image of humility. For most of them, the cloth was held in place by a crown of woven branches of sampaguita, the tiny white national flower, to simulate Christ's crown of thorns.

Their path led them to the edge of town, and each man in turn turned his back toward an older man holding a short wooden mallet embedded with small pieces of broken glass. *Oh my goodness*, I thought. It was obvious what was coming. The elderly gentleman sort of "popped" the glass against each flagellate's flushed back in several places, immediately releasing trickles of blood.

I was stunned, and my fists clenched. John had told us some

of what to expect, but seeing it happen just a few feet away was disconcerting. One by one the young men started back toward the town. Women of all ages, children, and older men lined the path; many observers urged the flagellants on as the men continued swinging the flails from side to side over their shoulders, first one, then the other, the flails further opening the tiny wounds on their backs, increasing the blood flow. Their upper arms also became bruised and bloodied.

Most of the flagellants were accompanied by another young man carrying a wooden paddle and a glass soda bottle. About every twenty steps, each bare-chested flagellant fell to the ground, face first, with his arms stretched out to his sides. *Ah*, I realized as I watched one particular young man, *now his body forms the shape of a cross*. His companion then beat him on his well-padded bottom—not his bare back—with a wooden paddle.[159] Between those "beatings," the companion spat or threw the liquid from the pop bottles. John quietly shared with us that it's usually a mixture of water and vinegar.

"It looks so terrible," I whispered back.

"It's meant to look terrible, and to hurt—part of the offering he is giving to God."

The blood continued to flow, and Dale pointed at the front of my skirt. I looked down. Droplets of blood had spattered my clothes. I had not expected that. Again, I felt dazed.

The men seemed very calm, and I murmured to Dale: "Perhaps that initial flailing before the cutting did hurt and then somewhat numbed their backs and upper arms. Maybe this doesn't hurt as much as I'm imagining."

The beatings we saw were not violent and not on bare flesh. The vinegar/water likely did sting—and cleanse. I believed there really was pain, but perhaps not as severe as it had seemed. The "beatings" became more frequent, and as we walked alongside, we saw that the

---

[159] Most of the young men we saw seemed to wear at least two pairs of jeans; in other locations, bundled reeds are used for the beatings.

procession was approaching a small church. At the door to the church, we were invited inside. The flagellants entered in single file, lay on the ground in that cross-shaped position, and received a blessing from the priest. Then they got up, one at a time, and walked out the back door, going a short distance behind the church to the waters of the bay, where they immersed themselves. *Salt water*, I thought. *Ouch!*

Pat, John, Dale, and I walked outside, away from the chapel, and quietly discussed what we had seen.

"It's very smart, really. The salt water will begin the healing process," Dale said.

John shared: "It also increases the likelihood of scarring. Proof of what they had endured. The scars will be important reminders to them and to their family that they have made this penance. Either they have promised God they would do this so they or someone they love can receive healing, or they are thanking God for an already answered prayer."[160]

We returned home sobered by the devotion shown by those young men, by what they had experienced. We talked about Christian and animist understandings of blessings and curses. In our experience the men were called flagalantees rather than flagellants.

On that trip to and from Navotas, we saw people walking along the road, mostly men but occasionally a woman, dragging large, heavy crosses, accompanied by groups of people. One arm of the cross was carried on the shoulder and the rest dragged behind in a slow and deliberate act of worship and contrition.

♦ ♦ ♦

In the heart of Manila is Quiapo Church, one of our favorite religious sites. Women were always selling healing herbs, twigs and oils,

---

[160] Karen J. Clayton. "Ritual Practices Surrounding the Celebration of Easter in the Philippines." Presented at the SW Commission on Religious Studies, Dallas, Texas, March 16, 1991.

amulets, religious candles and calendars, lottery tickets, novena booklets, or cards in the church plaza. As we entered, we saw on the wall of one chapel a Black Christ on a cross—the Black Nazarene; in another niche was a life-sized wooden sculpture of Christ kneeling on a platform and burdened by a huge wooden cross.[161] Each year, on January 9, "the image [is] borne forth in a ... procession to lead a massed throng of barefooted devotees down the back streets of the district. Men take turns pulling the carriage of the Black Christ, or struggle passionately to clamber over the rest for a chance to kiss its foot or lay a fervent hand on the hem of its robe."[162]

Walking inside the huge main sanctuary, our eyes adapting to the darkness, most of the people we saw seated or making their way on bare knees to the front were women. At the back of the sanctuary, men and women of all ages stood patiently in a line winding to and around a large glass coffin containing a replica of a tan-skinned Christ. As the people reached the coffin, most touched the toes or hands or hair of the Christ through openings in the glass on the sides and at the ends. Some touched the Christ with their hands or with the afflicted spot on their bodies. Many used a cloth hankie to touch the Christ, then pressed it against a part of their body or against a child accompanying them. The treasured cloth could then be folded and kept in a safe place as a reminder of their act and for further blessing and healing.

There are also customs about praying to have a child.[163] One of our students, Guia, told us she had been married five years and had not become pregnant: "This is a long time for a Filipino couple," she said. "I decided to take part in a novena."

---

[161] Small objects worn around the neck to ward against disease, bad luck, and other evil forces. http://www.marypages.com/novena-prayers.en.html and Acts 1:14. (Accessed February 19, 2024); Catholic News Agency staff. "What is the 'Black Nazarene'? Here's the fascinating history of this centuries-old tradition." https://www.catholicnewagency.com/news/250027/history-black-nazarene-philippines (Accessed February 19, 2024).
[162] Alfred Yuson in *Insight Guides*. (APA Productions, 1980, p. 138).
[163] Mallari, I. V. Vanishing Dawn: Essays on the Vanishing Customs of the Christian Filipinos. Manila: Philippine Education Co., 1954.

Usually, novenas are said for nine consecutive days; for eight weeks, Guia wrote her request on a piece of paper and put it in a basket in the Catholic church she attended. Each Wednesday, the priest announced the number of prayer requests he'd received for healing, for babies, for wayward children.[164] Then he led the congregation in prayer for these special requests.

"Now I am pregnant."

Guia believes the pregnancy occurred because of the novenas. There are customs about praying for a specific child—girls are valued, and still it is hoped that there will be at least one boy to carry on the family name and traditions.

◆ ◆ ◆

Philippine history includes the influence of Peking and Java man, Negritos, Indonesians who may have come via land bridges, Malay seafarers, Arab and Chinese traders as early as the thirteenth century, Spanish explorers (who later became Spanish occupiers), then Americans and Japanese. Each group brought its belief system—animism, Islam, Christianity, Buddhism, Shintoism, Judaism, and more—with its own view of the world and its perspective of ultimate things. Belief systems, religions, and other philosophies provide answers to the fundamental questions about life: Where did I come from? Why am I here? What am I to do? Where do evil and disease come from, and how do I manage?[165]

When a new belief system enters society, it is added to what has come before. Belief is never completely pure. It is learned and layered.

---

[164] The word "novena" means "nine" and special prayers to Jesus, Mary, the Trinity, angels, or specific saints are printed on small cards or booklets. Later, my Filipina American hospice patients or family members showed me novena booklets they had obtained on trips back home to the Philippines.

[165] Roman Catholic Christianity makes up 80.6 percent, Protestant Christianity makes up 8.2 percent, Islam 5.6 percent; the remaining 1.9 percent includes Hinduism, Judaism, the Baha'i Faith, Indigenous beliefs, other Christians and atheists. Religious Beliefs in the Philippines - WorldAtlas, https://www.worldatlas.com/articles/religious-beliefs-in-the-Philippines.html.

Mrs. Hernandez, our neighbor on the Silang campus, had become a Christian midlife. Her children were educated in Christian schools; one son became a Christian theologian and seminary professor. She was elderly when we met her, living with her son and his family. Whenever she washed clothes, dishes, or herself, she carried any used or extra water out to her lush green backyard and threw it on her flowers, fruits, vegetables, or the grass. But first she warned the spirits she would be tossing the water. She had done that as a child, believing she could keep the spirits in her yard from growing angry with her and possibly causing illness or bad luck. Her background had been influenced by animist beliefs in good and evil spirits (anitos), which can do favors or inflict harm. Mostly now it was a habit—it felt right to do it; her animist belief in good and evil spirits remained even within her Christian belief and experience.

In her book *Mai Pen Rai Means Never Mind*, author and teacher Carol Hollinger provides an important caution: "Despite the warnings of anthropologists, I am sure that most Americans, myself included, think that the slate Moses toted down from Mount Sinai really contained God's instructions as to the final, acceptable morality of *all* human beings. We are convinced that our idea of good is *the* Good and our idea of bad is *the* Bad."[166]

It has been helpful for me to attempt to see the positive ways humans respond to their understanding of ultimate reality. Many of the world's belief systems express the "Golden Rule" about our interactions with other human beings. Gautama Buddha stated it this way in the sixth century BC: "Don't do to others what you would not want done to yourself." Examining and understanding our paradigm is vital and determines our ability to know, value, and interact fairly and positively with others. All of that—the knowledge and the comparison and the trying to understand—enriches us and makes us more likely to learn from and communicate with others.

---

[166] Carol Hollinger, *Mai Pen Rai Means Never Mind*. Asia Books, John Weatherill, Inc., Tokyo. 1965.

My understanding of belief and finding answers is helped immensely by Friedrich Nietzsche: "One can stand any *how* of living if they have a *why*." Each person develops their own beliefs from their families, their culture, and their lived experiences.

Update 2020s

—Dramatic Easter celebrations continue. A *Rappler* online news article included a statement that the "Catholic Church frowns on self-harm or mortification as acts of atonement, but they continue."[167]

—The Far Eastern Division Seminary is now the Adventist International Institute of Advanced Studies, including a graduate school (business, education, public health, theology) and theological seminary. Its fiftieth founding anniversary was May 2–7, 2023.

—Spiritual behavior while grieving the death of a loved one: Knowing some Filipino customs surrounding death was helpful when I cared for patients and caregivers as a hospice social worker. The patriarch of a Filipino family was dying. I phoned to ask to visit the home; when I arrived, he had just passed. They were gracious and invited me in. I knew of their custom of gathering family and friends, sharing food, and not sweeping during the final days and hours to keep from disturbing any spirits. Also they felt a need for the body to stay in the home for a few days. I described the customs to our hospice director, who also respected their wishes regarding these important death-related customs. The deceased patient remained in the home as long as was allowed. The story is in my hospice book and is titled "We want his body here with us."

—The Catholic Church is building chapels in shopping malls.

---

[167] Joann Manabat. https://www.rappler.com/nation/luzon/pampanga-folk-cling-spectacles-church-disapproval-holy-week *Rappler* April 8, 2023 (Accessed February 19, 2024).

Father Reginald "Regie" Malicdem "serves as the mission station priest of Landmark Chapel" in the Landmark department store in Manila's posh Makati business district.[168]

---

[168] Paterno Esmaquel II, "Rappler Talk: Father Regie Malicdem on the mission of mall churches." *Rappler*, February 17, 2024.

———CHAPTER 28———

Independence Days and Masks
July 4 and June 12

Karen

> *"As iron sharpens iron, so one person sharpens another."*
> *—Proverbs 27:17*

Records of human bones indicate that people have inhabited the Philippine Islands for 30,000 to 40,000 years. Tribal groups were frequently challenged by invaders from Holland, Indonesia, Brunei, Malaysia, China, and Spain. Some say Filipinos wear a "mask"—smiling, gracious, welcoming, accommodating. The mask has provided protection while they stayed true to themselves through many kinds of serfdom. This is a common theme in poetry.[169]

American admiral George Dewey led the destruction of the Spanish fleet in Manila Bay in May 1898 and freed the Philippines after 327 years of Spanish rule. On June 12, 1898, General Emilio Aguinaldo, backed by his revolutionary forces, declared Philippine independence from Spanish colonization. The Philippine flag was flown and the national anthem played that day for the first time.

The US did not recognize the June 12 declaration of independence; decision-makers believed the Filipino people were unprepared to govern themselves. A Commonwealth of the Philippines was formed

---

[169] "We Wear the Mask" by Paul Laurence Dunbar; "Please Hear What I'm Not Saying" by Charles C. Finn; and "The Mask" by Maya Angelou, to name a few.

in 1934, but the Americans remained.

On July 4, 1946, the Republic of the Philippines was created, and the people of the Philippines were finally under self-rule. So, July 4 marked their independence from American rule and protection; however, their first declaration of independence on June 12, 1898, is more important to them. Their choice!

We expatriates on the Silang campus did not understand these historical facts. We should have. Meanwhile, the forty of us, mostly Americans, gathered each July 4 on our campus in the Philippines to celebrate US independence from Great Britain.

Cultural groups benefit from taking time apart to share their history and eat special food. The overseas workers did so about once a month.

Americans often treat the concept of a "melting pot" with the expectation that everyone will join together to become similar so they can have national cohesiveness and to ensure patriotism. In an Adventist Forum presentation titled "Melting Pot, Tossed Salad and Stew," I encouraged folk to remember the blessings of each heritage, mixed like a tossed salad, with each group retaining their particular characteristics and combining with other groups to create a delicious and beautiful whole.

Ray Holmes, who had American Finnish heritage, wrote about his impressions of the expatriate group on the Silang campus:

> The individuals in the group were very different from each other.... Some were naturally tender toward others, while some were more abrasive. Some were more colonial in their approach to the indigenous population than were others. One has to learn to live with such differences in personality and education.... The same people living and working in the US would probably have established far different friendships than those which emerged in our little community.... What we had was not an exclusive buffet of exotic dishes, but a very tasty

stew well-seasoned with gourmet thyme and a bit of Bohemian pepper. After two years of living and working together it was a well-cooked batch that had grown comfortable in the same pot. Like every stew, the flavors improved every time it was heated up. . . . It was one of the most enriching experiences of my life.[170]

Update 2020s

—**June 12, 2023,** was the 125th commemoration of the Philippine Declaration of Independence.

---

[170] C. Raymond Holmes, *Boiled Rice and Gluten: Vignettes on life as Missionary*. Self-published 1972.

CHAPTER 29

Mom and Dad Clayton and Other Visitors

Karen

"To travel is to take a journey into yourself."
—Danny Kaye

Dale's seventy-year-old father, who was visiting us on the Silang campus in 1979, was nowhere to be found. He had been gone several hours, and we were thinking of driving to look for him off campus when we spotted him trudging up the ridge road to our home.

"Martin, where have you been?" Dale's mom demanded. She had been worried and frustrated.

"I took the jeepney. I went to that city where they make the tablecloths and candy and sausage."

He'd been to his favorite place (and mine), Taal City, at least an hour's drive away by jeepney—in addition to the walk to and from the campus gate. We'd imagined all kinds of things happening to him, but here he was, happy and safe; he'd adventured and gotten back just fine and made friends along the way.

Taal City is a wonder. We loved taking visitors there partly because that meant we could visit again. The town had moved multiple times due to volcanic activity, and artifacts in the region date back to thirteenth-century Chinese invasions and reflect expeditions by the Malay. Taal City is known for delicately embroidered tablecloths and clothing, a delicious peanut-and-brown-sugar delicacy called panocha, *tapa* (a cured pork product), and—most interesting to Dad Clayton—"butterfly knives," known to us as batangas daggers.[171] Another term, *balisong* (*aling sungay*, meaning "broken horn"), is also the term for the place where they are sold. Carrying them is forbidden in some areas (e.g., Manila) because they can be made very small and disguised as a pen. A permit may be available. He bought several.

Mom Clayton enjoyed experimenting with new food, and I was thrilled to go to work and not have to think about supper, then come home to a meal she and Kimberly had fun preparing together. She also loved the crafts in the market, though she didn't purchase many. She was good at making her own—quilting, crocheting, making dolls for grandkids. She did get frustrated with Dale's dad accumulating fascinating artifacts, like the carabao horns he fell in love with on our way home from Baguio. The horns were covered with intricate carvings of village scenes: carabao, flowers, palm trees. A piece of carved wood connected the horns and filled the space between the horns. It measured five feet tip to tip, and he planned to take it back to Michigan!

Mom Clayton's response was an exasperated "Martin! Where in the world are you going to put that thing? How are you going to get it home?"

It almost fit in the trunk of the Blue Bomb. In an aside, Dad Clayton quietly said to Dale, "Could you just put that in your garage when we get to your place? Bring it home in your shipment." And we did. It now sits atop our library shelves.

Dale's dad, who loved fresh vegetables from his own garden. While in the Philippines, he planted cabbages for us; when they sprouted, he transplanted the little ones. We found lots of uses for cabbages. Dale's mom used to make sauerkraut to manage their huge annual cabbage harvest in Michigan.

---

[171] D. J. Rivera. "Batangas: Balisong: Few Things About This Famous Knife from Taal," https://www.pinoytravelogue.com/2017/08/balisong-taal-batangas-famous-knife.html (Accessed February 15, 2024).

Mom and Dad Clayton loved being with us and exploring the Philippines. When they left, they also visited Taiwan, but Dale's dad could not see the point of going to Hong Kong, yet another Asian country. He needed to get home. He was worried about the roof leaking with all the snow sitting on it in the winter months in Michigan. Never mind that his other son, who lived six miles from them, was keeping an eye on things. No, when he decided it was time to go home, it was time.

♦ ♦ ♦

We had many other visitors. Eugene Winter, a physical education professor from WWC, loved collecting rocks and shells. Ernest Booth, the grand old man of biology at WWC, especially loved and wrote books about birds. They vacationed at different times in the Philippines and stayed with us. We had a special treat for them: For each, we drove him to Tagaytay Ridge and took him down to the edge of Taal Lake, then rented a banca out to the little island to walk on the rough lava rock surrounding the active volcano—avoiding the steam venting through many openings. They both also enjoyed the beaches and PUC's wildlife-filled ravine.

Rosemary, Andy, Jamie, and Michelle Dressler, also friends from Walla Walla, were treated to the Tagaytay Ridge/Taal Lake trip. And they invited us to US Naval Base Subic Bay to visit Andy's parents; Papa Dressler was a civilian employee of the US military. Our kids still remember breakfast at their house there, where they were served a myriad of fabulous Philippine fruits and American cereals purchased from the post exchange (PX). What a treat! It had been a long time since they enjoyed Cheerios!

"This must be what heaven is like!" Kimberly said.

In addition to our personal friends, many visitors came to the Silang campus, as they had previously at Baesa. The campus hostess would make plans with various families to provide meals and places for the guests to stay. Sometimes the folks were "itinerating"—on assignment to provide guidance or evaluate the schools for academic accreditation. Some were on holiday. We often knew ahead of time when visitors were coming; sometimes we did not. Our cupboards always had the essentials for feeding guests.

The Americans who visited usually wanted "American food." My favorite meals to serve them were 1) potato salad, veggie sticks, and baked beans with molasses, or 2) lentil stew and cornbread. We almost always enjoyed these guests. However, it was tiring to constantly be ready.

Malcolm Maxwell, professor of religion from WWC and Dale's former academic dean, came as a special weekend speaker for our seminary students. We asked to have him stay with us, and it was a delight. I'd taken classes from him, Dale had sat in many meetings with him, and the children knew him from occasionally seeing him as a featured speaker and now knew him personally.

Young military men on leave from US Naval Base Subic Bay or Clark Air Base sometimes came for a weekend, wanting to partake of the Sabbath activities. One young man came several times and then invited us to Subic for an authentic American Thanksgiving feast: turkey, mashed potatoes and gravy, dressing, and pumpkin pie! He provided an even bigger treat and took us on a personal tour of the USS *Enterprise*, the first nuclear-powered aircraft carrier. We were awed that 5,000 people could live on that ship. That was about the population of College Place in Washington! The overall length was 1,123 feet, the width 253. The area of the flight deck was 4.47 acres. We took a picture of Kimberly sitting on one link of the anchor on the upper inside deck—each link weighed 360 pounds. Jeff especially loved that visit!

On both campuses, we entertained an interesting young friend, Dale Clark, who had been in the US military. After his discharge at Clark AFB, he stayed in the Philippines, taking freelance jobs in photography. He gave us meaningful insights about our temporary home, and it was fun for him to relax with Americans now and then.

"Kay, can you make me a really big, beautiful hamburger?"

"I sure can. But I thought you were a vegetarian."

"Yeah, well, I mean a 'shamburger.' The Food Factory has hired me to do some promotional photography. I want to start with a hamburger—I mean, 'shamburger'—made out of their veggie burger."

"Sure, I'd love to help, and the family would enjoy the burgers!" I mixed diced onion and celery, oatmeal, beaten egg, breadcrumbs, and ketchup, formed it into a hamburger lookalike, and "dressed" the bun with mayonnaise, lettuce, tomatoes, and onions. Then he misted the lettuce at the edges so it all looked fresh. I thought we were ready to photograph and eat it! But it was not quite right to Dale.

I asked, "What more do we need to do?"

"Well, it needs to look not just fresh but hot!"

"Well, it's not hot anymore."

"But we have to make it *look* hot. Don't tell your kids what I'm going to do." And he pulled out a pack of cigarettes, lit one up, puffed from behind the sandwich, and ran to the camera to get the "hot" shot!

"I'm not eating that burger, sham or otherwise," I told my friend. It was fascinating to learn photography tricks behind the scenes. When he was satisfied with the photo, we threw out that "sham" (and the cigarette) and finished putting the rest of the burgers together for lunch.

Friends had not warned me about another American regular, known as China Smith. The kids and I saw him coming down the dirt road and were not sure we wanted to answer the door. He was a tall drink of water, as similar folks are described in the movies. I greeted him at the door. He was soft spoken, friendly, and that first time he just asked for some cool water. We were a little overcome by his look; he wore clean but very old clothes, and his exposed arms were completely covered with tattoos. He described ports of call where he'd had too much to drink and had added to the canvas of his body. Later he told us the tattoos also covered his chest and back.

Hours later, when Dale came home, the kids were sitting at our visitor's feet, listening to his stories, and I said, "Honey, we have a visitor for supper. Meet China Smith. He's been in the Merchant Marines and lives a few hours from here with his Filipina wife. He says she usually stays home and works as a literature evangelist when he visits the campus and his American friends."

Following the appropriate exchange of niceties, I said, "Can you help me with something in the kitchen?" That statement, along with the raised eyebrows and head tilting toward the kitchen, was meant to convey nothing special to visitors but is well understood by spouses.

Once we were alone, I explained, "Dale, he's been here for hours. I'm trying to find out enough about him to see if we want him anywhere near us or our kids."

We examined the official-looking business card he gave us:

W.W.II————————————Indo-China
Donald A. Wagner
"China Smith" C.S.N.G. – U.S.A.A.F
U.S.M.M. SOLDIER OF FORTUNE – Ret.

We gave in, wanting to be kind. He stayed that night and then another. Over the next few months, China Smith stayed with us many times, usually for two or three long days. His stories went on and on and were often worth listening to. He craved American companionship; he was fascinating and frustrating and took up a lot of my time. We found a way to be courteous while not remaining occupied with him for too long. We would let him stay a couple of nights, then Dale would find a job that needed doing around our place, and he'd soon be gone, until the next time. His visits were less frequent once we moved to the new campus. We did get to meet his wife on one visit. She was a delight—and a very patient woman.

Sometimes there were visitors in the area whom we heard about but didn't get to meet. That was okay by us. Still, the one we almost missed caused us the most frustration.

I was in the lobby of the Manila Sanitarium and spotted some Americans being hosted by Filipinos. They were SDA officials from either the division in Singapore or the General Conference Headquarters in Silver Springs, Maryland. They wanted and needed to know how "the work was going" (e.g., whether the institutions were fading or growing) and were usually taken by Filipino SDA officials to various schools and offices, the Food Factory, and the Publishing House. These particular men were also supposed to connect with "overseas Americans." They made decisions that affected our pay, our holidays, our homes, our jobs.

I walked over to the Americans and introduced myself. The Filipinos were politely accommodating but had their own agenda and wanted to get on with it.

Addressing the officials, I said: "So pleased to know you are in the area. Will you be coming to the Silang campus?"

The officials looked at their Filipino hosts and said, "Will we be going there on this trip?"

"Oh, I'm so sorry. There is not time."

"Excuse me," I responded. "We've been hoping you would be coming soon. We have some things we'd like to discuss with you—things we *need* to discuss with you about our work."

"Sorry, I guess it's not possible this time."

"It is important," I continued, determined not to give up. "There are forty of *your* American employees and families on that campus. We can write you letters; we have done so. However, you are here, and we do have things we *need* to discuss with you *now*, on your trip here *this* time."

The Filipino hosts and the American officials conferred among themselves and agreed on a possible time the following evening.

"Ah, that is wonderful," I responded. "We are so pleased we can have some important time with you. And we will have a wonderful meal prepared for you and will see you tomorrow evening." I said: "Salamat po." And I thought of Harvard professor Laurel Thatcher Ulrich's comment: "Well-behaved women seldom make history." It became a favorite slogan of '70s women in the US.

We had a helpful meeting with them and, as importantly, made our point: "We know you are busy. We know the others create most of your itinerary. However, be sure to include us next time."

There were times I'd had enough of visitors. After I'd been asked regularly, often at the last minute, to help—feed, entertain, drive guests to Manila or somewhere else—I sometimes needed a break. I confess that more than once, when I wasn't expecting visitors and heard a car coming up that long, winding drive to the area of our Silang home, I would go back to my bedroom, not even answering the door if they rang. I wouldn't have done it if I knew there were no other Americans on campus; but I did do it—more than once. It's called self-preservation.

Update 2020s

—**The manufacture and use of the butterfly knife**, balisong, is shown on several YouTube channels.

―――― CHAPTER 30 ――――

Jeffrey and Kimberly

Karen

"Kids gain independence, confidence and creative problem-solving skills from experiencing places out of their comfort zone—thereby developing a sense of adventure sure to serve them well in life!"

—*The Koala Mom*[172]

We thought moving to the Philippines would be good for all of us—an adventure and a wonderful learning experience! Adults often want to do something bigger than themselves and their current world. When we first gathered as a family to discuss the possibility, it was hard for the kids to take in what this move would mean to them. What did they know of traveling by huge planes to multiple countries where people spoke languages they didn't even know about? That was 1978; we had *Encyclopedia Americana*, not the internet or Google Earth.

We said: "We will only go if everyone in the family wants to go."

They agreed to the challenge, and we helped them figure out what to take and what to leave with friends or give to the thrift store. Bikes and winter clothes were given away; they would need larger

---

[172] Bonnie Way. "How Traveling with Kids Fosters a sense of Wonder and Curiosity." https://thekoalamom.com/2023/07/traveling-with-kids-fosters-curiosity/ (Accessed February 19, 2024).

sizes of both when we returned in three or maybe six years anyway, and we wouldn't need boots, gloves, or mittens in the warmth and humidity of the Philippines.

The Playskool camper and ambulance and hospital were precious to Kimberly, but we thought she'd soon outgrow them, so she loaned them to younger cousins.[173] We also gave cousins Jeff's unique triple bunk bed with the center level for his trains, and Kimberly's dollhouse bookshelf went to a younger friend—Dale had built them both.[174] Then we focused on the excitement of the trip.

This chapter is really an overview of the experiences and consequences of moving to the Philippines when our children were adolescents, so I'm going to repeat some things here. The age kids travel with their parents on overseas assignments is crucial. We urge folks to only take very young children on this kind of move.

Getting to the Philippines was an adventure in itself. In Hawaii, we enjoyed the touristy Polynesian Cultural Center and the pineapple plantations, and it was a powerful experience to visit the National Memorial Cemetery of the Pacific. We tasted our first papaya there, played in the ocean, and saw our first mongoose when visiting Diamond Head. In Japan, we rode the 200 mph bullet train and stopped at Kamakura to see the Great Buddha and explore the fabulous Hasedera temple.

While walking to the temple, we stopped at a ballpark and watched Japanese men play American baseball. Jeff remembers purchasing his first Dr. Pepper there and seeing folks driving on the "wrong side" of the road. Frequently, Japanese folk wanted to practice their fine English. One young man asked me in perfect English, with a raised eyebrow and a smile, "Do you speak Japanese?" And this was the first place we saw large groups of students in school uniforms, each step now taking us further into Asian cultures.

---

[173] Later, it was fascinating to hear Kimberly, returning at age twelve and retrieving her Playskool camper from a friend: "Hm, I remember these being bigger than they are."
[174] Later, Kimberly and Dale would work together to create a dollhouse of another design for her and her children.

In Taipei we were intrigued by armed guards in tunnels, at the beaches, and guarding some important buildings; there was a focus on protecting citizens from the fear of imminent invasion by the Chinese. The National Palace Museum intrigued us all. The 100-horse panel painted on silk was stunning, as were the porcelain pieces, calligraphy, intricately carved ivory, bronzes, paintings, jades, and other artifacts.[175]

Jeff bought his first Eagles album in Taipei—pirated and very reasonable—and we purchased our twelve-record John Denver boxed set for $25. One evening, our hosts took us to Huaxi Street Night Market, also known as Snake Alley, historically a red-light district. Now men went there to watch a mongoose being dropped into a pen with a cobra. After much frantic activity, most times, the mongoose won. The snake was then tacked to a board and the blood drained and purchased by men who believed it was an aphrodisiac. I'm not sure how Dale explained *that* to Jeff. Bowls of soup with the meat of turtles and snakes and their organs were also available for purchase.

As soon as I realized what was happening on that side of the street, I took Kimberly to check out shops on the other side. We stopped at an apothecary. It was closed, but through the windows we marveled at the tiny glass-fronted drawers in huge floor-to-ceiling cabinets lining the walls. I described how those shops were important to the Taiwanese, as they believe many things could be prevented or healed with herbs, teas, insects, and more. Then we saw, taped on the window of that shop, photos of special healing available in a shop upstairs, including before and after shots of hemorrhoid treatment—all in living color! Again, I distracted my nine-year-old,

---

[175] Identified as one of the ten masterpieces of traditional Chinese painting, it was actually painted by Guiseppe Castiglione, an Italian missionary who became a court painter in 1723 during the Qing dynasty. https://archive.shine.cn/sunday/now-and-then/One-Hundred-Horses/shdaily.shtml (Accessed February 19, 2024); we learned that 20 percent of the 700,000 artifacts at the museum were transported from the Forbidden City with Chiang Kai Shek when he left the People's Republic of China and moved to Taiwan with the remnants of the Nationalist forces in 1948.

and we moved on to other fascinating things.

When we reached Manila, the kids enjoyed the minibus ride to the campus, the luscious new foods, and finding their own rooms in our home. That first evening, they met Julie and Jimmy Kneller, who were there just for the summer. I remember the four kids playing hide-and-seek, with various hiding places named Singapore, Bangkok, Hong Kong, etc. When it was time for the school year to start, the Knellers went back to their home in Singapore, and the American kids, Sandy and Scott, returned from their summer break. The four kids walked to the third house in the overseas-faculty section of campus and began school. Their teacher was eighty-year-old volunteer Molly Thorn. Kimberly has a warm spot for her—"She taught me to read!"—while Mrs. Thorn and Jeff didn't always see eye to eye.

Jeff was already quite enterprising at age twelve and got a job at the college bakery. Our helper, Becky, taught Jeff to shop at the local markets, and I always provided pesos for them to take the jeepney there and back. Sometimes Jeff shopped for our groceries by himself. The first time I saw him walking across the field between the market and our home while carrying net bags filled with fruits and vegetables, I said, "Jeff, oh my goodness. Let me help. I thought I gave you enough money to take the jeepney home."

He quietly explained that he'd given his jeepney money to the women begging outside the market, resulting in an embarrassing hug from his mom.

We all had a hard time with the glaring poverty experienced by many folks in the Philippines. Jeff was most bothered about the kids selling fried bananas or other fruit or wanting to wash our windshields when we stopped our car at busy intersections. Those kids were the main reason he didn't like going to Manila with us. Many adults and children lived near landfills, and their only income came from picking and selling what they found there. No school at all for those children.

Jeff explored our campus and the field where the cemetery was being developed. He was captivated by the activity there and the string of burials, which grew more and more frequent. He became friends with the men who dug the graves and the persons in charge of the funeral services. Some gravesites were already being used, and Jeff reported to us one day, "You know they have glass on the top of the coffins, and you can look right in and see the dead person."[176]

"Jeff, you went to a funeral there?"

"No, I just walked over when I saw a bunch of people walking with the coffin, and I walked with them. They didn't mind. They invited me to stay."

"That must have been amazing to see." I urged him to tell me more.

"They said I could go look in the coffin. One woman was wailing and hanging on to the coffin. I think it was her mother who died."

Filipinos love kids; Jeff was not noisy or bothersome, just curious, and they invited him to be part of that sacred rite of passage. He said he mostly stayed quietly at the edge of the groups, and they allowed him to observe the families as they gathered around and lowered the glass-topped caskets into the ground. The families seemed to translate his quiet fascination into respect for the deceased and accept him.

When we moved to the Silang campus, there were twelve kids in the eight-grade school, and it was all right for Kimberly but difficult for Jeff, who was six years older than the only other boy there. Jeff liked music and sports, and there were no organized sports and no band or other musical activities, no way to get music lessons unless you went to Manila. We wish we'd pursued that option.

Jeff spent much of his extra time helping in the motor pool—for fun, not for pay. He loved it: they allowed him to drive some of the big equipment used to move land and buildings. One was a D-18,

---

[176] Recently Jeff shared with me that he sometimes helped put the dirt back to cover the buried coffin.

which Jeff says was a "pretty good size dozer for a kid to be driving."

He was genuinely bored sometimes. He usually didn't want to go to town with us. He did like some of the malls and eating out. Neither Jeff nor Kimberly had been fond of pizza, but when they heard there was a Shakey's Pizza Parlor in Manila, they wanted to like it, and they did! It was fascinating to discover what helped us feel connected to home. We were extremely cautious about buying uncooked foods from vendors, but we sometimes ate the fried bananas, deciding they were safer because they'd been fried almost to a crisp. We made them at home, too—bananas with peanut butter or chocolate rolled inside a crispy wrapper and deep-fried.

Kimberly's best friends on the new campus were Carla Jones and her little sister, Janelle, a delightful sprite of a girl who looked forward to going to school soon. We had known their grandparents back in Walla Walla. Linda and Lisa Van Ornam—American twin sisters just Kimberly's age—were also playmates. One of the girls taught Kimberly to crochet, which became a lifelong joy for her. They had spent several years in Africa on a previous assignment and were good companions for her, thinking it normal to live outside America and create your own games. They'd learned many activities that didn't require American toys.

Our helper, Becky, taught the kids sungkâ, a game played on a carved wooden (usually mahogany) block about two feet long with seven small hollows (or pits) set in each of two rows with two larger hollows (or stores), one at each end.[177] There are ninety-eight game pieces, or counters, made of cowrie shells, pebbles, marbles, or beans, so kids can learn math and social skills. Filipinos play sungkâ tournaments and create fundraisers even when they live in other countries.

Many games were created using local materials—bamboo poles, coconut husks, circles drawn in the dirt. The kids played with the

---

[177] Similar to mancala, the national game of Africa. "Playing Sungka," https://mancala.fandom.com/wiki/Sungka (Accessed February 19, 2024).

woven bamboo *sipa* balls used to play a hacky-sack type of game. Filipino athletes also play sipa professionally. If the internet had existed then, we could have found more than forty traditional games that used native materials or instruments.[178] When you think about it, all cultures have simple games requiring only the players themselves. The Magna Kultura Foundation encourages teaching children to "play the traditional Filipino games, as it fosters appreciation of national culture and bring families closer together."[179]

Our first "out of country" holiday had been to Hong Kong: we rode the Star Ferry; visited Sha Tin, a Buddhist-style Lutheran monastery, study center, and porcelain-painting shop; took a bus, then walked a bit past well-tended duck ponds to see the actual border of mainland China; and followed the guidebook's suggestions for city walks. It was wonderful. Our second holiday was a "circle tour" of Thailand and Singapore. Jeff remembers "waterway taxis, incredible markets, brass castings, and hearing Foreigner for the first time." He also saw the film *Jesus Christ, Superstar*, Thai kickboxing, and "a very large, fat, very rich, encrusted-with-gold-leaf, lying-down Buddha."

Jeffrey and Kimberly say they remember being treated with respect, deference, and kindness everywhere they went.

The five sisters who had been born in Africa were used to the cloistered life on the campus compound, and they were not into American music or what was happening on the teen scene back in the States, instead spending much of their free time cooking, baking, and sewing at home. They excelled at music and handicrafts. They were quiet and reserved and excelled at music and handicrafts; they were somewhat shy around folks outside their family or in church activities, but adventure awaited. As soon as they reached ninth grade, they were off to boarding school in Singapore with other MKs for nine months of the year. There were only thirty students there,

---

[178] Wikipedia, "Traditional Games in the Philippines," https://en.wikipedia.org/wiki/Traditional_games_in_the_Philippines (Accessed February 19, 2024).
[179] Ibid.

and some already knew each other.

The eighty-year-old Mrs. Thorn became the assistant to Ms. Hemme, already in place on the new campus. Ms. H was an in-charge kind of woman. She meant well; she used her skills to the best of her ability based on having taught American kids in foreign lands for seventeen years. She didn't have children of her own.

We were pleased when we saw evidence of creative teaching. For example, when the time came to discuss the sixteenth president of the United States and our son was not prepared, Ms. H asked: "Jeff, I know you've read many of the books in our library. What have you learned about Abraham Lincoln that may not have been in our textbook?" Wise of her to give him an opportunity to show the value of his extracurricular reading and his exceptional memory.

The classroom was well ordered, and students were taught the subjects from an American perspective. When the teacher is so sure of herself, it is hard even for well-educated parents to know when and how to ask for creative additions to the curriculum. Many parents wanted our children to learn more about the Philippines' heroes and heroines and holidays and history and have more world geography and history in general. There were inexpensive Filipino books available to help with that.[180]

"Not enough time in the day or the curriculum to add one more thing" was Ms. H's immediate response to any suggestions. "And," she emphasized, "they need to be ready to continue in American schools and know North American history."

Jeff was unhappy in that classroom; we wanted to know how to help.

An international classroom with the children of the multiethnic seminary and university students operated nearby. Soon the kids from the two classrooms were having recesses together. The international students went on field trips and celebrated Philippine

---

[180] *Your Town and Mine* by Velasquez-Ty & Garcia and *Our Province* by Villamin and Juanson. See bibliography for details.

and other ethnic holidays. Ms. H finally saw the writing on the wall and began including some information about all the holidays, including learning more national and international history. Kimberly has pointed out that if the schools had done more together, there would have been enough kids to have teams and organized sports.

We parents were pleased that the children were being challenged and learning more about the world in which they traveled and lived. Colorful, noisy, inclusive activities were enjoyed by all. Teachers can continue to learn, too.

Jeff was happy to learn that two teens would soon arrive from the States. The Holmes family flew into Manila and were driven forty-five minutes by their host, a seminary professor, in the tinny, noisy, uncomfortable van to the Baesa campus to receive a feast similar to the one we'd enjoyed. It was late afternoon when the terrible seats-on-the-side van brought them an hour and a half along rutted roads to the Silang campus that same day.

They arrived after dark and were exhausted; we didn't even see them, and our house was next door. The next day, they got up very early and were driven back to Manila International Airport; the son left his father, mother, and sister to fly to his new boarding school in Singapore. Ray, Shirley, and Rhoda were then driven back to the Silang campus to settle into their new home.[181]

Much too much happened in a very short time for any young person—or family, for that matter. Many people and departments were involved in those *very bad decisions* for that family. Teens are especially vulnerable when moved from their friends and an active life in America to the isolation and limitations of life on a countryside campus. The young man knew no one at the boarding school and had a difficult time in Singapore.

Jeff was quickly approaching the age at which he would also be heading off to Singapore. The general arrangement was that the

---

[181] Ray Holmes is the author of the very candid *Boiled Rice and Gluten*, mentioned earlier.

teenagers would leave in August, come home for Christmas holidays, then go back to the boarding school until June. There were many positive aspects to the experiences there. Thirty teens from all over the Far East would live in a dormitory, take fascinating field trips, and spend lots of time with the faculty families.

But this wasn't what we wanted for our family, and it was too much adjustment for some kids; we knew of a few who had left midyear. We didn't want that for Jeff or Kimberly, so we decided to go home after three years in the RP. Also, my mother's cancer was advancing, and we wanted to be near her.

The new American girl, Rhoda, and Jeff became friends, and both seemed to focus on the many things they *didn't* like about being so isolated and "limited." We took trips snorkeling and doing other things we thought the kids would enjoy, but Jeff's behavior made it clear he did not want to be there; he wanted to go to the States.

Then one day he went missing from home—and the campus. We looked, we drove. We did not know where he was. Panicked, we drove to Manila, to our friend Dale's apartment. Jeff was not there, and he'd not seen him but said he would look. We prayed; it gave us courage but did *not* calm our fears. We drove to places we knew Jeff liked in that city of eight million people, to no avail. We finally returned to the campus, sure he would return on his own if he could.

What followed was three days of hell before our friend Dale brought him back to campus—and we learned that Jeff had slept in a mall, in a theater, walked the streets, and he reported that he was treated well. My stomach clenches as I write this. Manila is known for child trafficking, and Jeff was a handsome, blond, fourteen-year-old American boy.

Jeff's unhappiness meant more misbehavior. We all decided that the best plan for now was for Jeff to live the remaining six months of our tenure with Uncle Wayne and Aunt Jan just outside Detroit. He would finish his eighth grade with his cousins, Rod and Jeff, where there was a band and a sports program. The administrators of the overseas workers were very understanding and paid for Dale to fly with Jeff to Detroit, to get him settled in with Wayne and his family. While in the States, Dale visited three campuses offering opportunities for a position upon our return. More about that trip in another chapter.

One huge lesson for us and the other family with two teens was that the best time to go on foreign service is when children are very young. The entire Holmes family returned to the US after a few months; Ray returned later to teach another year with his family back home. It seemed a difficult situation.

When our end-of-term departure neared, Kimberly had a "pushmi-pullyu" feeling about leaving. She was an excellent traveler, and we had a wonderful trip home, traveling the rest of the way "around the world." Dale and I celebrated our twentieth wedding anniversary in Hong Kong—and ate at McDonald's because that was such a treat for Kimberly. Over the next seven weeks, we enjoyed travel in India, Egypt, Israel, and Rome, driving through portions of Italy, France, Switzerland, Germany, Belgium, and Lichtenstein, then flying for a week in London. We were sad Jeff was not a part of that trip.

One memorable incident on the way home involved a knife, Kimberly, and Israeli airport security. Kimberly was proud to carry a nine-inch carving knife, a gift from her dad, in her small purse. We had been told that Israeli security was especially alert, so we tried to do everything just right. But when the attendant ran Kimberly's belongings through the machines, she brought Kimberly's knife to her and said, "Honey, this can't go with you."

Oh, what a bad feeling! We assumed she would lose the knife and we might be in trouble. But the attendant continued, "The captain is going to hold your knife for you during the flight. You can have it when we land." Whew! Now it's a neat memory instead of a bad experience.

When the three of us reached the States, the first big thing was reuniting with Jeff in the Detroit airport. He'd brought his chocolate-loving mom a Hershey's bar!¹⁸² He knew I'd missed those. We visited family there, bought a car, and Dale drove the kids to our new home in Texas. Jeff was in ninth grade, and Kimberly in sixth. Texas was going to be "a whole other country"—the motto Texas boasted at the time.

The new campus was a welcoming place. The kids made friends. Fascinatingly, their closest friends were second-generation Filipino Americans. Neither of these new friends had been to the Philippines—so our kids taught them about the land of their heritage. Those friendships were good for both Jeff and Kimberly.

Update 2020s

—**Jeff's feelings about his Philippine experience now** are mixed with good memories and frustrating ones. His love of music and sports was not fostered there. But perhaps the interests that were— history, planes, inventions, and how things are made—are part of his adult success as a senior superintendent overseeing huge projects, such as for the US Post Office, shopping complexes, a four-story hotel, and a K–12 school on a ten-acre site. His biggest influence was and is his multitalented dad, who has built barns and furniture and skateboard ramps. Helping with construction projects on the Silang campus was challenging fun and a good learning experience. We've since learned that he made more than one trip to Manila alone.

—**When we ask Kimberly if she is glad she lived in the Philippines**, she gives an enthusiastic "Yes!" When we ask what she liked, she says, "Everything!" I remember there were times she missed her friends and Walla Walla, the only home she'd known before. She thought we'd go back there; instead, we went to Texas. She has said: "Every change meant some things would be lost forever and that

---

¹⁸² Hershey and other chocolates were occasionally available in the Philippines; often, though, they were very old and not tasty, a real disappointment after spending an exorbitant amount for them.

you could never truly go back. There can be great benefits, too. New experiences, friends, and wisdom, and seeing how creative and clever people around the world are, even with limited resources."

She loved the markets: "It was like stepping into Aladdin's cave. So many treasures I'd never seen before." She also loved "going snorkeling and the small sharks and exotic marine animals—aside from getting stung all over while snorkeling that resulted in spasms that night. Stopping at the side of the road to select the perfect pineapple from a huge pile at the edge of the field where it had just been harvested."

She's very skilled in many crafts, and I believe what she saw in the Philippines encouraged that interest. She is especially sensitive about people being treated kindly and fairly.

Now, years later, both kids will tell you it was a life-altering experience, and they have a wider view of the world and its peoples. Jeff has traveled to Haiti, Kenya, Amsterdam, London, and all but three of the states in America. Kimberly and Terry, her husband, and Kyrstin moved from Texas to New Zealand; Alec was born there, and they all moved to Australia and now are residents. They have traveled in the South Pacific and Europe.

—**Jeff reflects:** "No matter what you read, nothing can really prepare you—every day is an experiment. If I'd not had those experiences, I might not be what I am today." What he is, is a good person, an excellent worker, a responsible adult, father, and grandfather, and an exemplary son. He describes himself as a bit solitary and says he believes that comes partly from his experiences in the Philippines.

—**Kimberly says:** "Being taught to crochet by Lisa was a gift which enhanced a strong interest in textile crafts and has continued to bring joy and be useful ever since." Kimberly is a creative, kind, responsible adult, a wonderful wife and mother, a caring daughter, and she says her experiences mean she can make a home anywhere.

—**I say:** My learned experience is that the age children go to the mission field is vital—and the younger, the better. They can become bicultural as they learn about their new country and integrate what they already know from home and what they learn as they visit on furlough. The adolescent years involve so many physical and social issues; children may feel more able to integrate and learn and socialize in a stateside environment. The website Ask a Missionary provides helpful insights and suggestions.[183]

---

[183] "Ask a Missionary: How can I prepare my children for moving to the mission field?" https://askamissionary.com/family-single/preparing-children (Accessed February 19, 2024).

──CHAPTER 31──

Flight Attendants of 004

Dale

"Traveling. It leaves you speechless, then turns you into a storyteller."

—*Travel Poster*

I was flying with Jeff from Manila to Detroit, where he would live with my brother and his family for a few months while we finished our overseas assignment. I'd arranged for classes and labs to be covered in the Philippines and would be interviewing at three universities, planning for the next stage of our lives. It was a complicated and exhausting time—emotionally and physically. I found it hard to take Jeff there and hard to leave. I loved the Philippines and her people, but there is no place like home!

We listened to the flight attendant's instructions about oxygen masks and what to do if we ditched in the ocean, and soon we were airborne. The flight attendants hovered so unobtrusively that it seems rude to use the term "hover," and yet they were ever present, ensuring each passenger's comfort. They distributed warm, moist hand towels to refresh and relax body, mind, and soul. Snacks, drinks, and, in due time, dinners were served.

The flight attendants themselves were the icing on the cake. More than efficient servants, they were classy. Long hair was sculpted to form attractive coiffures, or it flowed in long tresses down their backs.

The dresses were of silky, colorful material and Asian in design. I recognized how much the Far East had intruded on me, how much I had come to appreciate its cultures. The flight attendants of China Airlines set me at ease, soothed my soul, and made me comfortable. This was a good flight.

There was a flight change in Taiwan, and we lost our Chinese flight attendants. The Taiwanese attendants were as classy but different, moving with an easy, simple grace, always present, always discreet. Their long dresses were made of a soft and flowing fabric, with an abstract botanical motif of blue and green with violet accents. Exquisite.

In Honolulu we changed to Pan American Flight 004. My initial reaction was that the American women did not measure up. Maybe it was the late night; but then, the other flights had been long, late night, and early morning, and the Asian ladies remained calm.

The American uniforms were navy blue, the skirts short. Some of the women had added scarves, boots, wide belts, and bold makeup. They were, comparatively, a ragtag group, loud and anything but demure. They chewed and popped their gum and giggled.

A baby two or three rows ahead of me was fussy, and the young mother's agitation did little to soothe him. This was an unpleasant experience in a long, confining, but mostly pleasant trip. Then, a flight attendant stopped by the mother's seat and was soon joined by another. In short order, a whole covey of attendants had crowded about the mom and babe, talking and giggling. One asked to hold the baby and bounced it gently. Another asked the mother if she was going home or just visiting. Another said, "Oh! Babies cry. Flying's not their favorite sport. Sometimes changes in altitude cause pressure in their ears and it hurts. They don't understand."

The baby was quieting down, the mother was smiling, and I was seeing a different side of the "loud" American flight attendants. These women were innovative. Friendly. These were the women to have around when there were good times to be had or problems to be solved. More than that, these were the women I understood—maybe; I thought I understood them. At any rate, they were like the girls I grew up with.

How could I have been so negative and now rise up as the grand defender of my native ladies? There are, no doubt, many correct answers. The Asian reserve and attention to detail gave those flight attendants an advantage. No doubt my living in the Philippines enhanced my appreciation of Asian cultures. No doubt the very long flights and lack of sleep set me up with a lowered tolerance and altered appreciation for my surroundings.

Elements of the culture I was reared in, whether I understood or not, proved an irresistible force. I sat in wonderment. My eyes were watery! I had trouble explaining my reaction, so I wrote my unfettered thoughts in a small notebook. When I finished, I signed my name, intent on tearing it out and giving it to one of the 004 flight attendants—but I feared they might be offended.

This is terrible poetry, but it was written from where I was, very early one morning:

Ode to the Stewardesses of Flight 004

You are the first American women
I have seen in a long time.
You are beautiful,
and I love you!
You bounce about the cabin,
unlike the Asian attendants.
You snap-smack your gum;
you are loud, you are untamed.
You are "all American"
and I love it.
You are black; you are white,
you are brown, you are a rainbow.
You play with babies,

and laugh with their mothers.
You are American ladies,
and I love you.
I am home at last.
Happy trip!

CHAPTER 32

Civet Cats, Owls, and Other Critters

Karen

"Until one has loved an animal, a part of one's soul remains unawakened."

—Anatole France

When we were looking at library books and pondering what life might be like in the Philippines, one beautiful image caught our attention: beautifully painted horse-drawn carts (*calesas*). They seemed to be leisurely moving through streets or picturesque countryside, carrying one or two passengers just out for a pleasant drive; some were transporting goods. The horses looked well cared for and beautifully groomed.

"Ah, I want to ride in those," I said to my own particular horseman, Dale. He and I have always loved horses and have owned several, ridden them, bred them, and trained and shown them.

The calesa looked intriguing, but we never rode in them. Likely there were places where they could be a pleasure; however, the calesa horses we saw in Manila were worked too hard, sometimes driven beyond their endurance. It made us sad.

One afternoon, I was shopping in a Chinese market in Manila, looking for items to decorate for our planned Lunar New Year celebration, and my companion said, "Kay, let's look over here." I turned to follow but soon realized that he was trying to divert my attention away from the terrible sight of a small, dirty, emaciated horse that had fallen in the gutter under his load, and he was still attached to the cart.

For similar reasons, we did not attend any cockfights (*sabong*). We could not support either industry. The beautiful gamecocks, *mga sunoy*, are well cared for by their owners, who train them to be aggressive, equipping them with razor-sharp spurs or blades. The matches are often fought to the death of one or both animals. Gambling is expected at most cockfights—called the national sport by some.

Dogs are trained to guard property and used for hunting in the provinces. Cats are valued for keeping mice and rats from attacking or robbing chicken eggs. As mentioned earlier, children are taught not to touch a cat or dog they do not know, as rabies is fairly common and the animals are typically not inoculated. There's even a legend about why dogs and cats fight, imparting negative qualities to both as, in the story, they fight about the cat's mismanagement of land owned by the dog.[184]

A neighbor's dog on our Silang campus bit Dale's hand severely. The owner did not seem concerned and certainly didn't want *his* dog quarantined. It was just "a little bite on the hand, after all." Dale endured thirty days of shots in his abdomen to avoid rabies. There are a few expensive dogs well cared for by their wealthy owners and sometimes kept for breeding.

Civets are small, nocturnal mammals closely related to the mongoose. They are said to be quite vicious, and most folks are afraid of them, so it's interesting that our most delightful and unusual pet ever was a tiny civet cat.

Boys of all ages brought all sorts of critters to Dale. Several students once brought us a python. They were proud to hold it aloft to show us its full eleven-foot length. We admired it and took a picture

---

[184] Leoncia T. Galicano and Josefina T. Tameta. *Philippine Legends*. Manila, Bookman, Inc., 1971.

of the boys bravely holding the snake, which they said had been run over by a car. We then asked them to release it in our backyard. It likely had a few broken ribs, but it slowly slithered toward the ravine.

One day, three young men stepped inside our living room door and handed Dale a tiny pasteboard box. The boys watched as Dale took the box and carefully opened the lid; the cloth inside moved, and under the cloth was a small, furry critter, black and brown and striped. A baby civet cat! He was such a beautiful and helpless little creature, and we fell in love with him immediately.

"I'll take care of him!" I announced.

Dale and I took turns feeding him every two hours for several days, beginning with mushed banana—the only thing he'd eat at first. I kept him warm, wrapping him in a towel, and even took him to work with me, keeping him mostly out of sight in a box under my desk. Dale created a nutrient solution, and we fed him from a blunt-edged syringe. "Civie" became one of our most cherished pets.

Soon we were being met at our door by Civie, who would make his little chortling sound, accompanied by our miniature apricot poodle, Pumpkin. They became close friends.

Kimberly remembers, "Civie used to climb onto my bed in the morning and tickle my nose until I woke up. One day I thought to play a trick on him. Waiting until he was up close and about to poke my nose, I drew in a slow, deep breath, and when he was really close, I puffed air in this face! He was so startled; he bit my nose and ran off!"

Civets, of the Viverridae family, are found in many parts of Southeast Asia, Nepal, and Sri Lanka. They are omnivorous, eating chickens and fruit, including coffee cherries. Most Filipinos are said to fear them. Some keep dogs to chase them away from their home and their chickens. Some folks prize coffee made from fruit left undigested and harvested after the civet passes it![185] It's called cherry or civet coffee (kopi luwak) and is quite expensive.

People could not understand why we would work so hard to keep

---

[185] https://www.allthingsnature.org/what-are-civet-cats.htm

a civet alive. They expected it would be mean and smelly as civets have a scent gland that exudes a pungent odor. The adult civets that folks see chasing their chickens can be aggressive. Later, for a short time, we had two adult civets we kept in a cage but decided to give them up due to their odor. We learned also that their musk is often used in making perfume.

Ray, our dear dour Finnish friend, was alternately funny and curmudgeonly. When he visited and sat in our rocker with his long legs stretched out in front of him, Civie scampered up them and curled in the crook of Ray's arms. They both loved it!

We planned to find out how we could take her home, but it turned out not to be necessary. When we needed to be away for a few days, a neighbor agreed to feed and water Civie and let him out in the house now and then. When we returned, he was dead in his cage. We were stunned and so sad. Without telling me—I'd have never agreed to it—Dale even did an autopsy and could not determine his cause of death. We have lovely memories of that dear little creature, and sad ones.

Dale built a cage just outside the stationary part of the sliding door of our dining room for Otis the owl. The Philippines has 200 endemic birds, and there are 17 endemic owls. Otis was brought to us by two boys who said they'd found him after he'd been knocked out of a tree by rocks, leading to a broken leg and wing. He was a fledgling screech owl, cinnamon colored and gorgeous. Likely he was a Philippine scops owl, *Otus megalotis*. Dale recognized he had not healed properly and could not live in the wild, fixed him up as best he could, and installed him in his special cage. We called him Otis after a friend who was education secretary of the Far Eastern Division of SDAs. And the genus name is *Otus*!

It was fun to watch Otis, and he was a delightful pet, but he was limited in his lifestyle—and he limited ours. He needed rodents, birds, snakes, insects. Initially we caught mice in the field, sometimes in the house. We caught small fish in the stream in the gorge. Finally we were purchasing snakes in the market, cutting them up, and putting them in our freezer until Otis needed them. A biologist's bride seldom realizes what lies in her future.

♦ ♦ ♦

There were numerous other species to fascinate us. Walking in the ravine one afternoon, we saw the green many-banded krait, known there as the "one-step" snake, so called because it's said you will die quickly if one bites you. Depending on the source, the deadliest snake in the Philippines is the pit viper or the Philippine cobra. Pythons are abundant; others to avoid are Wagler's pit viper, the equatorial spitting cobra, the Lake Taal snake, and the yellow-bellied sea snake. Many Filipinos are very cautious and reasonably fearful of all snakes.

We did not see some of the animals unique to the Philippines but still want to share information about them. If we'd stayed longer, likely we would have sought them out. The smallest monkey in the world, the tarsier (ranging from 3.5 to 6.25 inches long), eats insects and lizards. Its gigantic eyes help it hunt at night; its large ears make its hearing especially acute. We heard larger monkeys in the trees near some of the homes but almost never saw them. Other native animals include Visayan warty pigs, the Philippines mouse-deer, red-bodied swallowtails, Cebu flowerpeckers, Mindoro crocodiles, and the dome planthopper. And there are freshwater and saltwater crocodiles.

The Philippine eagle has a wingspan of two meters and is said to be found only around Mount Apo on Mindanao. It's also called the monkey-eating eagle, and its diet includes large snakes, lizards, hornbills, flying lemurs, bats, and pigs as well. We would have loved to see the green sea turtles come to lay their eggs on the seven small islands south of Palawan and the three islands of Malay. The eggs and the turtles have been a source of income for the folk in that area, though conservation movements have acted to create protected areas since 1996.

The animal we saw most was the carabao, an Asian water buffalo, the tractor of the Philippines and the source of livelihood for farmers—so prolific and so valued that it is known as the national animal. Sometimes it pulls a *paragos*, a wooden apparatus used to flatten land in rice fields, and it is adept at pulling logs in the forest.

In 1900, a unique organization was formed called the Military Order of the Carabao, created to "counter and satirize the very pompous Order of the Dragon ... funded by those who had defeated the very short-lived Boxer uprising in China." The carabao is said to "epitomize the camaraderie that grows among members of the armed forces who face the dangers and privations of extensive military service far from home."[186]

Carabao are loved and valued for their hard work and seen as faithful partners in life. Besides helping to plow the fields, they are used for meat, transportation, and milk for sweets and cooking; and their image adorns clothes, coins, and jewelry.

The tamaraw is a smaller water buffalo type found only on the island of Mindoro, south of the sizable northern island of Luzon. Tamaraw horns are distinctively V-shaped and each about fourteen to twenty inches long, contrasted with carabao horns, which form a "C" or half-moon and range from twenty-four to sixty inches in total length. They are both endangered species; currently there are about 350 tamaraw and 3.5 million carabao in the Philippines. Five conservation groups working to protect and preserve the tamaraw population have "deployed 4 camouflaged camera traps to the Mindoro's Iglit-Baco mountain range" and hope to increase the tamaraw population.[187] The story of Dale's lab assistant guiding

---

[186] Military Order of the Carabao. www.carabao.org (Accessed February 21, 2024).
[187] The Asian Wild Cattle Specialist Group (AWCSG) is working to bring together all initiatives. The groups include the World Wide Fund for Nature (WWF), Far Eastern University (FEU), the Department of Environment and Natural Resources (DENR), the Tamaraw Conservation Programme (TCP), and Hubbs-SeaWorld Research Institute (HSWRI); https://www.google.com/search?q=tamaraw+protection+groups+philippines&oq=tamaraw+protection+groups+philippines (Accessed February 21, 2024)

Dale and Jeff down to his home island of Mindoro on a fascinating adventure to find "the elusive tamaraw" is in the following chapter.

In the sea we enjoyed clownfish, seahorses, lionfish, harlequins, groupers, damselfish, angelfish, cuttlefish, saddleback fish, small sharks, and so many more in abundance! And in our house in Baesa were, of course, the unending geckos on the walls and ceilings.

Update 2020s

—**Civet Cats:** We likely would not have been allowed to bring our "Civie" home with us because they can harbor SARS and are carnivorous and nocturnal. Civet coffee is costly; civet musk is used to make perfume, cosmetics, and soaps, both as a fixative and fragrance, and for pain relief and as a sedative. Some say if you want to eat them, they're "best prepared by roasting them whole."[188]

---

[188] The Pros and Cons of Having A Civet As A Pet. https://www.patchpets.com/the-pros-and-cons-of-having-a-civet-as--pet (Accessed February 21, 2024)

——CHAPTER 33——

The Elusive Tamaraw

Dale

"Tamaraws are Critically Endangered according to the International Union for Conservation of Nature (ICUN) Red List of Threatened Species."

—*Kidadl Team*[189]

The mustang and the cow pony were indispensable, mystical companions to the Native American and to the cowboy. Draft horses are the workmates for farmers in the little farming village of Killmaster, Michigan, where I grew up. There is something wonderfully enduring about those bonds.

The carabao is the Filipinos' mystical companion animal and beast of burden. At first I thought the carabao was one of the most ungainly beasts I'd ever seen. They resemble the African water buffalo, an animal with a nasty disposition; but the carabao, as I learned, is very companionable. The Filipino farmer loves and holds the carabao in the highest regard, and I came to think of them much the same.

A carabao resided on the Baesa campus. He was kept on a grassy spot a short distance from my classroom and had a wallow, a depression in the ground that was generally wet and muddy; he loved

---

[189] "Fun Tamaraw Facts for Kids." https://kidadl.com/facts/tamaraw-facts (Accessed February 23, 2024).

to roll in the mud.¹⁹⁰ A lady faithfully brought buckets of water and poured them into the wallow and often over the reclining carabao. She scratched his head, and he seemed to like it.

I spent a few days at a student's home and observed the same behavior between my student's mother and the family carabao. She and the carabao took walks together, and she talked to the beast as I did with my horses. The Filipino farmer's wife often saw to the welfare of the carabao more tenderly than the farmer himself did. I began appreciating the carabao and considered it an interesting and valuable animal.

Johnny Guyo, my student laboratory assistant, told me about the tamaraw: "It has a nasty disposition, seems an incorrigible beast, and has never been domesticated."

Tamaraw are dwarf buffalo about four feet tall at the shoulders and are one of the eleven wild cattle species known. According to Global Wildlife Conservation, "despite their short stature, they are known for their big personalities."¹⁹¹

A friend in the Biology Department of the University of the Philippines, Los Baños, was the assistant director of the Tamaraw Project on Mindoro Island. I asked him about the university's field station and where tamaraw might be seen in the mountains of Mindoro. As luck would have it, he was planning a trip to that site and invited us to meet him there. We warped our academic schedules to fit his trip schedule, and Johnny, Jeff, and I left the Baesa campus on a Monday morning, taking a jeepney to Calamba, then a bus to the port city of Batangas on the south end of Luzon; there we boarded a small ship to San Jose on the southwest end of Mindoro.

We arrived Tuesday morning and spent time with Johnny's family, who owned a sari-sari store. Johnny's father was a handyman

---

[190] "Wallowing . . . is comfort behaviour during which an animal rolls about or lies in mud, water or snow." https://en.wikipedia.org/wiki/Wallowing (Accessed February 23, 2024).
[191] "Tamaraw Talks: Introduction." Global Wildlife Conservation, Dec. 20, 2018, https://www.rewild.org/news/tamaraw-tales-introduction (Accessed February 21, 2024).

with a gift for repairing broken things. One of his repair jobs grabbed Jeff's attention: Mr. Guyo was replacing a broken hammer handle for a neighbor. He took a tree branch that had cured for some time in his scrap pile and carved a fine handle to fit a man's hand and the hammer head. The end of the handle was slightly undersized for the hole in the head, but Mr. Guyo lit a small propane torch, picked up an old toothbrush from his workbench, and began melting the plastic toothbrush handle and dripping molten plastic into the spaces between the handle and the hammer's head. He compacted the soft plastic with the tip of a very small screwdriver. When he finished, the hardened plastic filled the spaces between the handle and the metal hammer head as securely as any larger handle could have. Jeff was impressed.

The next two days of hiking and finding the tamaraw would be grueling, so we went to bed early. Johnny's parents showed us to a bedroom. A generous mosquito net hung gracefully from the wooden framework above a bed. It dawned on me that Johnny's parents were offering Jeff and me their bed. They would suffer the mosquito bites that night because Jeff and I were their guests. I objected as gracefully as I could, but there was no way they could offer anything but their very best, in Mr. Guyo's words, "to a guest who has opened such opportunity to our son, Johnny." Johnny's parents placed great value on education.

Centuries ago, the tamaraw lived on several Philippine islands, but now it lives only on Mindoro. Its closest relative lives in Borneo, 950 miles of ocean southwest of Mindoro. It is believed that the tamaraw's ancestors rafted to the Philippines from Borneo sometime in ancient history. "Rafting" involves floating on materials, typically islands of soil and vegetation, from the original site to another. Many terrestrial plants and animals have crossed large expanses of seas in this way. This is usually associated with geological phenomena: earthquakes, floods, and other disturbances of landscapes that cause large pieces to break off and float to new locations.[192] After arriving in the Philippines, the animals evolved into a new species.[193]

The tamaraw was first described and named *Anoa mindorensis* by the French zoologist Pierre Marie Heude in 1888. It was unknown to science before the late eighteenth and early nineteenth centuries; most explorers and Filipino natives avoided Mindoro because it harbored excessive mosquito populations and virulent malaria. As effective antimalarial medicines and mosquito control were developed, more and more people visited and settled on Mindoro.

The genus and species names of the tamaraw were changed to *Bubalus mindorensis* in 1958. It is estimated that more than 10,000 tamaraw once occupied Mindoro, but hunting and habitat degradation had reduced the population to fewer than 500 in 1979.[194]

Morning came quickly, and we rushed to catch the bus north. It was unlike any bus I had seen, but we observed that it was common on Mindoro. It was a large bus missing its left side and windows. Several post-like supports reached from a long, horizontal entry step to the top of the bus, from the front seats to the back of the bus. This made it quick and easy to enter to find a seat and to exit when you reached your destination.

As we traveled farther north, the population decreased, and roads became narrow, rutted, and bumpy. We took a series of jeepneys, and they proved even more interesting than the bus because we were sitting closer together and the passengers were not all facing forward. Conversations flowed more easily. An old man facing us was very talkative. He had several US military friends during the Second World War, and he plied us with questions about how things were in the States today and why we were traveling the back roads of Mindoro. We told him that when we reached the point where the

---

[192] Oceanic dispersal - Wikipedia: en.wikipedia.org/wiki/.
[193] Brent Huffman. "*Bulalus mindorensis*: Tamaraw," https://www.ultimateungulate.com/Artiodactyla/Bubalus_mindorensis.html (Accessed February 21, 2024).
[194] "Tamaraw – Facts, Diet, Habitat & Pictures on Animalia.bio https://animalia.bio/tamaraw. (Accessed February 23, 2024).

jeepney turned around, we would take the trail up the mountain to the point where the University of the Philippines has a biological field station on Mount Iglit-Baco. This made him more engaged. He said: "You go mountain morning! Not night!"

His English was difficult to understand, and he worked hard to understand us. And he and Johnny spoke different dialects. He became insistent that we take a room for the night at a house where the jeepney route ended. Suddenly the old man began repeating himself: "I so sorry you Joe! I so sorry! I so sorry you Joe."

I asked Johnny, "What does he mean?"

Johnny said the man meant that he was sorry for us, but he struggled to comprehend the what and why of it. Finally, Johnny said he seemed to be repeating English words he'd learned from the GI boys who had courted girls in his village. By the time those GIs shipped out for new assignments or to go home at the war's end, many of them had set up "sweetheart relationships," and when they shipped out, they would try to explain and apologize for leaving. "I'm so sorry to leave you" or "I feel so sorry" seemed to have been frequent expressions that over time morphed into "I so sorry you." Now the phrases were used as expression of fear, regret, or undesirable happenings.

Trying to make sense of our new friend's message, we deduced that he was saying that he feared if we went up that trail in the darkness, bad men would rob and hurt us. He was so agitated that we decided it would be best to take his advice. He pointed to a house with a ROOMS FOR RENT sign, and we stayed there.

We woke early to a calm, cool morning. By 6:30 a.m., we had begun the eighteen-kilometer trek to base camp. The trail was narrow and steep but well worn and easy to follow, though the many side paths gave us pause. After an hour of hiking, we realized we had not filled our water bottles, and it would take most of the day to reach the field station. We didn't want to drink from the stream flowing down the trail.

Johnny said, "Don't worry. There is a trick we use to find fresh, clean water."

Before long he found what he was looking for—a patch of sandy gravel forming a narrow island. The stream split about fifty feet up the hill and ran along both sides of the slender island, which was about twelve to fifteen feet wide at its middle. Johnny dropped to his knees and started digging a pit with his hand in the gravely sand near its downstream end.

"The water in this hole," he said, "has been traveling downstream through all this sand, and almost anything in the water will be filtered out between the sand grains. The water here is purer than it was when it first started through this filter of fine sand grains—almost no creepy crawlies," he teased. Then he chuckled at his teasing. "But we'll wait just a bit. My digging may have released something, but soon this water will be as good as you can expect from a well."

We drank our fill, topped off all our containers, and headed up the mountain. We had walked perhaps two or three more hours when we detected three men in loincloths, one shirtless, peering from behind tree trunks.

Johnny said, "They live in these woods, very timid people. Most likely they are hunting." Suddenly they were gone, and Johnny said, "Likely they are Tau-buid tribe, nice people. Part of the eight tribes of the umbrella term 'Mangyan.' They are seen as the protectors of the tamaraw."

Jeff remembers that encounter vividly.

The forest became dense, and men abruptly stepped into the narrow trail in front of us. They fidgeted as we approached; as it turned out, we were just two small groups of curious persons on the same trail, fascinated with the others' differences. They wore loincloths as well—thin, ropelike, plant-fiber belts tied around their waists with narrow strips of cloth fastened front and the back. Handcrafted containers made from short sections of mature bamboo shafts hung from their belts. Fine braided strands of bamboo fibers strengthened and decorated the tops and bottoms. Exquisite! They contained betel nuts, tobacco leaves, matches, and a tiny clay pipe, hand-molded and cured in the ashes of a campfire. I wish I knew more about these men. The patina of those containers spoke of the paths they had traveled.

The Tau-buid people are pipe smokers from a very young age; valuing that over the betel nut, which they also use. The pipe smoke also keeps insects away! They "hunt animals using their *tulag* (spear), *gadun* (bow), and *silo* (spike trap)."[195] They also plant rice and other crops. We learned the children sometimes go with other Mangyan tribes, whenever there are schools or health missions. Our PUC Public Health Department created health missions for folks near our campus.

I traded two good-quality pocketknives for two small bamboo containers with belts. Each container held a clay pipe bowl and small pipe stem created so they could be separated to fit in the container. The men were delighted with the exchange. They would create new pipes and new containers. I would buy new knives. The containers were aged relics even then, and I have owned them for over forty years. What makes them so meaningful to me is the craftsmanship and the personality they reveal. Both bamboo cases rest today on the shelves of a bookcase beside Karen's computer, each holding the contents its owner added: tobacco leaves.

After another two miles, we stopped to rest where the trail passed between car-sized gray rocks. Jeff wanted me to take a picture of him jumping off one of them, but I failed to accommodate for how fast he moved through the air in that jump, so the photo was a blurred disappointment. The memory is still good, and I can follow his blurred path almost to the ground.

The stream formed a winding path between these rocks. We relaxed in the shade of some trees and were overtaken by three men

---

[195] "Ethnic Groups of the Philippines: Tawbuid," www.ethnicgroupsphilippines.com/ethnic-groups-in-the-philippines/tawbuid/ (Accessed April 4, 2024).

leading a young bull up the trail. The rocks made a pleasant spot to relax, and we figured we had about three more hours of sun and a half hour of trail, so we continued to relax as the men with the bull pressed on. From what we understood of their conversation, they were taking him up the mountain to butcher.

As we continued up the trail, we came across another collection of large gray rocks, but these rocks had large red spots on them. We sat to take another break, and I asked Johnny if he knew anything about these rocks and their red spots.

"Oh!" he responded. "This looks like a place where village elders gather and talk and relax and spit betel-nut juice. This is their office, their meeting room, so to speak. The elders solve village problems here."

The field station was a short distance from the rocks. There was a large, new, unfinished building with a roof and doors but without glass in the windows—likely a kitchen-dining building. Men were working on another building to the west of this one, perhaps the administrative building. Johnny told them we had arranged with the university to stay a few days to study the area and to look for tamaraw. They were good with that, and we retired to the large building to eat and relax. It had been a fascinating, long, hard day.

Suddenly, the workmen began shouting and laughing, and we rushed to the windows. Two men were up in a tree, but it was unclear what was happening. Feeling comfortable after our earlier interaction, we ran to join in the excitement. A rat was in the branches, trying to avoid the men, who struck at it with their tools. One man had a crowbar, the other a large stick. The poor rat didn't have a chance. It seemed not to want to jump to the ground, but the crowbar found its mark, and the rat fell, dead.

Johnny asked if the workers would let us have the rat to make a study skin. They seemed eager to please us and expressed a genuine interest in what we were up to. Soon the man who had killed the rat began talking, and Johnny translated, "He wants to know if he can have the rat's body back. He wants to cook it for his dinner."

I had difficulty understanding why this rat went to the tree when threatened, unlike any rat species I knew. But as I wrote this chapter, I began searching the literature on Filipino rats and discovered the Mindoro climbing rat (*Anonymomys mindorensis*). I am confident this was the rat I skinned, but I will never know because the study skin and skull no longer exist to verify it.

The next morning was bright and clear, and we set off in the direction the workers suggested we would most likely find tamaraw. We examined the proposed area and found narrow trails through dense bushes that flourished and spread unchecked except where tamaraw had trod. Passing through a somewhat swampy area tamped down with worn paths, we saw what we knew were tamaraw tracks. We were excited! Then we realized that this narrow, marshy trail might be a perilous place to meet the horns of a cantankerous tamaraw. It would be difficult to push through the thick brush to effect an escape.

As we exited the rampant bushes and walked further up the mountain, we spotted four or five tamaraw below us in an open meadow. We had binoculars and we were close enough to get good views and not be in real danger. We watched them in fascination for some time, even though they did nothing more exciting than graze. The object of our trip did not disappoint. They seemed congenial enough at this distance.

On the way back to the field station, we shared a path with two men—workers from the field station. They were friendly and curious. It was midday, and they invited us to eat lunch with them. Their wives had no idea we were coming! Still, they were most gracious. Our hosts suggested a faster trail back to catch the jeepney, which we took early the next morning.

A few kilometers down that trail, we came upon a village of seven houses; they were very simple structures with a single floor set more than a meter above the ground. One house had been burned. The other houses were abandoned, and Johnny told us that when someone dies of an illness, these folk burn the house, sometimes all the houses, and the villagers move to another spot to rebuild.

Perhaps a mile later, we came across several houses under construction, made of poles, sticks, and grasses. We learned that these were the folks who had burned the other house. They explained that a baby had died that morning, and Johnny told us they do not *have* to move if a baby dies, but they always move if an adult dies.

Several people were sitting on the floor of an unfinished house. A few other buildings had been started, but it seemed that construction had stopped. An adolescent boy was unconscious and resting in an improvised hammock at the far side of the developing village. Johnny said they feared he would die, and if he did, they would have to move again.

Hanging from a rope clothesline were several fish traps made of woven, wicker-like material. In cities, they are commonly purchased as room decorations by tourists, but these were authentic and functional; though beautiful, they were meant to catch fish. The villagers offered to trade the traps for clothing, medicine, food—anything we might have that they needed. We were low on food, but we pulled together what we had: apples, nuts, cookies, a couple of large bath towels, some of Jeff's and my T-shirts, cold tablets, aspirin, Band-Aids, vitamin C tablets, and a sewing needle I had carried for years, skewered in the inner leather of my wallet to use for clothing repairs. What a helpless feeling to not be able to share more.

As we moved down the trail, Johnny told us more about life in these mountains. If a baby dies, they burn the house and bury the baby, but they don't move to another site. If a mother dies in childbirth, they bury both the mother and the baby. If a mother has twins, they bury both twins because twins are a bad omen!

"That is a very hard thing, but that's what I've been told."

Life is simple—and difficult—for these mountain people. Death and sickness are treated matter-of-factly. Life seems on the surface to be cheap but, under it all, is precious to them. Our overt concern for the quality of life is engendered by the opportunities we have to improve it. For such opportunities we must be thankful.

We continued our uneventful trek to the spot where the jeepney picked up new passengers and began the journey back toward San Jose. Jeff and I had airline tickets to Manila in the morning. Johnny would follow by ship a few days later. I found the people in the backcountry of Mindoro more interesting than the tamaraw. The memories of those few days remain precious and vivid today.

Update 2018

—**Tamaraw under Threat:** Recent counts report only 523 individuals in the wild on Mindoro, according to one travel blog.[196]

—**The Tamaraw Conservation Program** (TCP) was established in 1979 through Executive Order No. 544, and the program started an off-site breeding facility; it has been largely unsuccessful—only one has survived, birthed in captivity in 1999. The travel blog explains, "The Gene Pool will not go to waste, however, as the new facility will be converted into the Mindoro Biodiversity Conservation, Research, and Education Center."

---

[196] Tamaraw under Threat: Here's how you can help. https://www.thepoortraveler.net/2018/11/the-tamaraw-is-under-threat (Accessed April 4, 2024).

—————CHAPTER 34—————

Study Tour by Ship: My Journal

Dale

"Culture and art and a taste for the beautiful must lead to goodness."

—Imelda Marcos, First Lady of the Philippines (1965–1986)

In the 1970s, the world was caught up in the Green Revolution. Benevolent dictator President Marcos's particular interest was the rapid disappearance of commercially important trees, such as mahogany, mangosteen, coconut, and guava and other trees, which represented a significant chunk of the gross national product. He issued a decree demanding that each Filipino citizen ten years and older plant one tree each month for five years.

> **Section 6 of the Decree:** Any person who violates any provision of this Decree or any regulation promulgated thereunder shall be punished with a fine of not more than one thousand pesos, with disqualification to acquire or enjoy any privilege granted exclusively to citizens of the Philippines . . . and for a period of five years be disqualified to hold public office or to graduate from any educational institution at all levels, to take any bar, board or civil service examination, and to practice any profession licensed and regulated by the Supreme Court or the Professional Regulation Commission.—Ferdinand Marcos, June 6, 1977

Expatriate professors and foreign students who were not officially citizens were granted an alternative way to serve the Philippines: the Student Travel & Exchange Program (STEP). PUC crafted a "study tour by ship" to meet the requirement, and we escaped tree planting by traveling from island to island, imbibing the culture and providing Filipinos with cultural insights of song, dance, and story from our home countries. As it turned out, the Filipino communities we visited were eager to entertain *us* with their song and dance. We loved it! It was a win-win.

Our group consisted of forty-nine international students from seventeen countries, thirty-five Filipino students, five Filipino faculty advisors, and myself. The Filipino people played a major role in the success of our trip: they were our translators, they knew where we were going and how to get there, and they made advance arrangements on each island for food, sleeping quarters, and performance venues. Some had hometown friends who advertised our tour and arranged entertainment for us.

Day 1. Baesa Campus to Manila Bay: Boarding the *Don Enrique*. *I awakened at 5 a.m.; left campus at 6 in Professor Fadre's jeepney. We arrived at Pier 12 in Manila at 7:15 a.m. and boarded the Don Enrique, a 768-ton ship built in 1942—traveling "lowest fare." While we were moving from the jeepney to the ship, someone relieved a graduate student, Titus Rore, of his wallet. Titus was ready to turn back to the campus, but others pledged to see him through financially, and he continued with us. We sailed slowly, with great noise of engines, through gray and hazy weather from Pier 12 into Manila Bay.*

As we traveled south, passing Batangas, Luzon, the sea became rough and choppy. Strong tidal currents run between Luzon and Mindoro Islands, and several students and staff were seasick and didn't eat dinner. I enjoyed the pancit served with a fish head and the half-inch of meat in back of the gills. I took a photo of the fish, and a Filipina student asked in a weak, puzzled voice: "Why, sir?" I couldn't decide whether she was shocked that I had wasted film on such a commonplace object or if I was making a negative statement by taking the picture.

Much of the day was spent sleeping as reading was not an option with the rocking ship and diesel fumes. Below deck there were 200 wooden double bunk beds with thin foam mattresses (about twenty-two by sixty inches) in an area about forty-four by fifty feet, loaded with people and their belongings—a bicycle and three guitars rested on top of one pile. I took some pictures and went for a bath, but the drains were plugged. The communal shower floor was covered with dirty, soapy water sloshing back and forth as the ship rocked. A discarded milk carton moved rhythmically with the water. As I brushed my teeth and looked in the mirror, a man urinated on the milk carton. I didn't take a shower—maybe tomorrow.

Day 2. Santo Niño de Cebu, Mactan Islands, and Ferdinand Magellan. At 4:30 a.m., most passengers were awake and milling about. A lady in the next tier of bunks had set up a shrine with carved figures at the foot of her bed. She seemed pleased that I was interested in her carvings of the holy Infant Jesus, St. Anthony de Padua, St. Martin de Porres (an African saint), and the crucified Christ. She insisted that I take pictures of her and the shrine. She was a businesswoman in charge of dessert sales for school lunches from Luzon to Mindanao. She offered her address and phone number and invited me to visit anytime I should reach Davao. She said she always prays before traveling, asking the saints for success, a safe journey, and a prosperous and safe return.

We disembarked on the island of Cebu. We had two tour guides from the Chamber of Commerce; they told us the average family size on Cebu was six children, the average income was 450 pesos a month (around USD 56.25), and warned us to remove our watches because "pickpockets are worse than in Manila."

We crossed a bridge from Cebu to Mactan island. Our guides said it's the home of most Filipino guitar makers and that the art is passed from father to son. Usually, the craftsmen barter for materials from companies that market the guitars, creating them in their homes and returning the finished product to the company. The price is based on the quality of workmanship and materials. I asked the guide why the artisans didn't market the guitars themselves. She said that without the company, the craftsmen don't have the capital for good-quality materials or the connections for marketing. At the Susing Guitar Factory, I bought a guitar for Jeff, paying 200 pesos (USD 25) plus 20 pesos for a case.

Magellan was killed on Mactan in 1521 by the Filipino chieftain Lapu Lapu. Most Filipinos were Muslim and had not accepted Christianity, but they were forced by the local Catholic priest to build a fort and a huge church. Magellan arrived and planted a cross near the church as a sign of Christian dominance, expecting to force the Filipinos to accept Christianity. Chief Lapu Lapu resisted, marshaled his forces, and personally ran the spear through Magellan.

I was fascinated by these historical facts and with a small, elaborately enshrined figure of the Baby Jesus (Santo Niño de Cebu). It was brought to the island by Magellan and survived the battles that burned Christian homes and the fort—but not the church—to the ground. The Santo Niño, with "strange and wonderful powers," became the patron saint of Cebu. A large, lavish Taoist temple added an additional religious tradition to the mix.

We purchased fruit for dinner and boarded our next transport, a small ferry, the Bona Conchita. Sleeping quarters were below deck and had the same small bunks with bare plywood, but no padding. The sea became rough off Siquijor island. Our cabin resembled a large diesel fuel tank. The fumes played with my head! I was nauseated, and sleep would not come, so around two o'clock in the morning, I went topside. The air was blowing wildly, and cots were so tightly packed that the only place to sit was on a stairway. There I slept leaning against the handrail. After my head cleared of diesel fumes, I spent the rest of the night on my ultra-firm bed. Most folk were up, about, and noisy by 4 a.m., wrapped in the anticipation of debarking.

Day 3. Mindanao, Iligan, and Cristina Falls. We docked on Mindanao, the southernmost and second-largest Philippine island, about 6 a.m. and boarded buses for a tour of Iligan. The first stop was city hall. A tour guide introduced the coordinator, who introduced an administrative assistant, who told about the city and introduced the city engineer, who provided most of the information. It was easy to determine "RANK"! Offices and titles are highly valued.

The municipal power plant was powered, we were told, by the 832-foot-high Maria Christina Falls. The mayor said, "Truth be told, it is really only about 600 feet high." We visited a vinyl pipe factory, a Pillsbury Foods plant, and other industrial sites. The inebriating diesel fumes and lack of sleep intruded on my concentration. We finally made it to the Maria Christina Falls, which were magnificent and rescued the day.

The Iligan Adventist Hospital and School of Nursing would be our headquarters for the next few days. Some of the girls found beds with the nursing school ladies; the rest of us settled for the library floor or its large tables. Someone hauled in a mattress and placed it on the table where my backpack lay. Everyone insisted that it was my backpack, my table—hence my bed. Who was I to complain? Filipino students' respect for and deference to teachers is palpable and sincere. Sometime in the night I woke to find Andy Ng sharing my table. Andy was a graduate student, an excellent fellow, but the worst of bed partners. I wish I could have known his dreams as he was most animated; his snoring was far less sweet than his violin.

Day 4. Lacida Beach, Enrique Pool, Gastronomic Orgy. *This was "picnic day," and plans included good food, snorkeling, shell collecting, and fun with friends. We caught a jeepney to a natural waterfall cascading toward Enrique Pool. The water was cool, refreshing, and crystal clear. Snorkeling in the nearby ocean was wonderful, and we found several nice shells and collected nine Ovum ovulate, beautiful, white, cowry-like shells about the size and shape of a chicken's egg, hence the name ovum cowry. Selmon cut himself on the coral. The cuts were extensive but not serious, more like deep scratches, but they lasted several days.*

After lunch, five of us caught a jeepney to Lacida Beach. The jeepney driver ripped us off, but when confronted returned some, but not all he should have. On the way back, another driver tried the same trick. This occurs in Manila, but not with this frequency.

Dra. Guerrero, the PUC campus doctor accompanying us, had been a physician for years in Iligan and made friends in high places. She met us as we returned to the nursing school with the good news that a group of us were invited to the home of one of her physician friends for dinner. Reflection on yesterday's industrial-tour celebrities and the value of rank explained our group: the doctora, myself, and the four graduate students—no undergraduates. Selmon, a graduate student, had been invited, but we couldn't find him. Too bad! Dra. Guerrero promised a gastronomic orgy. To this point in the trip, our meals had been, at best, second-rate ship fare.

An armed guard was at the gate this evening when we were admitted to the home of our host, reflecting the concern about the increasing incidence of wealthy folk being kidnapped for ransom in Mindanao. Wanting to be appropriate, we all removed our shoes except Dra. Guerrero. We should have followed her example. During dinner, one of the servants apologetically bought our shoes to us. I deduced that the upper crust of Filipino society does not, as a custom, remove their shoes indoors as we had seen in other Filipino homes.

Dinner was on the veranda, and a chunky, well-fed lad continued to ride his bike around and around the table in spite of his mother's protest. I think he has the makings of a business tycoon. He certainly had the brass and the proper lineage for it.

The dinner was exceptional! Our regret was our limited capacity to consume more of it, and the hostess was disappointed that she could not feed us more. The water was boiled, filtered rainwater. It was a pleasant change from the brackish water in the dormitory with which we filled our bottles each morning to avoid less reliable public sources.

When we got back to the library, the unfortunates who missed our culinary bonanza were eating lanzones—fruit from heaven; but I couldn't think of eating one, and it didn't seem entirely because of the overindulgence. Nausea! Somewhere near midnight and from the depths of my breadbasket, I parted with what had been a pleasant meal. I slept fitfully until morning and was revisited by the actions of my unhappy GI tract.

Day 5. Mountain View College, Cagayan de Oro City, Bukidnon Province. *Nausea! Lynn had been nauseous all night. Andy upchucked before finding sleep after midnight. Kimmo and Lisa did not escape the curse either. We suspected that the very tasty macaroni salad or the exquisite pancit held the secret. Selmon had shared neither our pleasures nor our afflictions. He had been trying to scare up a volleyball game when Dra. Guerrero found the rest of us and spirited us off to her friend's home. He had swallowed as much seawater as anyone, and yet he was disgustingly jolly and at the top of his game.*

We boarded buses and traveled toward Cagayan de Oro. The two buses had problems, and we were very late to several appointments. Scheduled to leave Iligan by 6:30 a.m., we were still trying to find dependable buses at 11. We passed through Cagayan de Oro at 2:30 p.m. with four and a half hours of unbelievable roads between us and our destination of Mountain View College (MVC), a sister college to our PUC. It was nestled on a 760-meter plateau on the side of Mount Nebo, near Valencia, in Bukidnon. The setting was rural and relatively unspoiled, a beautiful place of birdsong; but the birds went to roost before our arrival.

We fretted most of the trip that we would be late for our cultural exchange program at MVC. Mercifully, it was test week at MVC, and our program had been canceled. Communication was primitive. MVC communicated with the outside world by shortwave radio, a luxury we did not have at PUC. Nevertheless, the welcome was warm and genuine.

Day 6. Kaamulan Festival, Malaybalay, Bukidnon Province. *A very special day! Filipinos are traditionally animistic. Their world is filled with kind and malevolent spirits and countless mythical creatures that play roles in many Filipinos' lives and frequently intrude into the worlds of Filipinos who reject animism.*[197]

More than 95 percent of the population on Mindanao holds a mix of traditional animism and Islamic practices. New beliefs layer on top of the old, and distinctions and disagreements between ethnic groups persist. This

---

[197] Chapter 27, "Easter Celebrations: People Look for Answers," provides examples.

day we were going to the Kaamulan Festival, a local religious celebration on the scale of county and state fairs celebrated each year in the States. This promised to be fascinating and memorable.

Don Christensen, MVC president, invited me to breakfast. He had a meeting that morning in Malaybalay and offered to fly Andy Ng and me to the airstrip nearby. It was a very pleasant flight. The whole area around MVC was green with trees and grassy hillsides. Homes were spaced far apart, and the streams were clear. These mountains would provide gentle hiking and much animal life. What a lovely place to live. After just fifteen minutes of flying, we were back on the ground.

Don gave us directions to the festival and encouraged us to catch a ride if one of the locals happened by, as he said it was quite a hike. Andy flagged a jeep, and we climbed aboard; I remembered the kidnap-ransom stories, but we were already committed. The three men said they were working for the highway department and were very cordial. At one point we turned in a different direction than Don had suggested and onto a narrow, little-used back road. I said we needed to get out and go the other direction. "Oh no!" was the reply. "We will pass this way. It is shorter; a nicer road." Who was I to argue with the workers? Sure enough, we turned onto a nicely paved road that led swiftly to the heart of Malaybalay. A bus filled with students had just arrived from MVC after two hours of rough roads and bus trouble. Andy and I were thankful for the fifteen-minute plane ride and the time spent with jolly highway workers!

Our group was offered a part in the festival. Somehow the officials learned we were there as cultural exchange students. The theme of the festival was "Unity and Understanding through Cultural Development." It was truly wonderful. Our part was to be guests of honor and to sit in front of all other spectators. The dancers played to us, whirling around and about and at times behind us. Costumes were exquisite. Some were very old and held a special place in the hearts of the people as they spoke of history, community, families, belief systems, and special events in years gone by.

Mrs. Timoteo C. Ocaya, wife of the governor of Bukidnon, explained to us many of the happenings. Her husband eloquently led the festival and reflected the unrest between animists, Filipino tribes, Muslims, Buddhists, Taoists, and Christians, which has long been a problem on Mindanao.

She said, "In these searching times, it is befitting in our quest for national unity to put our part of Mindanao into good order by nothing less than a massive tribal gathering. Unity leads to identity and identity to patriotism, that precious element of any national character."

One event featured an old man holding a cock under his arm and chanting. Periodically, he took the cock from under his arm and swung it horizontally in an arc of 180 degrees. He did this several times to the right and an equal number of times to the left. Mrs. Ocaya explained that when he swung it to the left, he chanted, "May we have ten times good luck." When he swung it to the right, he was chanting, "May it be ten times more difficult for the evil ones." The rest of the chant was for "protection, prosperity and favor of the gods" toward people at the festival. His movements were quick, fluid, and graceful. They belied the age registered on his face, hands, and body. There was a quick snap of hands, and the cock's head was in his right hand, the wings flapping at the old man's left side. The cock was something of a ritualized sacrifice to solemnize a ceremony of petitioning the deities.

Events moved rapidly. It was wonderful! I snapped several rolls of Ektachrome film in the two hours of festivities.[198] Andy and I were fascinated by a group of men in warrior dress. The subjects were pleased to be noticed and photographed and requested: "Photo me, Joe!" They assumed stiff, formal poses, spoiling the charm of the scene. As soon as the picture was taken, they relaxed, and the charm returned. We devised a plan: one of us made a show of taking a photo and triggered the flash. When the flash occurred, they relaxed, assumed natural postures, resumed their jovial banter and facial expressions; the other photographer, standing to the side, got the photo we wanted.

---

[198] This was 1979, several years before digital cameras were available. In January 2000, Fujifilm released the FinePix S1 Pro with 3.1 megapixels for USD 3,995. As the prices of digital SLRs began to go down, Canon offered the EOS 300D in 2003 with 6.3 megapixels for USD 999. Ektachrome and other film media are little used and little known by today's younger digital photographers.

The Kaamulan Festival has been said to be the only multiethnic festival in the Philippines. It celebrates the cultural traditions of the seven ethnic tribal groups that originally inhabited what has become the Bukidnon province. The town officials of Malaybalay organized the first Kaamulan fiesta celebration on May 15, 1974. It was officially declared the regional festival by the Developmental Council of Region 10 on September 16, 1977— just two years before we, the students of PUC, were so graciously honored and entertained.

Day 7. A Day Off! *This was a day for relaxing and recuperation. Little of interest happened, which was providential because the next day was exhausting.*

Day 8. Marawi and Tamparan on Lake Lanao. *Peter Donton was our guide. Marawi is the capital city of the province of Lanao del Sur, and Tamparan is a mysteriously intriguing little city. Both are located on the beautiful shores of Lake Lanao. People of this province are called the Maranao. A popular style of house consists of one very large room with as many as ten families living in it. The political-economic mentality of the people causes them to see innovation (change) as a continued attempt to control their lands, homes, freedoms, belief systems, and economy. Infiltration of religious practice, moral concepts, economics, psychology, or social practices is considered a component of a holy war.*

Peter worked for five years as a chaplain at the Mindanao Sanitarium and Hospital, but his new ambition was to provide health care and education to the Muslim people around Lake Lanao. Peter is not a medical doctor, but his wife is, and together they operate a small hospital in Tamparan. Sanitation is poor and disease is rampant. Peter's clinic offers free vaccinations, but the Muslim parents fear that a side effect of the immunization is that their children will become Christians some ten years later.

There are fifteen Muslin doctors in Marawi, but Peter thinks they are ineffective and mostly interested in prestige and money. A high percentage of Marawi is illiterate. Many town mayors did not read or write, but they had private armies and great political power.

"The Marawi people are fierce and troublesome," Peter said. "Why waste time on these people?" He didn't answer, and it seemed he simply wanted us to ponder his question. He has ten young volunteers working at his clinic with parental consent. None of the staff had been hurt, but there have been four attempts to kidnap Peter.

Peter was working in a Boy Scout camp the last time he was kidnapped. As he walked from the camp at the end of the day, a husky fellow fell in step with him and said: "Dr. Denton, I am your friend." Peter replied that he was happy for that. Soon they were joined by another man. When they came to a side lane, Peter said, "I will leave you now. I must take my supper."

"No," they said, "let us pass this way," and by their gentle but persistent urging, Peter sensed he had no choice. Soon they came to a shed, and he was invited to enter and take his supper with them. As he entered, he was surrounded by twenty armed guerrillas.

"Okay, friends," Peter said. "What do you want?"

"Oh, you know," one of them said, "we need money." The guerrillas said they had been watching him from one to six that afternoon. Everything had been carefully planned.

The situation remained pleasant, and Peter tried to convince them that he had very little money. This they knew, but they also knew that the Mindanao Sanitarium and Hospital where he used to work did have money and also had strong connections with US organizations. It was the United States connections the rebels were most interested in.

Peter conversed easily with them about political corruption in government and local provinces. He was close with the governor and the mayors of nearby cities, so he knew the statistics and how much money was flowing where. He emphasized the need to get rid of the cinemas and liquor, and about other things that resonate with Muslim values. His captors were fascinated, and he continued late into the night. As the night wore on and individuals dozed off and the man at the door left to urinate, Peter stepped through the door and ran. It is not clear if they dropped their guard on *purpose or not. In any event, Peter was lucky and, now, more careful.*

Peter said that fighting between rebels and Philippine governmental forces resulted in 50,000 deaths in the five years prior to our meeting on this early October morning, and the rebels sometimes kidnapped foreigners for ransom to finance their struggle. On March 9, 1979, Dr. Lloyd Van Vactor was kidnapped from his office at Dansalan College, Marawi City, and held hostage by the Abu Sayyaf, also known as the Moro Army. Van Vactor had been an educational missionary of the United Church Board for World Missionaries since 1954 and president of the college since 1968. He wrote that the men who held him said they did not want to harm him, but he was to make it clear to President Marcos that there was still dangerous unrest in the Philippines.[199] He was released after twenty days. Most of our student group were a bit shaken by Peter's stories and chose to spend the day at the sanitarium and hospital rather than visit Tamparan, Marawi, and Lake Lanao. The rest were intrigued, fascinated, and Peter was confident we would be safe.

The drive to Marawi was mostly uphill on a narrow, two-lane road. Frequently, large rocks blocked one lane of the road for ten to fifteen meters, and then the other lane was blocked. This pattern repeated four to six times so that only one car could pass through at a time, and cars could not move rapidly or make frequent lane changes. A guard station with walls 2.5 meters high, half a meter thick, was located by the side of the road at most of these speed-control areas. They were made of woven palm-leaf mats or boards on both inner and outer surfaces and braced to hold the dirt packed between them. Few of the guard stations were occupied, but those that were housed two or more government troops. These guard stations were bunkers.

As we approached Marawi, there were command posts with similar but larger bunkers and heavy artillery sitting about. There were mortars, cannons, and other equipment mounted on wheels for ease of movement. I had expected more splendor in Marawi, like ornately painted buildings

---

[199] Lindy Washburn & Lloyd Van Vactor. *My Twenty Longest Days.* New Day Publishers. (Quezon City, Philippines: New Day Publisher, 1980)

and gilded mosques, but it was a rather shabby place. No doubt reflecting the disruption of life there.

The dress of the people was typically men wearing round, pillbox-type hats of woven grasses or of white cloth with fancy or simple stitching to give form, shape, and stiffening. Some wore an oval Nehru-type hat of cloth. Women, and some men, wore a tubelike wraparound garment called a malong. They simply slip into the tube and hold it up with a hand or make a twist at the top to keep it in place. Many women in our group purchased a malong; the colors and designs were beautiful. Selman showed them how women in his homeland of Bangladesh tie a similar tube dress at the shoulder, and it looked lovely.

The large houses Peter described were easily identified in Marawi and are characteristic of well-to-do families. They were very large and typically had a porch facade with a woven bamboo railing. Several bamboo posts held them one or two meters off the ground. The kitchen, used by several families, was at the rear and typically lower than the living area. The living area is a large open expanse without partitions and houses several related families. Sheets of cloth are put in place to afford some isolation for sleeping. This arrangement is thought to enhance kinship bonds. There were smaller, single-family homes also.

As we started toward Tamparan, Peter offered a brief orientation to what we might expect. Tamparan was a tiny city with a government-owned clinic where Peter spent most of his time. He was given authority to run all government programs because no one else wanted to do it. Peter is a Christian, but his objectives are clearly health care and education; and this has garnered him respect in this Muslim community. The city has a radio program on which he gives simple health lectures, and at specified times he speaks in the mosque. He teaches from the Koran and tells his listeners, "My God is your Allah!"

The Tamparan townspeople say, "Peter must be Muslim. He and the people of his clinic are kind and do what Mohamad and the Koran would have all of us do."

When we arrived in Tamparan, Peter contacted the mayor, and soon a *group was tuning up brass and wooden drums. We were entertained with rich, festive music and dance and treated to juice and black sticky-rice cakes rich with coconut milk. Delightful! The mayor gave a speech and chastised Peter for not informing him of our coming so the town could welcome and entertain us properly.*

Peter replied that we informed no one because we wished to avoid a welcome on the way. The mayor winked his understanding and continued: "Men of Tamparan give first fight to Japan in Philippines war. Several men killed in fight," he complained, "but central government, to date, no recognize history and gift of Tamparan and her brave men. Our brave people not fight Peter and his people; we fight to protect him."

The mayor continued, "We are honored by your coming. This first time my people see people from Africa, Malaysia, Indonesia, Thailand, Finland, and other countries you come from. Many old ones saw Americans and Japanese, but few go out of Province Lanao del Sur. One man goes to Mecca ten times."

It was Peter's turn, and he said, "We stay here and serve in the clinic to prove that Muslims are not thieves, traitors, dirty, or ignorant. Christians are too often branded with a bad image. They are believed to live immoral lives, to burn homes and shoot people. Sometimes these things are true, but we are brothers. We must help each other."

A Muslim man standing near me smiled and nodded as Peter talked. One of our students began singing, "No man is an island. No man stands alone," and everyone who knew the words joined in.

The clinic was simple, very bright, clean, and comfortable. A teenage boy lying on a cot had been shot in the foot while standing in the clinic pharmacy. I did not learn the details, but it was not an accident and illustrates the ever-present violence we had been warned about. Peter told the story of a young guerrilla who was wounded and carried to the clinic. He was shot in the upper-central part of his back and in critical condition. Government troops discovered where he was and demanded that he be released to them. Peter refused, and the soldiers said they were going up to finish him off.

"You have to go over me," Peter countered. "This is a private hospital, and you have no business here." H then argued that he was here to serve all patients equally. If one of the government troops were injured, he would help and protect them as best he could. "We are all the same here," he said. "We are all patients. We all need help."

The area near Marawi was patrolled by ten battalions of government troops. There were guard stations, called civilian assistance centers, about every half kilometer. They become less plentiful near Tamparan. Ambushes of government troops are infrequent but very carefully planned.

Peter said, "We were fortunate they don't know us and didn't know we were there. Foreigners are not kidnapped at random. We will not be on their list for today!"

We walked through town to a boat dock on Lake Lanao. Women and small children peered from behind slightly opened doors. Other children and men, very young to very old, flanked us. They were shy, reserved, friendly, and very curious. Small nude boys left their diving platform, and some hurriedly pulled clothing over themselves; they wanted their pictures taken like it was the best thing that could happen. Boys in canoes and small bancas paddled toward shore to have their pictures taken also. Everyone who wished to pose with the government soldiers were even allowed to hold the guns for effect.

On the way home, we passed back through Marawi, and several students begged to stop and buy curios they wished they had gotten the first time. Peter seemed less relaxed and more focused on the trip home.

"Always stay in groups." he cautioned. "We should not stay long." Apparently, he does not enjoy the same support from the people of Marawi as he does in Tamparan.

The return trip was uneventful and swifter as we were traveling downhill and the softening evening twilight added urgency to our return to the safety of Iligan and the Mindanao Sanitarium and Hospital.

Day 9. Ozamiz City and the Monster Truck: The Performance.
We were up at 4:45 a.m., preparing for a 1 p.m. departure by boat to Ozamiz. Caleb Querol, a student from my last year's Biochemistry class,

met us at the dock in Ozamis with a decommissioned six-by-six military dump truck, to transport us to Ozamiz City. This was a very capable transport but not what we expected. But given the task of transporting our large group, it was the best choice at hand.

Caleb's Decommissioned US Military-Surplus Dump Truck. —D. Clayton ©

We were scheduled to perform in the early evening; folks gathered and were very welcoming to our group, representing India, Malaysia, Australia, China, Indonesia, Thailand, Finland, Kenya, Russia, and the United States, including a proud Hawaiian. We were excited to present songs and poems that shared our cultural values and history—the ones from the US including "Yankee Doodle," "The Red River Valley," "Swanee River," "Don't Stand under the Apple Tree with Anyone Else but Me," "Love Me Tender," and "Back Home Again." Our Filipino students also entertained with songs and tinikling.

It was 10 p.m., and we were on board, ready to sail for Dumaguete City on the island of Negros—except for the three Kenyon students and Andy Ng. The sound of anchor chains rattled on the winch, signaling an eminent departure; then came the shout: "Andy is here! They made it!" We were due in Dumaguete at 4 a.m. It had been a long day.

Day 10. Dumaguete ("City of Gentle People") and Silliman University. *The ship's galley prepared a breakfast of rice and sardines. Almost no one had an appetite for it. Two Silliman University buses arrived shortly after 7 a.m. and gave us a tour of Dumaguete. The most interesting stop was at the Taoist Temple of the Bell. A diminutive lady and her daughter showed us about and explained the rituals and accoutrements of Taoist worship.*

The altar was a massive table constructed of concrete. Each of the four table legs was a stylized elephant head with trunk and legs resting on the floor. In front of the altar were four kneeling benches. She explained that the worshipper typically takes five incense sticks, lights them, kneels on the first bench, and prays to the virgin goddess, then places an incense stick in an urn on the altar. The worshipper then moves to the second bench and prays to the god who answers prayers and places a stick in the urn. On the third bench, the worshipper prays to the god who keeps one well and places an incense stick in the urn. On the fourth bench, the god of protection and security is addressed, and another stick is placed in an urn. Each of the four gods is represented by a carved figure in a large glass case behind the altar. The fifth stick represents a personal prayer, and our guide took a sixth incense stick and prayed to the god of land, as her family are farmers.

Our guide said that each week she donates forty pesos, and each day she offers prayers. Donations are not necessary, she assured us, but it seemed, somehow, that prayers without offerings are not worth as much. She prays for her eleven family members; six are men, and one of the men is a black sheep. She prays that he will become good.

Next, we were introduced to jō sticks, a collection of thin bamboo sticks in a hollow bamboo container. A question is asked, and the container is shaken until a stick falls out. Nelson Pallasa, one of our faculty advisors, asked if our return trip would be a safe one and shook stick 86 out of the container. He was directed to a series of little cubbyholes in a cabinet and drew a paper from cubby 86, which addressed categories such as travel, family, pregnancy, health, crops, etc. Fortunately, the translation of 86 was "Excellent for all categories."

The temple was a beautiful and educational place. Taoism is fascinating, and what seemed but a brief visit had morphed into much more.

Dumaguete is an intriguing, ecumenical city. The Taoists' temple is shared with Buddhists, who have no temple of their own there. There are also a large number of Muslims. Dumaguete is known as the City of Gentle People.

The Catholic Church has been a powerful presence since shortly after the Spanish occupation in the 1570s. We saw interesting little crosses on or above the doors of many houses there; and one of our Silliman University guides explained that the crosses were individual palm fronds taken by Christian worshippers and used to decorate churches for Easter celebrations. The worshippers folded the leaves into small crosses as a symbol of Easter, a season of victory. Catholic priests bless the crosses, and the people place them on their homes to ward off evil spirits.

Several Protestant denominations are also represented in Dumaguete. The most prominent are the Presbyterians, who established Silliman University in 1901. It was the first American institution in the Philippines.

Dr. David Sutherland Hibbard, the school's first president, describes the first day the university was in session: "There were fifteen boys that first morning. The equipment consisted of four desks about ten feet long, two tables and two chairs, a few McGuffey's Readers, a few geographies, arithmetic's [sic] and ninth-grade grammars. I was President and Mrs. Hibbard was the faculty."[200]

When Ferdinand Marcos declared martial law in 1972, Silliman University was closed, and it was one of the last universities allowed to reopen. Despite harsh consequences for violating martial law, Silliman students organized secret campus rendezvous class sessions in a room called "the Catacombs" in the basement of the Silliman Church. Silliman University has made a significant contribution to Philippine higher education and was designated a "national landmark" by the National Historical Institute on June 19, 2002.

---

[200] David Sutherland Hibbard. *The First Quarter: A Brief History of Silliman Institute During its First Twenty-five Years of Existence*. (Manila: Philippine Education Co, Inc, 1926).

All too soon, we were back at the docks, boarding the MV Misamis Occidentalist, a passenger-friendly cargo ship. Twenty to thirty cows were on the dock, waiting to be loaded. A simple rope halter was placed around their heads, and they were lifted by the neck, one by one, with a powerful crane over the side of the ship and laid onto the deck, twenty feet above the dock they had been standing on. That is certainly a fast and efficient way to load cattle, but I would not have thought their neck muscles and vertebral columns would support that much weight without serious damage. Each cow weighed six to eight hundred pounds. They struggled little and showed no panic when getting up. They were usually up and moving before the next critter was laid beside them. There were also several hogs already on the deck, huddling together against a barrier separating them from the cattle. Our next stop was Manila, and the animals were headed for the meat markets.

"**Waiting to Be Loaded**" by D. Clayton: Loading cows onto the MV *Misamis Occidentalist*, Dumaguete (City of Gentle People), Negros Oriental.

Day 11. Homeward Bound. Happy Day! *I was awake with most everyone else by 4 a.m. but stayed in the sack until 6:30. I went to the sundeck to see how the cattle and hogs were doing. They had butchered two of the hogs, and two more were dead and stuffed under a lifeboat, forward on the deck. Perhaps they were salvaging hogs that had died, or* perhaps they were for dinner. Perhaps they were readying them for rapid distribution to meat markets when we docked in Manila. That didn't make sense, as the meat would be on the ship the better part of a hot, humid day without refrigeration. But I had no better explanation.

Lunch was rice, a boiled egg, and a choice between a second egg or fish. I happily opted for the fish, fried rather crisply, and it was good. Dinner was a repeat of rice, an egg, and fish. This time the fish was terrible. It was canned and very "fishy." I had a Snow Bear (a hard, methyl candy) in my backpack, and it did a good job of clearing my mouth and head.

This was a very relaxed day—beautiful islands, calm seas, and a pleasant October sun. We arrived in Manila about 8:30 p.m. The unkempt dock looked pretty good! Karen looked best. We were home! Everyone was safe; and all was well with the world.

CHAPTER 35

String Beans and Other Tales

Dale

"Everything looks different through a foreigner's camera."
—*Ramon, a Filipino Friend*

I made a good and close Filipino friend soon after my arrival in the Philippines. Ramon worked in the campus maintenance and grounds department. One day, we were sitting at the dining room table, and I showed him some photos I had just developed of marketplaces and people. He looked them over with some care and amusement, and then he said, "Everything looks different through a foreigner's camera."

I pondered Ramon's comment a long time. I guess I still ponder it. What did he mean? I think he was saying that not only were the pictures I took not the pictures he would have taken, but that the market looked different in my photos than in his own experience. For each person, their culture, language, past experiences, and biases affect how they see things and which concepts they embrace.

"The longest bridge in the world is across a gorge in this province," Ramon told me.

I had trouble believing that.

He assured me, "It's true, because if you take an egg from my province and run as fast as you can, by the time you reach the other end of the bridge, the egg would have become a chicken."

I sensed that my leg was being pulled and asked for an explanation.

"Well," he said, "in my province, the word for egg is the same word as chicken in the province that starts on the end of the bridge."

The Philippines enjoys a relatively small landmass as countries go, but it is scattered over a large ocean. There are many islands and diverse tribal units, producing many dialects; in some cases, residents of different provinces and islands have difficulty understanding one another. Another friend, Ezekial, told me an even more interesting story of dialect confusion. More interesting because it really happened.

"My friend and I could not find work in our province, and we learned that a contractor was hiring in Pampanga, on another island south of my home in Bicol. We went to inquire and—so happy—we were hired!"

He explained that they found shelter in what was little more than a hut, but the rent was very cheap, and there was a dirty kitchen where they could cook. A "dirty kitchen" is better than you might imagine. It is typically a sheltered area outside the house with a woodstove that vents to the open air. There is a roof, but a side or two may be missing or sporting large window openings without glass. The floor is usually dirt or concrete. Even many elegant Filipino homes have a dirty kitchen outside. The smoke created in a dirty kitchen gives the food a pleasant smoky flavor common to the delightful Filipino food cooked in them.[201]

I apologize for the detour, but I didn't want you to feel sorry for these boys. They had work, a house, a dirty kitchen, and they were happy.

Ezekial told me that one evening, they decided to do some serious cooking and walked down to the village market. It was a typical open-air market with vendors hawking their wares. "We were attracted to one booth in particular because of some very nice string beans and a very attractive girl. We asked the price of her beans, and the girl

---

[201] Geraldine M. Daigler. "What to Look for in a Home." In *Living in the Philippines*. (Makati, The American Chamber of Commerce of the Philippines, 1980).

became very angry; her eyes flashed and were no longer attractive. We apologized for whatever angered her and asked again about her beans. She stood up from her chair, removed a rubber flip-flop caked with mud, as this was the rainy season, and struck my friend in the face."

They decided they did not want the beans after all and turned to leave, but a man from another market stall came over and asked the young men for an explanation.

"We explained that we simply wanted to buy some string beans. The man became as agitated as the girl. Then a policeman came to see what was happening. He asked the girl what we had done. Then the policeman became angry. We did not understand what the girl or the policeman were talking about because the local Pampangan dialect was not familiar. The policeman grabbed our arms and marched us off to the barangay police station."

Ezekial explained that the boys understood little more of the problem at the police station, except that now everyone was furious, and they were obviously in big trouble. The officer at the desk asked them to explain what had happened. They went through the whole thing. They had simply asked to buy string beans. This officer became amused, laughed, and asked more questions.

"Then the strangest thing happened. This officer gave a few belly laughs, then a gut-rending roar. He spoke through giggles to the others and explained that in the Bicol Region, where we were from, '*Magagon ang autak ninnyo. Pabakal ng antak ninyo*' means, 'Your string beans are beautiful. May we buy your string beans?' But in the dialect of the province of Pampanga, '*antak*' refers to female genital organs, not beans! In the girl's dialect, we had propositioned her. Everybody burst into laughter, hooted, and embraced us! Disaster was averted, and we were celebrities of sorts."

I asked if they ever explained this to the girl or bought her beans.

"Oh, yes! Oh, yes!" Ezekial exclaimed. "We became best of friends. My companion married her. They are very happy! He is a very lucky man. He is a very, very lucky man!"

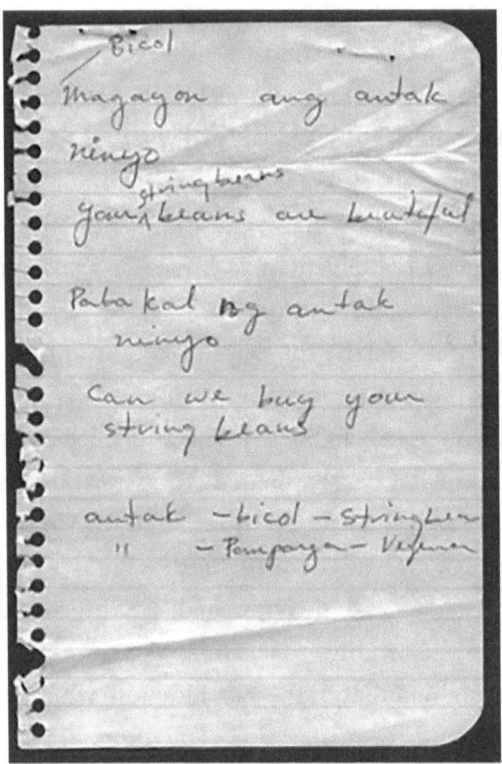

My notebook page on which Ezekial explained the different meanings of "antak" in Bicol and Pampangan.

—— CHAPTER 36 ——

Some of Our Favorite Places and Things

Karen

> *"Travel is more than the seeing of sights; it is a change that goes on, deep and permanent, in the ideas of living."*
>
> —Miriam Beard, Historian and Archivist

Hundred Islands

One holiday, three expatriate families traveled to Hundred Islands, four to five hours north of Manila near Alamitos City, Pangasinan. We arranged for a banca that accommodated eleven of us, and the two hired pilots took us anywhere we wanted to go—except for a few privately owned islands. It was glorious floating on and snorkeling in the clear water, dropping over the side to swim when we wanted, then anchoring at an island, setting up our blankets and coolers, and walking into the sea. The rock formations on the ocean floor were dramatic, covered in swaying sea grasses, unnumbered varieties of tropical fish gliding over brightly colored coral, sea anemones, starfish, and tube worms open in all their many-fingered glory. We swam to and through arches in caves on tiny islands and then to another where we could clamber up the rough coral to rest in the sun for a while. The price for the day for all of us? USD 11 (PHP 100).

A lovely reminder of that day is a large, delicate piece of still-supple black coral displayed in one of our many beautiful Filipino baskets.

When I see it, I remember a handsome, muscular teen walking toward us out of the water, holding out the coral for our delight and hoping we'd purchase it. The nonglorious part of that excursion was staying at the Last Resort—a thin-walled, many-roomed wooden structure uneasily grounded on the boardwalk to the marina.

Olongapo and the US Naval Base Subic Bay[202]

Olongapo means "head of the elder" in a local Philippine legend. Part of its fame is due to its position as the city closest to US Naval Base Subic Bay, fifty miles north of Manila.

The base was developed during the Korean War, became the home of the US Seventh Fleet, and was the largest of its kind in Asia at that time.

At the time of our visit, Olongapo was known as the largest "hostess" community for the US military, and it was fascinating to see the four-foot-ten Filipinas escorting six-foot-four American sailors to bars, restaurants, clubs, and other businesses.[203] There were also USO clubs sponsored by the USA. Here and throughout the Philippines there are Amerasian children left behind by military fathers.

The Las Pinas Bamboo Organ

Father Diego Cera built the baroque-style St. Joseph church in Las Pinas, at the edge of Manila, and was its first resident parish priest. He also worked for six years to construct the "Bamboo Organ"—902 of the 1,031 pipes are bamboo. It was completed in 1824, and we were able to stand on the elevated platform next to the organ, hear it played, and watch the hand-operated bellows. It was sent

---

[202] Subic Freeport Zone. Founded in 1607 under Spanish rule by Augustinian friars whose purpose was to Christianize the natives; the Philippines had been under Spanish rule since 1542; Americans established Subic Naval Base in 1899 and left in 1991 when the Philippine government refused to continue the lease.

[203] We were told there were 10,000 "hostesses" in Olongapo.

to be restored in Germany, returning in 1975 and honored in the International Bamboo Organ Festival a year later.[204]

Taal Volcano and Tagaytay Ridge[205]

From our Silang campus, we drove on the winding roads past coffee and pineapple plantations up to Tagaytay Ridge. The ridge outlines the original mountain, which was 18,000 feet before it erupted in 1572; it is now one-sixth that height. The original cone in the middle of Taal Lake is still active and at 300 feet above sea level is known as the lowest volcano in the world. The caldera runs north to south for fourteen miles; it is eight miles wide. In 1749, the volcano destroyed the entire Volcano Island and three nearby towns; another eruption in 1754 destroyed four more towns. An eruption in 1911 killed 1,334 people; its ashes reached Manila, fifty-five kilometers to the north. In 1965, twenty people were killed, and ash covered an area of sixty kilometers.

Twice with American guests we drove down the steep and rutted road from the ridge to the shore of Taal Lake, paid for a banca and its captain, and were taken out to the rocky area in the center. We picked our way slowly over the lava and were amazed and a little frightened at the steam escaping from below.

Tagaytay Ridge is known for many things: the markets, the resorts, the history of revolutionaries in 1896, and the Tagaytay Ridge Landing when Filipino and American guerrillas first cleared the area of Japanese forces. I wish I'd read more of the history of that area while we were there. We could have shared fantastic stories I'm just now learning."[206]

---

[204] Risa Also. "Las Piñas Bamboo Organ: A National Culture Treasure of the Philippines," https://www.tripzilla.ph/las-pinas-bamboo-organ/3985/2017TripZilla.ph (Accessed March 4, 2024).

[205] When two vowels are together, each is pronounced separately: Tagalog words usually emphasize the second syllable: *Taal* would be "tah-AHL"; Tagaytay is pronounced "tah-GUY-tie."

[206] 11tg Airborne Division Tagatay Ridge Airborne Landing Market, https://www.uswarmemorials.org/html/monument_details.php?SiteID=1397&MemID=1848 (Accessed April 4, 2024).

I drove to Tagaytay Ridge to shop in the multiple markets lining a portion of the rim and began seriously bargaining with one of the vendors. He dropped the price a bit; I persisted, and he said: "Ma'am, you see that bus over there? Japanese customers. I give you half price I give them. No more bargain."

"Salamat po!" I said, taking my bananas and happily paying the slightly reduced price.

Taal City (My Favorite Place)

When I wanted to really treat my visitors well or give myself a lovely short holiday, I drove out the front gate of the campus, up the winding road to Tagaytay Ridge, then west along the ridge road at the top of the ancient volcano's edge, stopping for a look at the South China Sea beyond and continuing south to Taal City. My favorite feature was the baroque-style Basilica of San Martin de Torres, consecrated in 1575 and only truly completed in 1878 and declared a national shrine in 1974. It was said to be the largest church in the Philippines, and we could walk up winding stairs to the top and view the entire city and beyond.

Many of the lovely handicrafts and foods found in markets around the Philippines are created in Taal City:

- Tablecloths: Tablecloths with what seem like cutouts creating a lace look are actually lightweight cloth with ten threads pulled at a time, then incorporated with more crocheting to create a look of cut holes. They come in all sizes, from doilies to tablecloths for twelve people. The one I purchased is embroidered with brightly colored fruits and vegetables.
- Dresses: Tiny baby dresses and dresses and barongs for adults, delicately embroidered.
- Panocha: Delicious! Better than peanut brittle. We watched the brown sugar liquid simmer in huge cauldrons in the

back of open-air sheds, then the peanuts were thrown in, and the stirring continued. The results were scooped up in large spoons and flung out onto wooden planks and shaped into six-inch circles, which settled and firmed up. Fabulous! Then we needed extras to take home. It's good for you since it's made of peanuts, of course.
- Sausages: We watched the ground meats mixed by hand, then stuffed into the packets of intestines and dried on multiple lines in the sun and air.

Pagsanjan Falls

We were rowed in a large canoe up the Bumbungan and Alanac Rivers by two boatmen to the dramatic 300-foot Pagsanjan Falls, passing many smaller waterfalls and fourteen rapids; the journey was exciting and quite safe. The trip upriver took two hours, and we looked from the canoe for a bit. The return downriver was complete in thirty minutes. It is also possible to walk up 500 steps and two vertical ladders from Cavinti in the Laguna province to reach the falls. Portions of Francis Ford Coppola's epic Vietnam War film, *Apocalypse Now*, was filmed on that river!

International Institute of Rural Reconstruction (IIRR)

We were invited to visit the IIRR campus by a graduate student's husband. Dave was part of the three-tiered program there focusing on people development.[207] First, a barrio was chosen, and several folks there were offered the opportunity to come to the center for a period of ten days or so, take classes, and learn how to help their own barrio learn new techniques in farming, fishing, sanitation, family clinics, and counseling. The second and third steps were happening

[207] "Yen Center: Eco Venue for Training and Conferences." IRRI https://iirr.org/about-yen-center/
(Accessed February 25, 2024).

simultaneously: we sat in a viewing gallery with two-way glass; in that gallery (with the acknowledgment of the adult students) were folk from other parts of Luzon, watching the villagers in their classes. The community leaders from other provinces were learning how to organize and conduct the classes so they could take the ideas back and put them into effect in their communities.

We met the founder and father of IIRR, Dr. James Yen, and his wife—delightful people in their eighties. Born in Sichuan Province, China, and graduating from Yale University in 1918, Dr. Yen became head of the Chinese National Association of the Mass Education Movement. He was a walking history himself, sharing stories of meetings with FDR, Truman, and Eisenhower. When the war broke out, he and his wife fled to Taiwan and played an instrumental role in its development. He came to the Philippines in 1952 and helped Filipino workers develop the Philippine Rural Reconstruction Movement; in 1960, the IIRR was established and now has outreach in Central America, Africa, India, and Thailand.

New Rice Green, Pineapple, Coffee, Mango Popsicles

"Oh, watch out!" And we'd turn to miss the rice drying on mats along over an eight-by-twelve-foot area on one side of the road—then swerve to miss the carabao cart coming at us from the other side. But such a lovely experience. We loved the "new rice green" color when rice was growing in the fields and the smiles and waves from the folk curious about what we were doing there. Delightful! I'm sure I enjoy coffee more having seen it growing in all the seasons, the beans changing from green to red to maroon, then brown. The pineapples we ate almost daily were so sweet and fresh—and cost us fifteen cents American. Along the road and in our yard, papayas grew ten to fifteen inches long; there were so many of them that we couldn't keep up, and Dale called them the "zucchinis of the Philippines." And mango season—so luscious and so prolific. Colleagues Denise and Larry made mango crepes, and we had them sliced into huge bowls to use with shortcake. We'd sometimes freeze them, then put a knife in the pit end, peel them, and eat them like popsicles. Yum!

Central Market, Divisoria, Pistang Filipino in Metro Manila

Many of our stories talk about escapades to various markets. We had a negative experience only once: It was just a few days before we left the Philippines to move back home, and we were doing last-minute shopping in the largest mall in Manila. I sat my book bag—which contained my extra shoes, water, cosmetics, and wallet—on the floor and walked to the other side of the table. I still cannot believe I did that after three years of being very cautious and wise! I soon had a sinking feeling, then panic! Sure enough, I'd lost my wallet with all my money and my one credit card: the card we had planned to use on our seven-week trip home through ten countries. We went immediately to the credit card office, stopped payment (USD 1,300 had already been charged for purchasing groceries, which we did not have to pay), and got a temporary new credit card. Oh, yes, and we had to borrow money from friends to have funds to leave the country.

Personal Day Off

Now is a good time for a confession. There are often mixed feelings involved when living in a foreign land. I'd always wanted to travel, and I wanted to be of service, to contribute to something bigger than myself. We chose to go to the Philippines to help in the area of education.

In order to help, it's necessary to listen and learn, to try to understand the people, their customs, and values, to immerse oneself in the culture, to give what one has to share. I did that most of the time—and then there were times I just wanted to be on my own, away from responsibilities and fitting into a role. Sometimes I would drive the Blue Bomb into Manila and disappear for a day, to be on my own—to eat in a nice restaurant, take in the culture, and treat myself. It was good for me.

My bubble burst just a bit when, after waxing effusive about an especially lovely meal—iced tea, dessert, the works—a friend said, "You know how we see huge blocks of ice on the street being broken into smaller chunks? That's where the ice in your iced tea came from."

White Sands Resort

Muted men's voices outside our nipa hut woke me the first morning. And I realized they were getting closer. The voices seemed excited. I looked out to see eight or ten men calling to each other. I admit I was frightened. Why? I'd had no reason to be fearful of anyone; it was just a woman's need to be alert.

The voices didn't come any nearer to our dwelling, so I got up, went to the door, opened it a bit, and there was the most beautiful sight. The men were forming a circle, beginning at the beach and moving out into the bay, each holding the edge of a huge net. Further out, a small boat assisted. We were hearing and watching a morning ritual: bringing in the fish. The night before, we'd had a memorable time swimming and floating in the warm water with a full moon above. During our daytime swim, we saw lionfish—one doesn't want to touch them—and many, many other colorful fish species. Then I swam away from a small shark. A lovely time and one of our best memories of the beauty of the Philippines.

Update 2020s

—"**Subic Bay was one of the largest US naval facilities in the world before it shut down in 1992** after the Senate of the Philippines terminated the base's agreement with Washington."[208] Negotiations continue between the Philippines, the US, and Australia as each eye the activities of China in the South China Sea.[209]

---

[208] "Subic Bay is one of the largest US naval facilities in the world…" Google (Accessed February 25, 2024)
[209] "US Navy Eyes Return to Subic Bay in a Commercial Deal," One News, May 12, 2020, https://www.adas.ph/2020/05/12/us-navy eyes-return-to-subic-bay-in-a-commercial-deal (Accessed February 25, 2024).

CHAPTER 37

They Came Ashore Right Here

Karen

> *"I recognized the spontaneous movement of a free people to resist the physical and spiritual shackles with which the enemy sought to bind them. It was a poignant moment."*
>
> —General Douglas MacArthur

World War II was still alive in the minds of the Filipinos we met. Many friends had terrible memories of the Japanese occupation and accompanying atrocities. Some memories were wonderful due to the final triumph.

Dra. Rasa invited us to spend a weekend in her family home in Anilao, Batangas, at the southwest edge of the largest island, Luzon. She used her home there for weekend getaways, and it was where she planned to retire. The home was elegantly simple, with native woods for floors and furniture and native grasses and palms for the roof. She loved her time back home. Still, there were difficult memories. She told us she remembers a day when the fathers, husbands, and sons were ordered to go to the cathedral for a special announcement from the Japanese occupying the area.

It was 1945, and the US 8th Army had landed "virtually unopposed" to support the liberation of Manila. The Japanese were nervous. The men were ordered inside the church, and the women and children were ordered to the grounds of the elementary school.

The Japanese locked the doors of the church and set it on fire. It's said not one person escaped that fire; the estimated number is 3,000 men who died. That was one way the Japanese controlled the rebellion of the population.[210] Then the Japanese were distracted by American airplanes flying low, and the women and children were able to escape.

"There were many widows in that town," Dra. Rasa mused. She said of the Japanese, "They behaved like Germans. They threw babies up in the air, and when the little ones came down squealing, the Japanese soldiers caught them on their upturned bayonets."

There was no way for her or for us to accept that unspeakably cruel behavior; during that time, folks lived in fear. Dra. Rasa wanted to share another significant memory with us: "Our father was afraid for our family, and he took us to his friend's atis plantation along the shore of Batangas Bay. Our whole family lived there with him for two years. We call him *Bapa*, or Uncle. Would you like to see that place and meet him?"

"Yes, very much so," I said. "What an honor that would be to meet him. And I'd love to see his plantation. My favorite Filipino fruit is the atis. I love it!"

Dra. Rasa drove us to the rim of the beautiful and infamous Batangas Bay.[211] We had picnicked and snorkeled there previously on a holiday weekend with Filipino friends. On the west side of the bay is Calumpan Peninsula and the town of Anilao. That city is thought to have originated scuba-diving in the Philippines; turtles, rays, snapper, and the blue-ringed octopus can be seen there.[212] Batangas is known for beautiful resorts and as the cattle-trading and atis capital of the Philippines.

---

[210] "When the Japanese Massacred Bauan's Male Population in 1945" https://www.batangashistory.date/2019/09/when-the-japanese-massacred-bauans-male-population-in-1945.html (Accessed February 25, 2024)

[211] There are fascinating accounts of American sabotage and diversion efforts in this area in *The War in the Pacific: Triumph in the Philippines* by Robert Ross Smith and "The Pacific War: Philippines Campaign, Phase 2" by C. Peter Chen. See bibliography.

[212] "Discover the birthplace of diving in the Philippines." www.underwaterasia.info/philippines/anilao-diving (Accessed February 25, 2024)

Dra. Rasa parked her car near the rim, and we walked along an irregular dirt path high above the bay, then followed the trail down to the water's edge. That walk and the beach held many memories for her, and she was uncharacteristically quiet. We reached a small home surrounded by fencing near the beach. An old man saw us and walked over to greet her. She introduced us to her bapa and told him a little about our family and that Dale worked with her. He responded with a smile and gestured for us to sit with him there on the beach. He did not speak English but understood a little, and while we squatted on the sand, Dra. Rasa told the story. Bapa quietly made comments to her now and then; mostly, he kept his head down, the smile gone, working some driftwood with his hands.

"Bapa has made his living from this atis (or sugar apple) plantation for many, many years. During two years of the occupation, we lived with his family. He also grew rice; and his rice and his fruit kept us all alive. One day, we became so frightened! We all saw a Japanese ship come into this beautiful bay.[213] Bapa had told us of hiding places when we first arrived; now he told us to go there. We hid—just there," she said, indicating a spot behind the rough fence with her typical chin gesture.

"We could see just a bit through the bushes. We watched the ship. It was covered with trees and grass; they were trying to make it look like an island. We were so afraid. Then we heard planes, and we could see US ARMY written on the planes. Eight planes, and they just kept circling up to the mountains, then flew straight for the ship, firing at it. Holes ripped open in several places. It received a lot of damage. The men on the ship were yelling, and we saw some of them jump into the sea. The planes would circle up and back again—*zoom, zoom, zoom!* They went around maybe ten times. Oh! It was wonderful!"

---

[213] This was likely at the time of the "reconquest" of the Philippines by the 6th and 8th Army operations on Luzon and would have occurred in 1944 or 1945. See Smith, Robert Ross in bibliography.

Dra. Rasa believed most of the men on the ship died there, "but there were two Japanese who made it to the shore."

"Both of them were badly injured," she continued, "and when the people saw them—we had come down to the shore when we saw that the Japanese ship didn't fight back—the people were so angry. You know what they did?"

Bapa looked out into the bay, remembering with his sad eyes.

At this critical moment in the story, Dale and I looked at each other, wondering if Jeff and Kimberly should hear this. Our children were enthralled, quiet, listening intently. We agreed with our eyes that it was important for them to hear it out.

Dra. Rasa continued, standing up now, pointing and using dramatic arm gestures: "We could see they were hurt, but they kept walking toward us. They were about to come ashore. We children were peeking between the boards of that fence over there. If they got to shore, we knew that Bapa—and the rest of us—would be made to help them. It was the war. They were occupying us, and we'd been afraid for so long, heard such terrible stories. The people tied big stones to the legs of those men and threw them back into deeper water! I'll never forget that."

Bapa closed his eyes as he listened to Dra. Rasa. Then he opened them and pointed toward the bay and said in Tagalog: "They came ashore right there."

Dra. Rasa sat back down near us and was quiet. Then she said, "He knew—we all knew—that it was wrong to kill those men. They had families, too. They were doing what they had to do. It was wrong. Still, Bapa saved many lives that day; he saved my family. I love this man," and she put her hand on Bapa's arm, looking at him tenderly.

The dear old gentleman met her gaze and again looked down and was quiet. My family will never forget this day, that story—and the contrasts: the beauty of the place and the horrors we heard. And Bapa and Dra. Rasa's father planted rice and bananas and fed their families to supplement his atis crops. At the end of the story, he climbed trees behind his small home to find the best, sweetest, largest atis for all of us.

The motion picture *MacArthur* (1977) has since given us a more comprehensive picture of what was happening in the Philippines during the war. It is also good to somewhat understand what it must have been like when the Americans fought the Spanish and then left the Philippines. Japanese occupation followed; thousands became part of the Bataan Death March, including Ferdinand Marcos, and others became guerrillas. There were 100,000 slaughtered in Manila alone in December 1941, immediately after Pearl Harbor was bombed, then more in Baesa. Then the planes move north to Baguio. In many places Americans were targeted and killed or imprisoned in inhumane conditions. The Philippines would likely not have survived to become free had it not been for the guerrillas—Americans and Filipinos—preparing the way for MacArthur's return to Leyte.

We have also learned much about the guerrilla activity of Filipinos and Americans working together to protect and defend the Filipino people from Ira Wolfert's excellent *An American Guerrilla in the Philippines.*

An American teacher at PUC in the 1940s was one of the prisoners; he visited our campus and told us of his rescue by Americans on landing crafts in Laguna de Bay, not far from Batangas and our home in Silang, Cavite. His story appears in the next chapter.

These stories helped us understand why so many people smile and wave the "V for victory" sign at Americans or call any White man "Joe." Americans stayed or came back after the war for many reasons: to train at Clark Air Base and Naval Base Subic Bay, to create elementary schools, to teach at universities, to help with land development, to create NGOs to help Filipinos; one taught folks how to make soap out of coconut oil again instead of buying soap from China in the sari-sari stores.[214]

Now Japanese tourists visit the Philippines. We were moved

---

[214] This process is described in the appendices.

when we visited the memorial to the kamikaze pilots of WWII on Clark's Mabalacat Airfield.[215] The area was small and stark, cement and plain. On a flat area in front of the monument, Japanese tourists leave small gifts, tied in bamboo or silk, to honor the pilots who took off from the airfield at the memorial site to purposely fly into US battleships. The ships they hit were severely damaged, and sometimes they sank; the kamikaze pilots almost always died. They knew this was their fate and volunteered for those missions, some of which occurred in the Batangas Bay area.

The term "kamikaze" is from "God" or "divinity" (*kami*) and "wind" (*kaze*). Author Anu Garg notes in *A.Word.A.Day*, "In Japanese folklore, kamikaze was the divine wind that destroyed a Mongol invasion fleet under Kublai Khan. Today Westerners use that word for persons who behave recklessly and/or in a self-destructive manner."[216] Filipinos have vivid memories of the Japanese involvement in their land. They love to sell their crafts, fruits, and vegetables to the Japanese visitors but often do not bargain as much with them as with other tourists; the memory of the war is still raw for both.

Many challenges have faced the Philippines throughout its history of invasions by the Dutch, Indonesian Muslims, the Chinese, the Spanish, the Japanese, and the United States. José Rizal's 1912 memoir and call to arms, *The Social Cancer*, was also surprisingly helpful. His book provides a background on living under the colonization of the Spanish for 330 years. Some persons who cooperated with the Spanish were highly favored and rewarded. But many Filipinos were seen as "Indians" and worthy of contempt. One touching description by Rizal of this phenomenon stays in my mind. He was embarrassed to describe his exquisite Filipino home, which was an unusual sight given the way most Filipinos were demeaned

---

[215] The kamakazi movement is described in *The Divine Wind*, by Rikihei Inoguchi and Tadashi Nakajima, two Japanese pilots of the former Imperial Japanese Navy, and American Roger Pineau. See the bibliography.
[216] Anu Garg. "A.Word.A.Day with Anu Garg: Kamikaze," https://wordsmith.org/words/kamikaze.html (Accessed February 25, 2024)

by their Spanish occupiers: "We mortals in general are very much like tortoises: we are esteemed and classified according to our shells; in this and still other respects the mortals of the Philippines in particular also resemble tortoises."

Update 2020s

—**Batangas:** The Philippine Statistics Authority (PSA) officially released the Provincial Product Accounts (PPA) report for the Calabarzon region (Cavite, Laguna, Batangas, Rizal, Quezon) covering the period from 2018 to 2021. The report shows that the economy of the Batangas province increased and grew by 12.5 percent in the year 2021 from a negative 14.4 percent rate in the year 2020.

After the series of trials and the effects of the eruption of the Taal Volcano, the crisis caused by the COVID-19 pandemic, and the passing typhoons, the province showed the "fastest economic recovery" in the entire Calabarzon region.[217]

---

[217] Jojo C. Magsombol. "Batangas 'fastest' in economic recovery—PSA" https://journalnews.com.ph/batangas-fastest-in-economic-recovery-psa/ (Accessed February 25, 2024).

CHAPTER 38

Richard Hammill, POW

Dale

"We buried our wedding silver at the base of a tree near the barracks."

—Richard Hammill, POW, Religion Professor PUC, President of Andrews University

Richard Hammill and four other members of the accreditation committee were settled uncomfortably with me in the Blue Bomb. It was definitely an overloaded midsize automobile. At the intersection, I headed into the swollen stream of jeepneys, buses, motorcycles, and other conveyances, observing the cardinal rule of the Philippine highway: "If your fender is in front, you have right-of-way."

"Whoa!" bellowed Winton Beavon after a particularly frightening almost-encounter: "We almost made the back page!"

The "back page" is an alias for the obituary section of *The Review*, a monthly publication that shares news, inspirational stories, awards, retirements, and deaths in the worldwide SDA monthly journal. We were in a jolly, excited mood. It was like taking a group of early teens on a junior-camp outing. In actual fact, this was a bunch of SDA's "first-string executives" come to our campus to evaluate the collegiate program—and, of course, me. They represented the evaluating organization that controlled a significant source of our budget.

Richard Hammill was the president of my alma mater, Andrews University, and a scholar and a gentleman. This was a good group: Leslie Harding was dean of the Far East Seminary, Molly Harding was a gracious and accomplished lady, Malcolm Maxwell was a valued colleague of mine at WWC, and Winton Beavon was a friend, a professor, and an administrator. Just now, we were all bouncing about, violating one another's personal space, and having a great time en route to the University of the Philippines (UPLB) campus in Calabarzon, one of eight UP campuses.

Dr. Hammill had spent several years as a teacher, first in Viet Nam and then in the Philippines in the 1940s. When the Japanese invaded, many Americans were sent with expatriates to various POW camps, along with government officials and other sorts who were suspected of troublemaking. Dr. Hammill, his wife, and his son were sent to the Japanese internment camp in Los Baños, then called the UP College of Agriculture and Forestry. It was a sixty-acre site between Laguna de Bay and the foothills of Mount Makiling.

At our entrance of what is now UPLB, we asked two campus policemen about the route to Baker Memorial Hall. Built in 1927, it was about all that remained of the old campus as Dr. Hammill remembered it. We explored the grounds, and Hammill told his story; it was riveting. The scribbled notes I made form the basis of this story.

◆ ◆ ◆

Baker Hall was an old gymnasium on the UPSB campus used to house a large group of prisoners, mostly those without families. Hammill was held with his wife and preschool-age son in a barracks for about a year. The Japanese were not cruel and did not mistreat prisoners as long as they cooperated. He showed us where the camp's perimeter fences had been placed and one spot where a man had cut through the fence and escaped.

Unfortunately, that fellow got soused with native liquor and, in a fit of bad judgment, returned to camp. He retraced his steps, singing and expressing his joy in the new freedom he had achieved. The guards watched him struggle back through the hole he had made in the fence and then shot and injured him as he stood up. About an hour later, they executed him where he lay and garnered a new level of respect and cooperation from the other inmates.

Dr. Hammill said the food had consisted mainly of soft corn gruel in the morning and rice with a few greens in the afternoon. Both quality and quantity deteriorated as the internment wore on; in the last few weeks, Hammill dropped to 111 pounds.

Not long after the Hammills were moved to Los Baños, their small son came home with his pockets bulging with corn. A Japanese soldier had taken a liking to the lad, perhaps remembering his own son, and loaded his pockets with corn from the kitchen as a gesture of kindness and friendship. Hammill planted some of the corn, and the rich soil yielded him good returns.

Every morning, the prisoners were lined up for roll call, standing four wide per column to facilitate counting. They were standing in this formation in the early dawn of Friday, February 23, 1945, just as the sky began to lighten. Suddenly, the shadowy forms of planes and the hum of their engines filled the northern sky. The dark shapes dropped steadily toward the prisoners standing in rigid formation outside the gymnasium. Parachutes popped open as the planes headed toward the horizon, and the Japanese guards began shooting. It had dawned on the captives and captors alike that the Americans were intent on more than strafing that day. Filipino guerrillas firing from carefully chosen positions taken during the night near each sentry post silenced the Japanese guns.

Whether by plan or miscalculation of the winds, the paratroopers drifted past the camp and fought their way down the mountain and into the internment camp. The liberation took everyone by surprise.

Housed in barracks on the first rise of the foothills near the camp's southern edge, Hammill ran there to view the battle as GIs fought down the slopes. One GI would move downhill to draw fire while the others watched and eliminated the snipers. The strategy was to run a few yards, fall flat, and fire in the direction of the enemy. It is difficult to believe there were only three military casualties and none of the 1,122 POWs were lost.[218] The mother of Hammill's friend Blake died three days later of malnutrition, old age, and stress.

The success of the attack was due to the cooperation between American paratroopers and Filipino guerrillas who covered their advance on the camp. Two or three days before the GIs dropped in, there had been increased heavy strafing from gun emplacements around the periphery of the campus and back in the hills. Hammill said there must have been heavy Japanese artillery in the foothills of Mount Makiling above and to the south of camp, because the US planes had concentrated their bombing and strafing in that area during those earlier sorties.[219]

As the GIs and Filipino guerrillas moved down the mountain, amphibious tanks advanced from the large freshwater lake, Laguna de Bay, to the north. The tanks rolled into camp, firing on Japanese troops, and American soldiers instructed the prisoners to get aboard. By the time Hammill and his family reached a tank, it was full, but the soldiers promised to return. Hammill pleaded for them to take his wife and child. A GI grasped his wife's arm and pulled her and the child into the tank. Hammill jumped onto the sloping front of another tank and clung there as it rumbled for the lake shore. Japanese snipers in the coconut palms kept firing on the tanks, and the tanks returned their fire.

As rounds struck the tank, Hammill and a paratrooper who jumped on beside him dove over the rim of the tank's turret and

---

[218] Numbers from *World War II* magazine, published online, June 12, 2006. This article also reported the rescue of 3,500 POWs at the Santo Tomas University in Manila and 500 POWs from Cabanatuan prison.

[219] Mount Makiling is the highest peak at 1,090 meters and is also one of eighteen sites identified for preservation of biodiversity in the Philippines.

onto the mass of prisoners huddled there. By this point he had only a tattered pair of shorts, the remnants of trousers. He recalled the burning sting of the hot brass cartridge casings as the tank's machine gun spat them from its magazine onto his bare legs and torso. As they moved out into the lake, the firing lessened, and the sounds behind them seemed far away in both time and space. Everything had happened so rapidly that the reality and consequences of the events took a while to register.

The remaining American troops gathered the last of the POWs and moved them to the vicinity of the gymnasium. From there they marched to the lake and waited for the return of the amphibious tanks. Some of the POWs recall seeing an American flag on the tanks rolling out of the lake to free them, whereas Hammill told us, "You couldn't see the lake from the camp." That seemed to be the case as we looked at it that day.

No doubt both versions are true. Prisoners in the first group saw their rescuers dropping from the sky, and the second group saw only the amphibious tanks returning from delivering the first group. Hammill's name is recorded with the rescued in Bruce Henderson's book *Rescue at Los Baños*.[220]

Hammill told us: "We buried our wedding silver at the base of a tree in front of the barracks." There was, of course, no time or motivation to unearth it in the early dawn of February 23, 1945. Thirty-four years later, Richard Hammill told us he wondered if he might be able to locate the tree and retrieve what most likely had become useless scraps of metal; but precious reminders of love, marriage, adventures, and memories grow dim with time.

The site was covered with banana trees, and houses now dotted the hillside where none had been. The older trees had been cut. As the tanks rumbled into Laguna de Bay, Hammill had turned and observed the barracks engulfed in flames, so he knew that landmark

---

[220] Bruce Henderson, *Rescue at Los Baños* (New York: Harper Collins, 2015). P. 312 Hammill's name.

would be missing. The prospect of locating anything now was indeed remote, and Hammill suddenly seemed the least interested of anyone in our group.

He became remarkably calm as we walked about the campus. We listened as he recalled events in low, even tones. He seemed eager to return to the PUC campus before sunset, to leave both the joy of memory and the sadness behind him. This day had taken a visible toll on his energies. As we left the Los Baños campus, he expressed a desire to visit the lake, to see if he could determine where the tanks came from and where they had entered the lake. When we reached the beach, which was but a few minutes' drive, Richard Hammill was fast asleep, and we turned without speaking, homeward.

Lunch had been many hours before. In my mind, I was already at the banquet awaiting us back on campus—smelling the pancit and lumpia and tasting pineapple fresh and ripe from the field; but Richard Hammill was back on the Los Baños campus and far away, in another time.[221]

Update 2020s

—UPLB is said to house "one of the highest concentrations of scientists and researchers in the Philippines. They provide technical expertise in agriculture, forestry, natural resources management and conservation, biotechnology, environmental management, and related areas to farmers, entrepreneurs, and investors; government, non-government, and civil and people's organizations; and to R&D agencies and the country's policy makers."[222]

---

[221] Richard L. Hammill, *Pilgrimage: Memoirs of an Adventist Administrator*. Berrien Springs, MI: Andrews University Press, 1992.
[222] University of the Philippines, Los Baños, "Research Centers," https://uplb.edu.ph/research-and-extension (Accessed February 25, 2024).

CHAPTER 39

The Farmer's Daughter in Makati

Dale

"Very young, very clean. Very nice and pretty."
—Iti, the One Who Finds Customers

I finished shopping and sat on a bench to watch the night-lights work their magic as evening claimed Makati—one of sixteen cities that make up Metro Manila. It has the highest concentration of multinational corporations, major banks, department stores, elegant shops, and foreign embassies in the Philippines. It is also the cultural and entertainment hub of Metro Manila. With daylight, Makati becomes the Filipino world of business; and with the setting sun, it becomes a strange mix of high and low culture.

The night was young, shades of red and purple intermingled in the sky, and a soft breeze swept off Manila Bay. An attractive young woman stopped and faced me. She was slender, sensual, and strange.

"Maybe you like me?" she asked.

I was speechless.

"Maybe you like me?" she asked again; and then, "Or maybe you like girl better?"

Ah! So, that is the strangeness. This young person is male. I managed a feeble, dismissive hand motion, and he was gone. The encounter was unsettling.

Suddenly, he returned. "I have very nice girl. Very young, very clean, very nice and pretty. I leave her with you." And he or she was gone again, but the girl remained. She was young, skinny, and ill at ease. I was at a loss for words.

"Are you hungry?" I asked. That was a strange thing to say. I was not collected, but in retrospect, she looked like she had missed a few meals.

"Yes," she said. "Yes, I am."

We found a table in a festive little café, and she ordered a large bowl of steaming pancit. Her name was Aveline. She said she was seventeen. She was a farmer's daughter, which added humor to the situation. She told me that her father had a couple of small rice fields that supported the very basic needs of his family, but there was little money left for extras, like education.

Her dream was to be a nurse. Like many young adults, she left home to get a job and make her way in the city. And like many others, she could not find a job that would feed her, house her, and pay her tuition; so she shared a room with several girls in similar situations. The crossdresser who had solicited for her was a "friend," her pimp, living in the same building.

Why, I asked myself, *am I sitting here, talking to this very young prostitute?*

Patrons of our little café seemed more than casually interested in our table. She was a young Filipina wearing her working clothes—a light, revealing blouse and a very short skirt. I was forty-something and Western. We each finished our steaming bowls of pancit, and I suggested that we sit and talk outside. She was a bright, interesting girl who had recently reset some boundaries, and she intrigued me.

"You like go hotel now?" she asked.

"No," I replied.

"Oh! Room free!" she said. "Juan rent room, and friends share turns."

"Let's just talk," I said. "I have a nice wife and a family."

"Oh, I understand," she said, face averted. "I have good family, too."

We sat on the steps of an upscale boutique, closed for the evening, and compared our lives with openness and honesty, uncritically. It seems so surreal now. We talked about her family, rice farming, education, nursing, and about prostitution. Mostly, we talked about nursing. She was searching for the courage to enroll in an A and P course in Manila if she could only save up the money.

"The Anatomy and Physiology textbook is your owner's manual," I said.

That was a good description for my students in the US, but the humor was lost on Aveline by the time I explained about new cars and the importance of "owner's manuals" for their operation, care, maintenance, and longevity. This farmer's daughter had limited exposure to owner's manuals.

Suddenly, Nelia walked past; she was the proprietor of a camera shop I visited frequently to buy film, photo paper, and developing chemicals. She stopped, squinted, and said, "Dr. Clayton?" and quickly moved on. That was not the friendly, cordial greeting she gave me in her camera shop. I hoped for a chance to explain the real situation to her.

That was embarrassing! The evening had lost some of its charm, and I offered to take Aveline home. She accepted, eager to avoid the interest she would generate on late-night public transportation. We drove for some time through darkened, unfamiliar streets, and finally, at last, she said, "Stop here!" The street narrowed ahead, and tenements seemed to close in.

"Stay here," she said. "Make lights to shine down there until I wave; and then I'll be home and safe."

She slipped from the car, closed the door softly, and ran swiftly down the center of the street, leaping potholes, waving as she dissolved into darkness. I had made and lost a friend in less than two hours.

The night was dark, and I was not sure where I was. I tried to recall the many turns and to calculate a resultant angle for retracing my path. I soon found a familiar landmark and was on my way back to Silang, Cavite, to the campus and home.

Three days later, a guard from the campus gate knocked on our door and said someone at the gate wanted to see me. I drove with him back down to the gate, and there she was, prim, proper, and pretty in a denim skirt and a cotton blouse—the farmer's daughter. She had a companion, a girlfriend. Filipinas seldom travel or move freely about public places without a companion, and as is the custom, they rarely let go of the other's hand.

I invited Aveline and her friend back to our home and introduced her to Karen. I noted that they were eager to hold her hands, which I interpreted as a gesture saying, "Whatever else you think you know about us, we are your friend."

Karen put them at ease, happy to meet the girl I'd told her about who wanted to be a nurse. She told them nursing was an interesting and exciting profession, a helping profession—similar to Karen's plans of being a social worker. And so it went. We encouraged the girls to pursue their education. We had a snack and we talked. I showed the girls a bit of the campus, and they were eager to catch a jeepney to be back in Manila before dark.

I think back on the events of that night in Makati and recount our disparate circumstances and the respect we found for each other. I was a college professor, and she was a hooker dreaming of being a nurse. I never saw her again, but I think of her and hope she became the nurse she desired to be. I wish I could know how she is today.

Friendships depend on mutual respect and boundaries. When you know your own values and respect another's boundaries, even though they differ from your own, you can form friendships and memories that last a lifetime.

As Karen met Filipinas and accompanied them in downtown Manila or to the local markets, she enjoyed their presence and tried not to be embarrassed by their incessant hand-holding; hand-holding is a symbol of sincere friendship and security in an insecure environment, and she came to appreciate this practice. Filipino men who are close friends also hold hands when they walk together, with the same inference as a Westerner's handshake, without the connotation of homosexuality, simply friendship. Those who may be LGBTQA would not be noticed as the hand-holding behavior is accepted.

Updates 2020s

—**Don't call them prostitutes:** some of the preferred terms are GRO (guest relations officer) or dancers. It's easy to find websites or newspapers advertising available women with names like Cherry Blossoms. Many want to marry and come to the US. And there are "sex tours." Forced labor in the sex industry occurs and is estimated at 99 percent female, of which 21 percent are children. Makati is one of six cities where sex tourism is advertised in the media. But don't call them prostitutes; many will say they are Filipino bar girls.[223]

—**Many women are "victims"** due to poverty and social change, and there is now a movement to "rescue" rather than prosecute girls, according to a research article in the *Journal of Tourism and Hospitality in 2019*.[224] In 2022, research on violence against women in the Philippines revealed that one in four have experienced gender-based violence, and 41 percent don't seek help.[225] The Philippine Commission on Women also reported on these issues.[226]

---

[223] "Filipina Bar Girls—Don't Call Them Prostitutes!!" Accessed February 25, 2024, https://www.philippinesluv.com/2017/07/25/filipina-bar-girls-dont-call-prostitutes.
[224] Mark Gabriel Wagan Aguilar, *Journal of Tourism & Hospitality*, 2019, Volume 8, Issue 5, Tourism and Hospitality Management Programs. South Mansfield College, Philippines.
[225] "Violence against women in the Philippines: barriers to seeking help," www.ncbi.nlm.nih.gov.
[226] "Violence Against Women – Philippine Commission on Women," pcw.gov.ph (Accessed February 24, 2024).

CHAPTER 40

Where Do We Go Next?

Karen

"Texas! It's Like a Whole Other Country"
—The Official Motto of Texas in 1981

Living in the Philippines was a marvelous adventure—challenging and satisfying. Near the end of three years, it was time to return to the US to be with Jeff again and with my mom, who was bravely battling advancing cancer. Our friends on campus knew that Dale had opportunities at several universities in the States, in Tennessee, Massachusetts, and Texas. We had a "reveal party." When friends arrived and saw the centerpiece on our dining room table—a Philippine-made straw cowboy hat placed brim down, the curved surfaces filled with corn chips—they realized we were moving to Texas!

The school where Dale would teach and where I would finish my bachelor's degree was in the tiny town of Keene, about forty miles southwest of Fort Worth and fifty miles southwest of Dallas. Since 1893, the founders of Southwestern Adventist University (SWAU) have focused on "providing students with a holistic education that centers on Christ and equips them to positively impact society."[227] SWAU has been identified as one of the most diverse colleges in Texas; its motto is "Knowledge, Faith, Service." There was an Adventist elementary school for Kimberly and an Adventist high

---

[227] Southwestern Adventist University, https://swau.edu/.

school for Jeff. Dale was asked to be the chairperson of the Biology Department. Hopefully there would be time for research, too.

We had left much of our furniture and belongings in Walla Walla when we left for the Philippines. Three friends each had one of our horses. Friends can be amazing. Here's part of a letter we wrote to Larry and Linda, who were managing our fourplex:

> *Dear Friends,*
>
> *Well, it is time to start thinking about rounding up our worldly goods and start them on their trek toward Keene, Texas. The first time we could go to WW would be Thanksgiving Vacation; we'll get the horses then. In the meantime, we need the furniture and stored boxes, so we will ask the movers from the Texas Conference to take them to Keene. I'll write to the seven families who each have some of our things; however, we need to ask you to coordinate things there on the day the movers arrive. And I hope we can schedule them to be in WW before you leave for the summer at the biology station on Fidalgo Island for the summer. Thanks so much! Hugs . . .*

On the Silang campus, we sold our piano, our drapes, and some other household items. We had purchased sala sets, two Imelda chairs, and two collections—lovely baskets and fish traps of many shapes and sizes.[228] All of them would be shipped to us. At least they were lightweight.

The night before we left, Dale and his friend Pat had packed all night, and I crashed at one point and stopped for a nap on a bare bed. Around 5 a.m. we heard music. Twenty students and faculty were at our front door, singing. We invited them inside, and they sang some more, and we shared sad goodbyes. As we rode down the winding

---

[228] Living room/family room furniture sets of wicker and rattan, including a sofa, two chairs, two end tables, a coffee table, and a large footstool—about $400 US, but "very dear" in Filipino money.

road in the lovely school van for the last time, people came to the windows to say farewell.

I told Dr. Roda, "I don't want to go."

He said, "We don't want you to."

Becky went to the airport with us. It was very hard to part from her. We vowed to keep in touch.

Updates 2020s

—**Beauty remains throughout the Philippines; and there are important social issues:** limited access to good education, high poverty, overpopulation, imbalances in the food supply, high unemployment, corruption, sexploitation of women and children, climate change, air pollution, deforestation, water pollution, destructive fishing, management of solid waste, and rising sea levels, to name a few.

—I read daily updates about events in the Philippines through Maria Resa's *Rappler* online newspaper. Becky and I keep in touch via Facebook and texting. And two of Dale's students from Silang in 1981 are friends in the US—one in Washington and one in California. We also have a Filipina friend in New Zealand. It feels good to be in touch with our Filipino home.

CHAPTER 41

Reverse Culture Shock

Karen

"We had to move to another part of the country, to a completely unfamiliar place—Texas—whose culture was different from our previous home in Washington State. So technically, we weren't even home."

—*Kimberly*

The day we left the Philippines, June 11, was our twentieth wedding anniversary, and Hong Kong was our first stop on a fabulous trip home. *We'll have a wonderful anniversary dinner at a great restaurant,* I thought. We could have; however, we knew it was a strange time for Kimberly, with the pushmi-pullyu feelings of again moving someplace where she did not know one soul. She had been waiting a long time for a McDonald's, so that's where we ate our anniversary dinner. It's a great memory, especially for Kimberly.

We could write another book about our trip home. Suffice it to say that we traveled for seven weeks and enjoyed several days in each of these countries in this order: Hong Kong, India, Egypt, Israel, Italy, France, Switzerland, Lichtenstein, Belgium, Germany, and England. We flew between some countries and also rode the storied Indian trains from New Delhi to Agra and back, then Mumbai (Bombay) to Poona, where we visited an Adventist college. Back to Mumbai, then we flew to Giza and drove to the pyramids and the underground burial sites of the royal elephants, flew Nefertiti Air (truly!), to Israel, including an unforgettable Friday evening at the Wailing Wall. We flew to Rome, spent a week, then flew to Cologne, spent a weekend, then drove to Geneva, devoured fondue in the town of Gruyère, slept in the lower level of a *Zimmer* (bed-and-breakfast) right next door to the stable, visited the home of Dürer in Belgium, explored Windsor Castle, Madam Tussaud's Wax Museum, and a small portion of the British Museum of Natural History, and ate fish-and-chips with vinegar in London. Seven weeks. All fabulous!

Jeff greeted us at the Detroit airport and handed me a Hershey's bar. Also greeting us were Dale's two brothers' families, Dale's parents from Alpena, and mine from Battle Creek. It was a great reunion. Jeff had been living with his uncle Wayne, aunt Jan, and cousins Jeff and Rod, attending school there for six months prior to our return. Our Detroit family—Gary and Pat, Wayne and Jan—created excellent feasts. And it was great to see our parents, who had visited us in the Philippines and still were concerned for our health and safety. Interestingly, no one seemed to want to hear stories about the Philippines and the three years that changed our lives. No one asked anything specific about any of it. Amazing to us and disappointing.

Dale, Kimberly, and I had been in London just a couple of weeks before the wedding of Charles and Diana, so the first night and morning back in the States, Kimberly and I stayed up to watch the ceremony. I'd watched Charles's mother's coronation with my mother in 1953 in Battle Creek.

As I was saying goodbye to my parents in Gary and Pat's backyard, Dad said, "Your mom is having surgery next week; more problems with the trochanter [the head of the femur]—weakness, possibly more cancer."

And I replied: "Well, then I guess I'm not going to Texas right away." A few days later, I was in Battle Creek for the surgery and stayed for part of her recovery.

Dale drove the kids to Texas in our new "woody" Plymouth

station wagon. Our shipment had gotten there before them and had been unloaded in the house we were renting from the school, so they had the job of unpacking. Dale needed to get started in his new position as chair of the Biology Department and get the kids enrolled in their schools. It was a crazy time; busy for them and emotional and surreal for me, being at my folks' instead of Texas. Still, it was a precious time with my mother.

When I did go to Texas, I took the train from Battle Creek, Michigan, traveling two quiet, relaxing days. I wanted and needed time to myself before another significant beginning.

My arrival gave me several jolts: I disembarked Amtrak in Cleburne, and we ate at K-Bobs, a huge, Western-themed restaurant accompanied by country music. Not my favorite, but *Hey, this is yet another cultural experience. Enjoy it.* Then we went shopping at K-Mart, and I had a hard time understanding the overhead Blue Light Special announcement: "Ah'll sev'n, git yer twelve-pack a' pipper talls."[229] And everyone said, "Y'all have a good day now!" And they ran everything over a little plastic screen on the counter. It beeped, and the price showed up on a screen. Amazing! And the choices! I'd not seen these many things or these many brands in, ah, yes, three years. It felt like too much all at once.

While shopping on aisle 7, the kids let slip that our mare had foaled; we had a little filly! What a delight. But, oops, that mare was in Washington State, and we were in the great state of Texas. And school has already started.

Then Jeff shared, to the frustration of his father: "Dad's going to Washington to get Trinket and her new baby."

"You don't think you're going to do that without me, do you? How exciting. How do we go? The kids are in school. Where do we get a truck and horse trailer?"

"Slow down," Dale cautioned. "Let's talk about this when we get home. I've got it all worked out."

---

[229] Translation: "Aisle seven, get your twelve-pack of paper towels."

When we got home, somewhat settled for the evening, I found out he did have it all figured out: "School has started, but LeRoy has a truck and four-horse trailer; we can get the classes for Friday covered. We'll leave Thursday night after labs and drive twenty-four-seven to Aileen's in Wyoming to get Zeke, then to Walla Walla to pick up Trinket and the baby, and be back here for classes on Monday."

"What? Who's LeRoy? And I'll help drive."

"LeRoy is one of the biology teachers, and his wife, Jeannie, is going, and she can drive, too. We'll put sleeping bags in the bed of the truck. It's September; it's warm. It'll be fine!"

It worked out and was quite an adventure. Our kids stayed with LeRoy and Jeannie's kids in their house, with a graduate student overseeing things. This was a running start to our new life. And it didn't slow down. Dale had talked with the chair of the social work department at Southwestern and had all the necessary information for me to register and begin classes as soon as we returned from retrieving our horses. She told him I'd finish my degree in eighteen months—and I did.

The kids' school was going well. But I was adamant that they not look like MKs (missionary kids). I asked Kimberly if things were all right at school. Did she have the right socks—did we need to buy something?

She said, "Mom, I'm fine. If the kids don't like what I wear, tough!"

She did seem to be fitting in. She had several friends already, one a young Filipina who had never been to the Philippines and loved learning about it from Kimberly. Jeff's new Filipino friend Ivan also had never been to the Philippines!

Kimberly describes returning home: "Reverse culture shock or repatriation is just as challenging, if not more, than going to live in another country. Even after only three years, it was sometimes difficult to fit back into my own society where I had missed many American events and history. To top it off, there hadn't been a job for my father at Walla Walla College. That meant we had to move to another part of the country, to a completely unfamiliar place—Texas—whose culture was different from our previous home in Washington State. So technically, we weren't even home. I imagine the adjustment was even harder for Jeff, being a teen and in high school. I was only on the cusp of teenhood, still in primary school."

Jeff wore jeans and shirts and was not one to worry about clothes anyway. However, he decided he wanted to attend public high school in Cleburne, so we helped him make that shift.

Texas was indeed "like a whole other country," with accents we got used to but never adopted and friendly, openhearted people—some very loud and opinionated. In our work environments we found colleagues we admired, and we enjoyed school and work.

Interestingly, folks often started conversations with "So, you've been in the Philippines. Did you like it?" We were ready to describe in great detail some of the things we saw and learned and enjoyed, but no one asked more than that. Only once were we asked to give a presentation about our life, work, and school in the Philippines. I wanted to do that more and share our experiences; I was so disappointed. We had a life-altering experience, and I was eager to give folks insight into travel and mission work. No one seemed interested.

Then I learned that the young woman teaching English as a second language had lived in Thailand for a few months. I went to meet her. Poking my head into her office, I said: "I hear you've worked in Thailand."

She nodded in the affirmative, and I said, "Can I just talk to you for a few minutes?" She welcomed me, and I learned she'd lived in half a dozen countries and traveled to more. I had found a sympatico friend; we have stayed close and travel together now and then.

Dale was extremely busy. There were only three biology teachers in that accredited university, preparing biologists and premeds, predental students, nurses, occupational therapists, physical therapists, and teachers. After three years he chose *not* to be the chair.

Each summer, the three professors took twelve students on a

three-week study tour to Florida, Hawaii, or Costa Rica/Honduras. Sounds like a vacation, but it was hard work with a lot of responsibility involved. Still, it was quite wonderful. Some summers, he also taught at the WWC marine biology station where we'd spent eight summers before our trek to the Philippines. The kids and I went with him unless I was working full-time. Then Jeff went into the Marines and missed those summers.

One year after we arrived in Keene, we moved from the rental to a small, five-acre farm just outside town. We had three horses with foals every other year or so. This was a busy time. Our parents visited frequently, and Dale's sister and her family moved to Arlington, about twenty miles from our home.

My mother's cancer continued to progress, and she spent three months living with us, enjoying our family and our minifarm with the horses and chickens. It was a precious time, with all of us helping to make her life the best it could be. She enjoyed our little farm with the horses, wild turkeys, and a dog, and especially loved the bantam rooster and hens and chicks, which came to her guest room door. She was there to see me graduate from college at age forty-three! Three weeks later, Dad came down and drove her back to Michigan. I continued as an intake worker at a residential treatment center for adolescents. In another three weeks, my mom became much worse. I flew home and was there for the last few hours before she died. I couldn't imagine a world without my mother in it.

I began graduate work in sociology at the University of Texas at Arlington. My first course was Cross-cultural Communication, and I pursued my interest in belief systems, taking Anthropology of Religion, Sociology of Religion, Folklore and Mythology, and Stratification—all informed by my experiences in the Philippines and our other travels. Just before I graduated, I was asked to prepare a presentation about our mission experience for the SDA Union Conference employees. Listening to my radio on my way to that presentation, I heard that Corazon Aquino had won the snap election called by Marcos in 1986. A huge change was in store for that country.

Our travel experiences, my social work, and my sociology education gave me a good background for doing medical social work at John Peter Smith Hospital and the Episcopal hospitals in Fort Worth—Huguley Hospice and the American Cancer Society—and for teaching cross-cultural training and sociology part-time.

Jeff attended high school, then joined the Marines! Talk about seeing the world. When he came back from the Marines, he began his career in construction, doing roofs, framing, installing glass, and eventually was responsible for major projects like building two post offices valued at four million each, supervised by him from the ground up. His career is very successful; he married and has two stepchildren. Now his partner, Tammy, and he live in Stockton, California, and enjoy a good relationship with his son, Ryan, and five grandchildren—all in Texas.

Kimberly finished high school in Keene, then attended Southwestern, majoring in communication. There she met and married Terry Johnson, also an MK and a world traveler, and they've lived in Texas, Michigan, and New Zealand and are now living in Australia. They have two children, Kyrstin and Alec.

Dale accepted a position teaching at La Sierra University (LSU) in Riverside, California, after twenty years at SWAU. I retired, sort of: I spent a third of my time "nesting," a third teaching in the adult degree program, and more than a third volunteering as education curator at the Stahl Center Museum of Culture on the LSU campus. We both loved it there; we met more delightful people and worked with folk we knew in the Philippines!

Dale retired from LSU in 2006, and we moved to the place of our dreams: Whidbey Island, halfway between Seattle, Washington, and Vancouver, British Columbia, and ten miles from the biology station on Fidalgo where Dale taught in the 1970s. He has continued his research in a home lab he built and published some of his work. We write, read, walk, and enjoy this wonderful place. Eight other families we worked with at WWU have retired near us. It's a great retirement. We get together whenever we can with Jeff and Tammy; and we enjoy traveling to see Kimberly's family in Australia.

We have traveled extensively and created sixteen homes—six of which we've owned. Every two weeks we meet with our Oak Harbor Writers' Group. We enjoy an amazing life.

——POSTSCRIPT——

Karen

"We were blessed to live in the Philippines."

The need for learning and critical thinking continues everywhere. Our purpose in working in the Philippines was to help increase young people's opportunities through good education, preparing them to be productive in a challenging world.

Being invited to go to the RP, making all the decisions required (leaving our home, jobs, friends, not knowing where we would come back to), traveling to places I thought I would only read about, experiencing the new country and culture, and learning about myself have been vastly influential. We tried to do things correctly and to be helpful. We wanted it to be a wonderful experience for our children and help them understand more about the peoples of the world. We made precious friends we treasure to this day.

We did many things right. We listened and learned and read. We worked hard at doing our jobs well. The few simple words we know help us meet and interact with Filipinos in our other travels and in the US. Filipinas especially love to hear our greeting in Tagalog; one young woman said: "Oh, you make the hair on my arms stand up. You know my language."

I replied: "Conte lang" (Little bit only). And we both smiled, understanding, and I told her I lived in her country and loved it and the people there.

We did not learn Tagalog. We wish we had; we would have learned so much more about the country and its people, communicated more meaningfully, and they would have known we cared enough to do our best. We did learn many helpful words and phrases and tried to pronounce words correctly. For example, when there are two vowels together, both are pronounced (in what we hear as a Spanish accent). Most Americans over fifteen have heard of Bataan because of the Bataan Death March in WWII. We notice that most American pronounce Bataan as "Bah-THAN." We know it should be pronounced "Bah-tah-AHN." It makes a difference—to Filipinos and to me, now.

After we came home, I was attending an international meeting in New Orleans and recognized three lovely Filipinas walking toward me. I'd known them only casually, and it had been a while since I'd spoken Tagalog. Quickly I searched the "Philippines" file in my brain so I could greet them appropriately.

"Magandang hapon," I said with a friendly smile. (Good afternoon.)

"The word you used means 'Japanese,'" responded one of the women, obviously offended.

So I learned the pronunciation "hah-POON" means "afternoon." I had put the emphasis on the first syllable, "HAH-poon," and had used it incorrectly for three years in the Philippines. My mistake was not a simple mispronunciation but truly an insult! I felt so bad, and they walked past me before I could explain, defend, or do whatever it took to make things right.

As I look at what we've chosen to share in these stories, I wonder what we've left out—or should have. We want to honor our host country and be honest about what we saw and felt and learned. We wish we had been more sensitive to how hard it was for Jeffrey and tried harder to find creative ways to make it a better experience for him. But both Kimberly and Jeffrey are now thriving.

One of my gifts is organizing events. It would have been helpful to everyone on the national and expatriate faculty and staff at Philippine Union College if I'd created a monthly occasion to learn from the Filipinos about the history and culture of the Philippines while sharing our own backgrounds, interests, talents, and reasons for working outside our home countries. Perhaps I'll approach the Mission Institute folk with that idea and help make it happen!

POSTSCRIPT AND DISCLAIMER

Dale

Written while still in the Philippines:

I am going home soon, and the world I will live in is different from this one; but always, afterwards, wherever I go, the joy and the sorrow, the courage and the generosity I have known these last three years in the Republic of the Philippines will make my life richer and more beautiful.

Palm trees lashed by typhoons, interesting mixtures of vegetables and meats steaming on rice, tropical sunsets flaming over the bright-green rice paddies, and junglefowl crowing in the dawn's first glow made life more remarkable. But it is the Filipino people who made me laugh with joy and catch my breath in admiration and wonder. They have made my heart beat a little faster. They have made me glad I came to these islands in the sea and experienced the shock and joys of their culture.

I accepted an official call to teach at Philippine Union College. "The call" is terminology for an invitation from our church headquarters to go to a new assignment. It invokes the concept of divine intervention and carries something of an obligation to answer; I have no real quarrel with that. Strange happenings occur all the time, and some are very often blessings. How can one account for that? One possibility is the positive influence of positive expectations. Another possibility is the wrestling with the positive and negative aspects of choices and choosing positive outcomes. An interesting possibility involves mystery. That smacks of adventure, and I like it!

Not everyone answers the call. Dr. Ernest Booth—my teacher, mentor, and friend—told me that when he received a call to teach biology at a high school in Honolulu, he was thrilled and felt blessed, thanking his lucky stars and divine intervention for the prospect of sunshine and sandy beaches. The academic administration in Hawaii was equally excited. It seemed a match made in heaven, and then the other shoe dropped. Booth learned he would also teach chemistry. He was a field biologist, a naturalist. He loved all creatures great and small. He knew their innermost secrets, where they lived, and how they reared their babies; but the role of chemistry in their lives was not a part of his fascination or his expertise. Sadly, he concluded, this particular call was not a divine intervention in his life.

The Philippines was and is considered a mission field by many religious organizations, including the SDA church. In fact, I received an official card for my wallet identifying me as a missionary. My parents were proud. I was amused.

I value my Christian heritage and enjoyed my friendships and colleagues at WWC. I had a lighter teaching load there and colleagues I enjoyed and admired. It was the best job I had ever had. So, why would I do this?

Adventure! I had never had an opportunity like this to look forward to with hope or backward to with memories. I could regale my grandkids with it. I loved teaching, and I would be teaching at PUC. But it was not the teaching that motivated me; it was learning—learning about the lives of people so like myself and yet so different. Karen, a sociologist, says, "People are more alike than they are different." True. But to a scientist, differences are more intriguing. Vive la différence! How could I not have done this?

BIBLIOGRAPHY AND SUGGESTED READING

Alamar-Phoenix. *Reading for Learning and Living Series.* Quezon City, Philippines Phoenix Publishing House, 1973.

Ancheta, Celedonio A. *Triumph in the Philippines: 1941-46 – The Saga of Bataan and Corregidor.* Volume III of a Series: Historic Documents of World War II in the Philippines, Vol. III. Manila, Philippines: Navotas Press, 1978.

Blair, E. H. and J. A. Robertson, Ed. *The Philippine Islands, 1493-1898.* 55 Volumes. Cleveland, Ohio: The Arthur H. Clark Company.

Bundor, Pedro and Jaime Alipit Montero. *Democracy among the Mountaineers.* Manila: New Day Publishers, 1973.

Burnham, Gracia with Dean Merrill. *In the Presence of My Enemies.* Wheaton, Ill: Tyndale House Publisher, Inc, 2003.

Chen, C. Peter. "The Pacific War: Philippines Campaign, Phase 2." World War II Database.

Clayton, Karen J. "Ritual Practices Surrounding the Celebration of Easter in the Philippines." Paper; SW Commission on Religious Studies, Dallas, TX. March 16, 1991.

Clark, Nick, Editor. *"Practical Information: Education in the Philippines," World Education Service, World Education News & Reviews,* Vol. 22, Issue 1, 2009.

Climo, Shirley. *Tuko and the Birds.* New York: Henry Holt and Co., 2008.

Colin-Jones, Graham and Yvonne. *The Essential Guide to Customs & Culture/Culture Smart!* Philippines. London: Kuperard/Imprint of Bravo, Ltd., 2008.

Clymer, Kenton J. "Not so benevolent assimilation: The Philippine-American War." *JSTOR Reviews in American History.* Vol. 11, No. 4 (Dec., 1983), pp. 547-552. Review of Stuart Creighton Miller's Book (see below).

Dickerson, Roy E. *Distribution of Life in the Philippines.* Manila: Bureau of Science, 1928.

Evangelista, Patricia Maria Susanah Chanto. *Some People Need Killing: A Memoir of Murder in My Country.* New York: Random House, an imprint of and Division Penguin Random House, LLC, 2023.

Flavier, Juan. *Doctor to the Barrios.* Quezon City: New Day Publishers, 1970.

Fontanilla, Conrado. "Philippines Political and Social Issues." 2013. https://hubpages.com@conradofontanilla.

Francia, Luis HJ. *A History of the Philippines from Indio Bravos to Filipinos.* New York: The Overlook Press, 2014.

Frost, Robert. *Selected Poems.* New York: Gramercy, 1992.

Frankl, Viktor. *Man's Search for Meaning.* Boston: Beacon Press. 2006 Edition.

Galicano, Leoncia T. and Josefina T. Tameta. *Philippine Legends.* Manila: Bookman, Inc. 1971.

Gray, Luke. *Three-Ring Circus: Life as a Missionary Kid in a Family of 11.* Bloomington, IN: Westbow Press, 2014.

Henderson, Bruce. *Rescue at Los Baños*. New York: Harper Collins Pub., 2015; p. 12.

Hoefer, Hans Johannes, et al. *Philippines: Insight Guide*. Hong Kong: APA Productions, 1980.

Hollinger, Carol. *Mai Pen Rai Means Never Mind. An American housewife's honest love affair with the irrepressible people of Thailand*. Tokyo: Asia Books, John Weatherhill, Inc., 1965.

Holmes, C. Raymond. *Boiled Rice and Gluten*. Self-published, 1972.

Huke, Robert E. *Shadows on the Land: An economic geography of the Philippines* (including Philippine legends). Manila: The Bookmark, Inc., 1963

Rikihei Inoguchi, Rikihei and Tadashi Nakajima with Roger Pineau. *The Divine Wind: Japan's Kamikaze Force in World War II*. Annapolis, Md.: US Naval Institute, 1958.

International Institute of Rural Reconstruction (IIRR); https://www.iirr.org.

Iyer, Pico: *The Global Soul: Jet Lag, Shopping Malls, and the Search for Home*. New York: Vintage Departures, 2000.

Johnston, Madelyn Steel. "Early Withdrawal of Overseas Workers." MA Thesis, Andrews University, Berrien Springs, MI.

Jones, Gregg. *Honor in the Dust: Theodore Roosevelt, War in the Philippines, and the Rise and Fall of America's Imperial Dream*. New York: New American Library, 2013.

Karnow, Stanley. *In Our Image: America's Empire in the Philippines*. New York: Ballantine Books, 1989

Lawson, Don. *Marcos and the Philippines*. New York: Franklin Watts, 1984.

Lopez de Araneta, Victoria. *On Wings of Destiny: A Novel on the Life and Times of Jose Rizal.* Manila: White Cross Inc., 1940

Mallari, I. V. *Vanishing Dawn: Essays on the vanishing customs of the Christian Filipinos.* Manila: Philippine Education Company, 1954.

Marcos, Imelda Romualdez. *The Compassionate Society and Other Selected Speeches.* Intramuros, Manila: National Media Production Center, 1973.

Maynard, Mary McKay. *My Faraway Home: An American Family's WWII Tale of Adventure and Survival in the Jungles of the Philippines.* Builford, CT: The Lyons Press. 2002.

Miller, Stuart Creighton. *Benevolent Assimilation: The American Conquest of the Philippines, 1899-1903.* New Haven: Yale University Press, 1982. Cf. Clymer.

National Historical Institute. *Aguinaldo Shrine.* Manila, 1978.

Newman, Yasmin. *7000 Islands: A food portrait of the Philippines.* Melbourne: Hardie Grant Books,

O'Brian, Thomas J. M. M. "Philippine collision course." In Maryknoll/Philippines. Volume 78, Number 2. Also, multiple articles re belief and oppression. Maryknoll, NY, Leo J. Summer, MM, Feb. 1984.

Quezon, Manuel L., III "Punditry. Politics. History. Commentary." https://www.quezon.ph.

ANC/YouTube: Coverage of the Marcos Inaugural, June 20, 2022; more coverage. https://www.quezon.ph/w2022/06/30/anc-coverage-of-the-marcos-inaugural/

Papineau, Aristide J. G. *Papineau's Guide to the Philippines.* Pedrosa, Carmen N. Sept. 20, 2009. "Paternalist racism." In: *The Philippine Star*, 1976.

Pazzanese, Christina. "How an authoritarian wields social media." Cambridge, Mass., *The Harvard Gazette* Nov. 18, 2021.

Perez, D. P. *Valente Villegas, Ph.D. Carabao Husbandry.* Manila: Oriental Commercial Company, Inc., 1932.

Ramos, Maximo. *Tales of Long Ago.* Manila: Alip and Sons, Inc., 1952.

Ressa, Maria. Winner, Nobel Peace Prize 2021. *How to Stand Up to a Dictator: The Fight for Our Future.* Foreword by Amal Clooney. New York, NY: Harper/Collins Pub., 2022.

Rizal, Jose. *The Social Cancer (Noli me Tángere).* Philippine Education Company/Open Library, 1887. Translated-published independently Charles E. Derbyshire, 1912.

Romulo, Liana. *Filipino Celebrations: A Treasury of Feasts and Festivals.* Tuttle Publishing, 2012.

Santos, Alfonso P. *Heroic Tales: For Character Building in the Changing community.* Diliman, Quezon City: Allied Printing & Binding Co., Inc., 1970.

Santos, Alfonso P. *Heroic Virgins and Women Patriots: Female Patriotism during the Japanese Occupation*, Diliman, Quezon City: University of the Philippines Press, 1977.

Schraff, Anne E. *Philippines.* Minneapolis: Learner Publishing Group, 2009.

Sharp, Larry W. *Missions Disrupted: From Professional Missionaries to Missional Professionals.* Peabody, MA: Hendrickson Publishers; 2023.

Simons, Lewis M. *To Tell the Truth: My Life as a Foreign Correspondent.* Lanham, MD: Roman and Littlefield Publishers, 2022. Pulitzer

Prize for International Reporting in 1986, "for exposing the billions that the Marcos family looted from the Philippines."

Simmons, Deborah Tuhy. *Stepping Off the Edge: Faith and Fiasco in a Philippine Mission.* Columbia, MO: Compass Flower Press, 2017.

Smith, Robert Ross. "War in the Pacific, Triumph in the Philippines." Dept. of the Army, 1963.

Spence, Hartzell. *Marcos of the Philippines: A Biography.* Cleveland: The World Publishing Company, 1969.

Takaki, Ronald. *Strangers from a Different Shore: A History of Asian Americans.* Boston: Little, Brown and Company, 1989.

Vagara, Maria Isabel Sanchez, *Little People, Big Dreams: Corazon Aquino.* Beverly, MA: Frances Lincoln Children's Books/Imprint of The Quarto Group. 2020.

Velasquez-Ty, Catalina and Tomas P. Garcia. *Your Town and Mine.* Manila: Ginn and Company. Social Studies Series, Grade Three, 1965.

Torrevillas-Suarez, D and Juliano D. Raymundo. *Vendors of Manila.* Quezon City, RP: New Day Publishers, 1972.

Tupas, R., B. P. Lorente, "A 'New' Politics of Language in the Philippines: Bilingual Education and the New Challenge of the Mother Tongues." In: Sercombe, P., Tupas, R. (eds)

Language, Education and Nation-building. Palgrave Studies in Minority Languages and Communities. London: Palgrave McMillan, 2014.

US Department of Education, *Country Studies/RP.* Wash, DC: Library of Congress.

Velasquez-Ty, Catalina and Tomas P. Garcia. *Your Town and Mine.* (Social Studies Series, Grade 3). Manila: Ginn and Co., 1965.

Villa, Jose Garcia. *Footnote to Youth.* Short Stories, 1933. https://lifewithkrich.com/footnote-to-youth/.

Villamin, Araceli M. and Ceferina G. Juarison. *Our Province.* Alemar-Phoenix Reading for Learning and Living Series. Quezon City, Manila, RP.: Phoenix Press, Inc., (Written in line with the Educational Development Decree of 1972; Grade Three), 1973.

Welch, Bob. *Resolve: From the Jungles of WWII Bataan, the Epic Story of a Soldier, a Flag, and a Promise Kept.* New York: Berkley CA, 2012.

Wolfert, Ira. *American Guerrilla in the Philippines.* New York: Simon & Schuster, 1945.

Wolff, Leon. *Little Brown Brother: How the United States purchased and pacified the Philippine Islands at the century's turn.* New York: History Book Club, 1960.

Woolsey, Raymond H. *Flying Doctor of the Philippines.* Hagerstown, MD: Review & Herald Pub. Assn., 1972.

World War II Magazine; see especially June 12, 2006. Available for purchase online ebay.

Young, Hon. James Rankin with J. Hampton Moore. *History of our War with Spain Including Battles on Sea and Land, etc.* Washington: Office of the Librarian of Congress, 1898.

Yuso, Alfred. *Insight Guides: The Philippines.* APA Productions, 1980. *Aguinaldo Shrine.* Manila: National Historical Institute Publication. No date given.

APPENDIXES

A. Demographics: Republic of the Philippines
B. How to Learn about Another Culture: Karen
C. The Challenges of Cross-Cultural Work: Karen
D. A Historical Timeline of the Philippines and SDA Work
E. A Brief History of the Philippines: Dale
F. NGO—Bringing Folks Back to Their Roots: Karen

APPENDIX A

Demographics: The Republic of the Philippines

The Philippines Is an Archipelago

In 1978, there were 7,107 known islands, of which 466 were inhabited.

As of 2022, there are 7,641 known islands, of which 2,000 are inhabited.

Location

The Philippine Sea is to the east.

Taiwan is to the north across the Luzon Strait.

Borneo is southwest across the Sulu Sea.

Viet Nam is west across the South China Sea.

The islands of Indonesia are across the Celebes Sea and to the south.

Volcanoes

The Philippines is part of the Ring of Fire, which comprises 200 active volcanoes. Taal Volcano in the Cavite province is the lowest volcano in the world at 300 feet above sea level.

Main Crops of the Philippines

Cereals: rice, maize, sorghum, corn.

Legumes: mung bean, peanut, cowpea, soybean.

Vegetables: tomato, eggplant, lima bean, bottle gourd, sweet and hot pepper.

Root Crops: cassava, sweet potato, taro.

Fiber Crops: cotton, manila hemp.

Tobacco

Plantation crops: coconut (second-largest producer in the world), cacao, coffee, sugarcane, banana, mango, pineapple, cassava, palay, rubber.

Leading crop: sugarcane comprises 23.46 percent of all crops.

APPENDIX B

How to Learn about Another Culture

1. **Learn the appropriate words.** "Hello." "Thank you." "Where is the CR (bathroom)?" etc.
2. **Read.** Read histories, poems, scriptures, nonfiction, fiction.
3. **Study the country's gestures.** Learn what is positive and helpful and what is offensive.
4. **Keep a notebook of helpful printed information.** Maps, basic words and translations, etc.
5. **Listen.** Be respectful and learn the correct pronunciation (e.g. Bataan: Bah-TAH-an).
6. **Watch videos, YouTube, films.** For example, *American Guerrilla in the Philippines*.
7. **Ask questions.** Do so kindly and cautiously.
8. **Use public transportation.** Do so with guidance from a local and with caution.
9. **Protect your valuables.** Don't wear expensive or glitzy jewelry.
10. **Take pictures.** First, learn what subjects or behavior may be offensive or sacred and should not be filmed.
11. **Study maps.** Carry a printed map with you. Even better, carry a map in English (for you) and one in the local language (for those you want to ask for assistance). Also, use your phone maps.
12. **Develop a personal friend within one of the nationals.** It will benefit you both.
13. Read about the religions/belief systems.
14. Find out about traditional healing methods.
15. Get plenty of rest.
16. Keep a journal every day at first.

17. Be kind to yourself and others.
18. **Find specific details in Country Studies.** https://countrystudies/rp: history, geography, climate, the society, the economy, and government.

APPENDIX C

The Challenges of Cross-Cultural Work

Karen

Cross-cultural Communication was the first course in my master of arts in sociology program at the University of Texas. My research paper for that course was on cross-cultural training. It was clear that persons *not* well prepared for overseas work often cost their employers and themselves financially and in work not completed or done poorly.

The emotional cost to employees can be great without suitable preparation. Continued stress makes work harder, one's professional career can be damaged, and failure is always a possibility. Madelyn Johnson of Andrews University conducted a study on SDA foreign service employees, reporting that persons who attended the training institute offered by Andrews University were less likely to return early from their assignment.

There are also costs to the nationals (in-country residents), who may lose valuable time and resources when projects are handled unprofessionally or not concluded satisfactorily. Misunderstandings and inappropriate behavior cause difficulties and damage relationships between workers, organizations, and sometimes governments.

Huge monetary costs are involved in placing foreign service workers in their assigned country: travel and shipping, housing, salary, medical insurance, subsidized private schooling, and supervision. Industries that place personnel overseas estimate setup costs alone to be between $50,000 and $200,000 for a family of four (figures from 1980). There is no way of assigning a monetary value to the emotional and personal losses when persons are unsuccessful in their assignment. Some researchers believe it is better not to fill a position than to send someone who does not have the qualities necessary for an effective overseas worker.

Children learn much about their world when traveling or living in another country. Parents must consider the effects overseas assignments may have on their children. Very young children are much more likely to fit into a new environment; middle and high school children are at a disadvantage when appropriate schooling and extracurricular activities are not available or they are required to live in another country a large part of each year for their education. There are many successes, but some participants have been damaged by the experience.

Some mission organizations require a visit to the prospective mission site to experience a bit of the weather, the food, the people—the culture of the place. Regions Beyond Missionary Union requires several weeks. Luke Gray, an American who grew up in a large missionary family in the Philippines, reports his parents spent five and half weeks in their prospective worksite in the Philippines, then were asked for a four-year commitment. After those first four years, missioners are regularly given a yearlong furlough in their home country; then another four-year commitment is expected as they continue their service. See *Three-Ring Circus: Life as a Missionary Kid in a Family of 11*, Westbow Press, a Division of Zondervan, 2014.

———APPENDIX D———

Historical Timelines:
Events in the History of the Philippines, Filipinos in the US, and SDA Activities in the Philippines

According to the Nations Online Project, "the Philippine archipelago was populated at least 30,000 years ago by migrations from the Indonesian archipelago and elsewhere."[230] At that time, Filipinos lived in houses, cultivated crops, fished, and developed tribal customs, and laws placed women on an equal footing with men in many respects; monogamy was practiced. There were oral and written languages.

900 BCE: The Laguna Copperplate Inscription, a document written in the Philippine language, was created.[231]

1500: Immigrations by Chinese traders and Indo-Malays.

1521: European traders came, led by Ferdinand Magellan, on their search for the Spice Islands, claiming to have "discovered" the islands. They named them the Archipelago of San Lazaro. They brought the concept of the infant Christ, called Santo Niño, and urged Christianity on the residents; Magellan was killed by a poison arrow on Mactan, now the Philippines.

---

[230] Nations Online, www.nationsonline.org/oneworld/History/Philippines/ (accessed Mar. 20, 2021).
[231] Antoon Postma. "The Laguna Coper-Plate Inscription: Text and Commentary." https://www.jstor.org/stable/42633308 (Accessed March 4, 2024).

1542: Ruy Lopez de Villalobos led a Spanish expedition and claimed the islands for Spain, naming them "Philippines" after Prince Philip, later King Philip II of Spain.

1565: Beginning of Spanish rule: Spaniard Miguel Lopez de Legazpi interacted with native chiefs, treaties were established, and missionaries arrived, encouraging "the growth of literature, art, science ... industry ... schools and colleges ... libraries and museums, and [setting] up printing presses ... hospitals, asylums, and orphanages." Spain's biggest legacy to the Philippines is Roman Catholicism. The Spaniards ruled the Philippines for 300 years.[232]

1587: The first Asians to arrive in California, US, worked on the Manila galleon trade.

1756–63: The British East India Company captured Manila and occupied that area for a time.

1763: Filipino immigrants called Manilamen settled in Louisiana and were said to have revolutionized part of the shrimping industry.

1800s: The Filipino elite class, the Ilustrados ("enlightened ones"), fostered nationalism.

1886: Physician, scientist, scholar, and writer José Rizal and his books awakened many; he lived in exile and wrote significant books about the possibilities for Filipinos.

1896: Nationalist leader Rizal was executed for his role in the Katipunan rebellion.

---

[232] Janrex Karl Raelagmao, "Summary of Spanish Colonization in the Philippines," March 10, 2016. WordPress.com.

1897: New republic was established by General Emilio Aguinaldo in Bulacan.

1898 (April): The Spanish fleet was defeated under Commodore Dewey in Manila Bay.

1898 (June): Emilio Aguinaldo declared the Philippine Republic an independent state.

1898 (August): US troops occupied Manila.

1898: Philippine revolutionaries led by Aguinaldo declared independence.

1898 (October): Commodore Dewey entered treaty negotiations with the Spanish in Paris.

1898 (December): Spain ceded the Philippines (and Guam and Puerto Rico) to the US and recognized Cuban independence. The US gave $20 million to Spain.

1899: The US Senate ratified the treaty, enforcing US "sovereignty" against the "insurrection." According to Leon Wolf, "Filipino revolutionaries had already destroyed Spanish military power in much of the Northern and Central Philippines."[233]

1898–1902: The Philippine–American War took place, leading to "approximately 4,500 US deaths. Filipino forces suffered approximately 20,000 losses," and "an estimated 250,000 Filipino civilians lost their lives through violence, starvation and disease."[234]

---

[233] Leon Wolff, *Little Brown Brothers: How the United States Purchased and Pacified the Philippine Islands at the Century Turn.* New York: History Book Club, p. x, 1960.
[234] Ibid, pp. ix–xi.

1902: US president Roosevelt declared the war with the Philippines over; the US colonial period in the Philippines began.

1917: Ferdinand Marcos was born September 11, 1917, in Sarrat, Philippines.

1936–1946: Commonwealth of the Philippines was established.

1941: On December 8, the Japanese attacked, and they occupied Manila on January 2, 1942, setting up an "independent republic." President Manuel Quezon established a government in exile in the US.

1942: The Filipino People's Anti-Japanese Army (Hukbalahap, or "Huks") arose as a resistance force.

1944 (October): Allied forces led by General MacArthur landed in Leyte with little resistance; Quezon died in exile, and VP Sergio Osmena assumed the presidency.

1945: Tagaytay Ridge became the site of the first parachute landing in the RP, executed by the 511th Parachute Infantry Regiment, 11th Airborne Division, 8th Army, USA.

1945: The Japanese surrendered to General MacArthur (September 2).

1946: The RP declared independence from the US; Manuel Roxas y Acuna became president on July 4.

1947: The RP signed a bilateral treaty with the US, which agreed to provide military aid, training, and material assistance to the Philippines to combat Huk guerrillas challenging the government.

1953: The Nacionalista Parta elected populist Ramon Magsaysay as president.

1957: Carlos P. Garcia, vice president, was elected in his own right; his theme was "Filipinos First." An agreement was reached with the US to relinquish areas no longer needed militarily.

1965: Ferdinand Marcos, Nacionalista Party leader, became president.

1967: The Philippines became a founding member of ASEAN, the Association of Southeast Asian Nations.

1969: The Liberal Party rival leader Benigno "Ninoy" Aquino was jailed; Marcos's power began failing.

1972: Marcos declared martial law on September 21, after a new communist insurgency threatened; it was reported that some government agents were provocateurs.

-1,000,000 are said to have died in guerrilla warfare.

-65,000 were detained in military prisons and campus

-Amnesty International focused on the Philippines.

1972–83: Marcos and his wife, Imelda, built a power base.

1978: The Claytons arrived in the Philippines.

1981: There were reports of political detainees murdered or disappeared. Communist activity increased.

1981: The Claytons returned to the US.

1983: Returning to the RP after medical treatments in the US, Aquino was assassinated.

1986: Marcos declared a "snap" election; there was a bloodless coup titled People Power Revolution, also known as the EDSA Revolution or February Revolution, and Marcos was deposed. One of the strong activists was Jaime Cardinal Sin, thirtieth Roman Catholic archbishop of Manila and the third Filipino cardinal.

1986: Corazon Aquino, Ninoy's widow, was declared president. She had the support of the People Power Movement, a populist group of priests, nuns, and citizens.

1989: Marcos died in exile in Hawaii.

1992: General Fidel Ramos won the election.

1998: Joseph Estrada, Ramos's vice president, became president and then was forced out of office in 2001 following accusations of bribery and impeached.

2001: Gloria Macapagal-Arroyo was inaugurated as president.

2016: Rodrigo Duterte, whose grandfather was Chinese, was inaugurated as president.

2021: The Nobel Peace Prize was awarded to Maria Ressa, journalist and now CEO of *Rappler*, along with a Russian journalist.

2022: Ferdinand "Bongbong" Marcos was inaugurated seventeenth president of the Philippines on June 30; Sara Duterte, daughter of the previous president, was inaugurated as vice president.

Filipinos in the US

1763: Filipino sailors settled in Louisiana, first to settle in the US—called Manilamen.

1587: First Filipinos landed in October on a Spanish galleon which docked at Morro Bay, CA.

1910: The Filipino population in the US was 406. They were considered American nationals, from a US territory.

1920: The Filipino population in the US was 5,603.

1930: The Filipino population in the US was 45,208 (25 percent service workers, 9 percent fisheries, 60 percent agriculture). Workers arrived in San Francisco, hired taxis to Stockton, and established "Little Manila" there; some stayed, and others disbursed to jobs in California and Hawaii.

1934: The US Congress passed the McDuffie Act, establishing RP as a commonwealth, to become independent in ten years. The purpose of the act was Filipino exclusion. Now residents of a country deemed "independent," they no longer had unrestricted entry. Filipinos in Hawaii could not remigrate to the mainland and were classified as "aliens" and ineligible for New Deal or Works Progress Administration employment or assistance from the Relief Appropriation Act.[235] Filipino immigration dropped from 11,360 entries in 1929 to 1,306 in 1932.[236]

---

[235] "Every Cause Has Its Effect," Filipino Nation, July 1931, p. 5; Senator Tydings, in Wallovits, *Filipinos in California*. IN Takaki, Ronald, *Strangers from a Different Shore*, 1989. Little, Brown and Co: Boston, p. 332.
[236] Ibid. Takaki, Ronald, p. 332

1945: The War Brides Act encouraged an increase in Filipinas.[237]

2015: The Filipino population in the US reached almost four million, according to Pew Research.

2021: The Filipino Population in the US reached 4.2 million, according to Pew Research.

Excellent sources detailing the life of Filipinos in America and pertinent organizations:

- "A Filipino American Story (since 1587)."[238]
- "A look into the rich history of Filipino Americans in Stockton and Little Manila."[239]
- Filipino American National Historical Society (FANHS): fanhs-national.org/filam.
- Filipino American Physicians: www.theappa.org/contact.
- "Little Manila, Stockton, California," Wikipedia.

Philippine Union College History

1917: The Philippine Union Academy, Pasay Campus, opened in Manila; college classes were added in 1925.

1927: The Philippine Union Junior College (PUC) opened in Baesa, Caloocan, on the north edge of Metro Manila.

1932: PUC became a senior college.

---

[237] Parrilla, Katherine. "Undiscovering the Hidden Histories of California's Filipino Community." *Smithsonian Voices.* October 4, 2022. (accessed March 3, 2024
[238] "A Filipino American Story since 1587." Oct. 1, 2021 #FAHM2021 #FAHM https://www.facebook.com/nextdaybetter (accessed March 3, 2024).
[239] Anada Rochita, ABC10 "A look into the rich history of Filipino Americans in Stockton and Little Manila."; https://www.abc10.com/article/news/community/race-and-culture/history-of-filipino-americans-in-stockton-and-little-manila/103 (accessed March 3, 2024).

1972: PUC purchased 165 hectares in Putting Kahoy, Silang, Cavite.

1981: All PUC students moved to the new Silang campus.

1996: PUC became the Adventist University of the Philippines (AUP).

APPENDIX E

A Brief History of the Philippines

Dale

Archaeological records of Buddhist and Hindu artifacts suggest that the Chinese were in the Philippines as early as the ninth century. Their interest most likely lay in trade and exploration. Buddhism probably did not have as significant an effect on Indigenous animist beliefs or tribal cultures as did the later arrivals of Muslim and Christian invaders. The Chinese (Buddhist) population of the Philippines is little more than 1 percent today.

The Muslim population of Mindanao represents the first significant immigration to the Philippines and to its Indigenous tribes. The first Arabian trader reached the southern Philippines in 1380, and in 1390 Prince Rajah Baguinda began spreading Islam through the islands. The Muslim invaders (the Moors) were a fierce and troublesome people.

In the 1570s, the Spanish sailed into Manila Bay to the large northern island of Luzon. Three rajahs—Sulayman, Matanda, and Lakan—resisted the intrusion, but the Spanish forces were superior, and the period of Spanish colonialism and Christian proselytizing in the Philippines began.

The Spanish treated both the Muslims and the Filipino animist tribesmen harshly and forced them to become Christians. They came with the cannon behind the cross. This backfired for Magellan on Mactan island in Cebu when he was killed by the Filipino chieftain Lapu Lapu.

Entrance of the United States into the fray was highlighted by Admiral Dewey's victory in the Battle of Manila Bay, May 1, 1898—the decisive battle of the Spanish–American War. The United States paid Spain $20 million to annex the Philippine archipelago on December 10, 1898, sparking the Philippine–American War. The Filipinos who had fought beside Americans to defeat Spain were outraged at being bought. Filipino general Emilio Aguinaldo declared Philippine independence on June 2, 1899. Although many casualties occurred, the war was officially over on July 4, 1902.

With the Tydings-McDuffie Act (1935), the Philippines became a self-governing commonwealth, a status designed to prepare the country for independence in 1945. Unfortunately, World War II intervened, and in May 1942, the defeat of General MacArthur on Corregidor Island placed the Philippines under Japanese control. MacArthur returned in October 1944, landing on the island of Leyte, and the Americans and Filipinos fought side by side until the Japanese surrendered in 1945 (see chapter 24, "Richard Hammill, POW"). On July 4, 1946, the Philippine Islands finally became the independent Republic of the Philippines.

The history of the Philippines has not been conducive to development of stable governance. To make matters worse, the Christian north (Luzon) and the Muslim south (Mindanao) have different religions, cultures, and agendas; they distrust one another. The central government is located on Luzon, and political power is necessarily disproportionate. As in any nation-state, politicians have enhanced knowledge, connections, and power, the combination of which breeds corruption. Politicians and entrepreneurs, both Filipino and foreign, have been exploiting the resource-rich island of Mindanao for centuries. A multitude of factors has resulted in cycles of violence and peace talks between the government and the Moro Islamic Liberation Front, an organization that has sought to establish an independent Islamic state on Mindanao.

APPENDIX F

Bringing Folks Back to Their Roots

Some nongovernmental organizations (NGOs) and other advocates are helping to bring Filipinos back to their roots with crafts and skills used in their history—and they are less expensive than soaps sold in sari-sari stores and other markets.[240] Making coconut soap is one example.

Ira Wolfert wrote this description based on the account of Ensign Ilif David Richardson, US Navy, about his service in a patrol torpedo squadron while helping build the guerrilla movement in the Central Philippines between 1941 and 1944:

> [They would find or make] a wooden wheel and handle with a rope belt connected to a spindle that was mounted in a bracket. The spindle had a pulley on one side of the bearing and on the other side a scraper of the fruit-juicer variety. The scraper was used to extract and shred the meat of coconuts. Then the shreds were boiled and coconut oil floated to the surface. After the water boiled off, an extract of hardwood ash was added to it. The extract was made by running sea water through the ash. The ash and the oil were then stirred and boiled together. It thickened, hardened, and became soap. The product would then be cut into 1-pound cakes.[241]

---

[240] https://www.bing.com/search?q=ngo+making+soap
[241] Wolfert, Ira. *American Guerrilla in the Philippines*. New York: Simon & Shuster, 1945.

Filipinos continue making coconut oil soap in a similar fashion; it is much less expensive than the soaps sold in the markets and sari-sari stores.

―――ACKNOWLEDGMENTS―――

This book exists because we adventured to the other side of the earth and the people in our new home in the Philippines welcomed us, taught us, and were patient and kind. Students and colleagues—Filipino, American, Finnish, Caribbean, Canadian, Japanese, Indonesian, North Korean, Thai, Singaporean—we thank and honor each of you.

We want to acknowledge close friends and travel companions John and Pat Jones, Larry and Denise Herr, Ray and Shirley Holmes, Ralph and Marie Kneller, and Janet Miller, who traveled with us in the islands, played music with us, read us stories, empathized with our frustrations, and joined us in our joys of acculturation. Thanks also to Jean (the friend who found my dressmaker and led me into the best shopping), and Jim Zachary, my seminary boss and friend; thanks to Barbara Van Ornam, who sent the valued list of dos and don'ts and guided me to cotton clothing and great markets. Don Van Ornam kept us organized and on track; and Sam Robinson introduced Jeff to the world of big machines and building!

Salamat po to Rebecca Bea (Becky), our exceptional helper and friend, who continues to be a valued friend and keeps us updated on life today in the Philippines. You helped us manage practical things and understand so much!

Salamat po to Marjorie Reyno, manager of the clinical labs at LLU in Loma Linda, California, and David Evangelista, MD, physician in the Tri-Cities area of Washington State. Thank you for bringing your families to our home in Washington State. We appreciate your thanks and memories of Dale teaching you in Silang, Cavite, from 1980 to 1981. It was a joy to experience the physical and academic rewards of his work.

Thanks to Larry McCloskey, Linda McCloskey, and Andy Dressler, who assisted us in very practical ways in College Place while we were in the Philippines.

Thanks to our Oak Harbor Writers' Group, begun by Kelly Gust in 2013. Each chapter was read, often more than once, then commented on, with encouragement, suggestions, and corrections given in the long process of bringing words to publication. Many thanks to Bill Walker, Erika Jenkins, Ina Orme, Kelly Gust, Pat Craig, and Harry Anderson.

Thanks to our friends who read and helped us refine the stories and show the value and meaning of our work: Terese Thonus, Marjorie Reyno, Don Abbey, Luke Gray, and Don Abbey.

Koehler Books has brought this book to publication. Thank you to the owner, John Koehler, who oversaw the whole process; Lauren Sheldon, our "go-to" person for most things—her graphic artistry is much appreciated; and the detail and expertise of senior editor Hannah Woodlan has guided us so skillfully. It's true, editors and graphic artists make the finished produce attractive and correct, and owners get it to the public. Thank you!

Thank you to Nancy Rosenfeld, our agent, of AAA Books Unlimited. Her expertise and guidance have been invaluable. We appreciate her offering our books to publishers and working with them toward the final product. Thanks to her for representing me in publishing my hospice book, *Demystifying Hospice: Inside the Stories of Patients and Caregivers*, to Rowman & Littlefield Publishing Group, which published it in 2018.

Thanks to our parents, Larry and Naomi Crandall and Martin and Cora Clayton, for providing a Christian foundation for our lives and our work. Each is a beautiful example of a supportive parent, guiding us to love learning and travel. We are especially grateful that they visited us in the Philippines so we could share our adventure with them and relieve their minds that we were thriving and helping.

Our children, Jeffrey and Kimberly, get the biggest thanks for accompanying us on this Philippine adventure and other travels, learning together about the world and its peoples. This experience was formative in their lives, and they are glad they lived in the Philippines for a time.

—— ABOUT THE AUTHORS ——

Dale and Karen, both born in Michigan, have indulged their love of travel, visiting twenty-three countries so far. They have two adult children: Jeffrey is a senior construction supervisor living with his partner, Tammy, in Stockton, California, and Kimberly is a K–12 administrative assistant living with her husband, Terry, and two children, Alec and Kyrstin, in Melbourne, Australia.

Dale's academic training, teaching appointments, research, and publications have focused on biology, genetics, and physiology, with a special interest in animal behavior and circadian rhythms. He received his PhD from Michigan State University after a master's degree from Loma Linda University and a bachelor of arts from Andrews University. He was awarded the Zapata Award for

Excellence in Teaching and was chair of the Department of Biology at Southwestern Adventist University for three years, teaching there a total of twenty years. He has also taught at Michigan State University, East Lansing, MI; Walla Walla University, College Place, WA; Philippine Union College, Silang, Cavite, RP; and La Sierra University, Riverside, CA, and continued his research and publishing in retirement. He is also a fine woodworker and storyteller. Dale is completing a memoir of his childhood in a tiny town in Michigan titled *Killmaster Kids*.

Karen earned a master's degree in sociology from the University of Texas, Arlington, with a special interest in cross-cultural communication, diversity, and belief systems. She was a licensed social worker and has worked in adoptions, residential treatment for kids, hospital discharge planning, hospice, and as the director of patient services for the American Cancer Society in their Fort Worth regional office. Karen volunteered as education curator for the Stahl Center Museum of Culture at La Sierra University, Riverside, CA; and she has taught sociology at the University of Texas, Arlington; Southwestern Adventist University, Keene, TX; in the Tarrant County Junior Colleges in Fort Worth and Hurst, TX; and at La Sierra University, Riverside, CA.

Karen's book about hospice patients and caregivers, *Demystifying Hospice: Inside the Stories of Patients and Caregivers*, was published by Rowman & Littlefield in 2018, with a paperback edition released in 2020. It is in 719 libraries, according to WorldCat, and has been rated as one of the twenty best hospice books by Book Authority. Her next book, one of essays and poetry, will be titled *Discovering Myself*.

www.ingramcontent.com/pod-product-compliance
Lightning Source LLC
LaVergne TN
LVHW041743060526
838201LV00046B/895